GCSE 9-1

geography

AQA

SECOND EDITION

Revision Guide

Rebecca Tudor

Tim Bayliss

Catherine Hurst

SERIES EDITOR

Bob Digby

OXFORD
UNIVERSITY PRESS

OXFORD
UNIVERSITY PRESS

Great Clarendon Street, Oxford, OX2 6DP, United Kingdom

Oxford University Press is a department of the University of Oxford. It furthers the University's objective of excellence in research, scholarship, and education by publishing worldwide. Oxford is a registered trade mark of Oxford University Press in the UK and in certain other countries.

© Oxford University Press 2023

Series editor: Bob Digby

Authors: Rebecca Tudor, Tim Bayliss, Catherine Hurst

The moral rights of the authors have been asserted

First published in 2018

Second edition 2023

British Library Cataloguing in Publication Data
Data available

ISBN 978-138-202914-8

Ebook ISBN 978-138-202911-7

10 9 8 7 6 5 4 3

Paper used in the production of this book is a natural, recyclable product made from wood grown in sustainable forests.

The manufacturing process conforms to the environmental regulations of the country of origin.

Printed in India by Manipal Technologies Limited

Acknowledgements

The publisher and authors would like to thank the following for permission to use photographs and other copyright material:

Cover: watchara/Shutterstock; **p8:** Chris Wildt/Cartoonstock; **p11:**Bob Digby; **p12:** Stocktrek Images, Inc./Alamy Stock Photo; **p21(l):** MARTIN BERNETTI/Getty Images; **p21(r):** Manish Swarup/REX/Shutterstock; **p22:** Tim Bayliss; **p25:** Harvepino/Shutterstock; **p27:** imagegallery2/Alamy Stock Photo; **p28:** Neil Cooper/Alamy Stock Photo; **p29:** Apex News and Pictures; **p30:** SWNS/Alamy Stock Photo; **p31:** Crown coyright (2017) Ordinance Survey; **p32:** David Moir/REUTERS; **p33:** NASA; **p36:** EDF Energy; **p37(t):** Jack Sullivan/Alamy Stock Photo; **p37(b):** Pix/Alamy Stock Photo; **p40:** Land and Water Services ; **p42:** Travel Ink/Getty Images; **p43(t):** Mint Images/Frans Lanting/Getty Images; **p43(b):** Bazuki Muhammad/Reuters; **p44:** © Eye Ubiquitous/Alamy; **p45:** pyzata/Shutterstock; **p46:** Brian Bailey/Getty Images; **p48(l):** Franck METOIS/Alamy Stock Photo; **p48(r):** Tibor Bognar/Getty Images; **p49(t):** Bartek Wrzesniowski/Alamy Stock Photo; **p49(b):** Soltan Frédéric/Getty Images; **p50:** Avalon/Photoshot License/Alamy Stock Photo; **p51:** Eye Ubiquitous/REX/Shutterstock; **p52:** © Eye Ubiquitous/Alamy Stock Photo; **p53(t):** Frans Lanting/Getty Images; **p53(b):** Tyler Olson/Shutterstock; **p54(t):** Renato Granieri/Alamy Stock Photo; **p54(m):** Dmitry Chulov/Shutterstock; **p54(b):** © Rolf Adlercreutz/Alamy Stock Photo; **p55:** © ASK Images/Alamy Stock Photo; **p56(t):** © Robert Harding Picture Library Ltd/Alamy Stock Photo; **p56(b):** MarcAndreLeTourneux/Shutterstock; **p64(b):** Mike Charles/ Shutterstock; **p64(t):** dbphots/Alamy Stock Photo; **p65(l):** Crown coyright (2017) Ordinance Survey; **p65(r):** Angie Sharp/Alamy Stock Photo; **p67(l):** Mick House/Alamy Stock Photo; **p67(r):** Westend61/Getty Images; **p68:** © Environment Agency 2017; **p72:** Paul Heinrich/Alamy Stock Photo; **p74(t):** Washington Imaging/Alamy Stock Photo; **p74(b):** Crown coyright (2017) Ordinance Survey; **p76:** David Angel/Alamy Stock Photo; **p81:** David Robertson/Alamy Stock Photo; **p82:** Crown coyright (2017) Ordinance Survey; **p83(tl):** Simon Ross; **p83(tr):** Jeff Morgan 08/Alamy Stock Photo; **p83(bl):** Yorkman/Shutterstock; **p83(br):** ©Natural Retreats; **p84:** Terry Abraham; **p88:** America LLC/Alamy Stock Photo; **p89:** imageBROKER/Alamy Stock Photo; **p92(t):** Peter Treanor/Alamy Stock Photo; **p92(m):** antonio di paola/Alamy Stock Photo; **p92(b):** imageBROKER/Alamy Stock Photo; **p93:** Peter Tsai Photography/Alamy Stock Photo; **p94(t):** lazyllama/Shutterstock; **p94(b):** Mario Tama/Getty Images; **p97(l):** urbanbuzz/Istockphoto; **p97(r):** Doug Houghton/Alamy Stock Photo; **p98(l):** Pictorial Press Ltd/Alamy Stock Photo; **p98(r):** Russell Binns/Alamy Stock Photo; **p99(r):** Scott Hortop Travel/Alamy Stock Photo; **p100(t):** pjhpix/Shutterstock; **p100(b):** Jane Tregelles/Alamy Stock Photo; **p102(t):** Jeff Morgan 04/Alamy Stock Photo; **p102(b):** Courtesy of Leese and Nagle; **p103(b):** Bennett Dean /Eye Ubiquitous/Getty Images; **p104(l) :** Bristol City Council; **p104(r):** Crown coyright (2017) Ordinance Survey; **p105(t):** PLEIADES © CNES 2016, Distribution Airbus DS; **p105(b):** Populous Arena Team; **p106:** Hemis/Alamy Stock Photo; **p107(l):** LOOK Die Bildagentur der Fotografen GmbH/Alamy Stock Photo; **p107(r):** Rolf Disch Solar Architecture, Germany; **p107(b):** Daniel Schoenen/LOOK-foto/Getty Images; **p108(t):** allOver images/Alamy Stock Photo; **p108(b):** PETER PARKS/Getty Images; **p114:** © Jenny Matthews/Alamy Stock Photo; **p115:** Kjell Nilsson-Maki, cartoonstock.com; **p116:** Nick Turner/Alamy Stock Photo; **p117:** © Danita Delimont/Alamy Stock Photo; **p118(t):** Design Pics Inc/REX Shutterstock/; **p119(t):** © flowerphotos/Alamy Stock Photo; **p119(b):** FAIRTRADE; **p120:** Majority World/REX Shutterstock; **p121(t):** Andrew Park/Shutterstock; **p121(b):** © robertharding/Alamy Stock Photo; **p124:** epa/Shutterstock; **p125:** Eye Ubiquitous/Alamy Stock Photo; **p126:** Unilever Nigeria; **p128(l):** Sipa Press/REX/Shutterstock; **p128(tr):** Peeter Viisimaa/Getty Images; **p128(br):** Nick Turner/Alamy Stock Photo; **p129:** © jordi clave garsot/Alamy Stock Photo; **p131(t):** Corbis; **p131(b):** robertharding/Alamy Stock Photo; **p132:** www.morecobalt.co.uk; **p133(l):** © Construction Photography/Alamy Stock Photo; **p133(r):** Image courtesy of AGGREGATE INDUSTRIES UK LIMITED; **p134:** Shutterstock; **p136:** Peel Ports Group Ltd; **p138:** Paul Lovelace/REX Shutterstock; **p139:** Cameron Spencer/Getty Images; **p146(t):** Abbie Trayler-Smith/Panos; **p146(b):** Images of Africa Photobank/Alamy Stock Photo; **p147:** Maya Pedal; **p149:** Jim West/Alamy Stock Photo; **p163(t):** Newzulu/Alamy Stock Photo; **p163(b):** Bob Digby; **p165:** Andy Slater; **p167(l):** Hannah Peters/Getty Images; **p167(r):** Nigel Spiers/Alamy Stock Photo; **p168:** NASA; **p176:** Shutterstock; **p177:** Bob Digby;

Artwork by Aptara Inc., Mike Connor, Barking Dog Art, Simon Tegg, and Q2A Media Services Inc.

Although we have made every effort to trace and contact all copyright holders before publication this has not been possible in all cases. If notified, the publisher will rectify any errors or omissions at the earliest opportunity.

Links to third party websites are provided by Oxford in good faith and for information only. Oxford disclaims any responsibility for the materials contained in any third party website referenced in this work.

Contents

Contents

Unit 2 – Challenges in the human environment

Contents

Guided answers are available on the Oxford Secondary Geography website:
www.oxfordsecondary.com/geog-aqa-answers

Please note this revision guide has not been written or approved by AQA. The answers and commentaries provided represent one interpretation only and other solutions may be appropriate.

Introduction: Helping you succeed

If you want to be successful in your exams, then you need to revise all you've learned during your GCSE course! That can seem daunting – but it's why this book has been written. It contains key revision points that you need to revise for your AQA GCSE Geography exams.

Your revision guide!

This book is one of five OUP publications to support students studying AQA GCSE 9–1 Geography. The others are:

* Student Book (second edition), alongside which this book works. All page links in this book refer to the Student Book.
* Exam practice book targeting grades 4–6
* Exam practice book targeting grades 7–9
* Fieldwork book.

How to use this book

The AQA GCSE 9–1 Geography specification has three units (1–3), and units 1 and 2 are split into sections (1A, 1B, 1C, 2A, 2B, 2C). In this book, these units are split into these sections, and then again into topics (1.1–24.9), and contains the following features to help you revise.

Introductions to each of Units 1–3

These contain outlines of:

* the three exam papers you'll be taking
* the key ideas and content of the specification.

Revision content for Papers 1 and 2

Each topic (1.1, 1.2 etc) in this Revision Guide exactly matches the content for each topic in the AQA GCSE 9–1 Geography Student Book. The content covers what you need to know for Papers 1 and 2. Each double-page topic in the Student Book has been summarised in a single page in this Revision Guide. Some pages also focus on practising geographical skills.

Each page contains the following features:

* *'You need to know'* – at the start of every page. It summarises all you need to learn for each topic. Some pages are linked to *'Big Ideas'* which help you to understand key concepts, such as 'sustainability'.
* *Main content* – a summary of the content found in the Student Book for each topic.
* *Six second summary* – a summary checklist of the essentials that you need to know.
* *Over to you* – activities to help you learn content for the exam.

Guidance on Paper 3

Paper 3 deals with skills rather than content. This book contains two features to help you with Paper 3:

* Issue Evaluation (pages 182–192), which includes a resource booklet, just like the one you'll get before your exam. The exam will test your skills in analysing the booklet.
* Fieldwork skills (pages 193–201), to help you revise your two days' fieldwork and prepare for the exam.

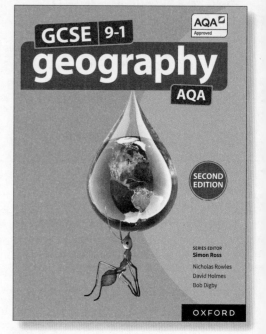

Figure 1 *The AQA GCSE Geography Student Book*

Unit 1 Living with the physical environment

This is assessed by Paper 1 in the exam. It has three sections, each with different topics.

- **Section A** *The challenge of natural hazards* includes topics on Tectonic hazards, Weather hazards, and Climate change.

- **Section B** *The living world* includes topics on Ecosystems, Tropical rainforests, Hot deserts and Cold environments. You have to know about Ecosystems and Tropical rainforests, and **either** Hot deserts **or** Cold environments.

- **Section C** *Physical landscapes in the UK* includes topics on UK physical landscapes, Coastal landscapes, River landscapes, and Glacial landscapes. You have to know about UK physical landscapes and **any two** of Coastal, River or Glacial landscapes.

In addition, there'll be questions on geographical skills (e.g. how to interpret statistics, maps, diagrams or photos) in every topic.

Complete this for Unit 1!

The three *Living world* topics I've studied are Ecosystems, Tropical rainforests and

_____

The two *Physical landscapes in the UK* I've studied are

_____

_____ and

_____.

Unit 2 Challenges in the human environment

This is assessed by Paper 2 in the exam. It also has three sections, each with different topics.

- **Section A** *Urban issues and challenges* includes topics on a case study of a major city in **either** a low income country (LIC) **or** a newly emerging economy (NEE), **and** a case study of a major UK city.

- **Section B** *The changing economic world* includes topics on a case study of **either** an LIC **or** an NEE, **and** Economic futures in the UK.

- **Section C** *The challenge of resource management* includes topics on Resource management, Food, Water and Energy. You have to know about Resource management and **one** from Food **or** Water **or** Energy.

Like Paper 1, there'll be questions on geographical skills (e.g. how to interpret statistics, maps, diagrams or photos) in every topic.

Complete this for Unit 2!

The major city I've studied in **either** an LIC **or** an NEE is

_____

The major city I've studied in the UK is

_____.

The LIC or NEE that I've studied is

_____

I've studied Resource management and

_____

Unit 3 Geographical applications

This is assessed by Paper 3 in the exam. It has two sections:

- **Section A** *Issue evaluation* will be based on a pre-release booklet that you will receive a few weeks before the exam. You will study this booklet in class time.

- **Section B** *Fieldwork* will be about your two days' fieldwork (one day physical, one day human), including questions on links between physical and human geography.

Complete this for Unit 3!

My *Issue evaluation* enquiry topic is

_____.

The two days of fieldwork that I've done are

Physical geography:

_____

Human geography:

_____

However you look at it, revision can be dull! But it helps if the revision you do is **active**. This page will help you develop useful ways of revising.

Revising in groups

Working as a group is always better than alone. Try these ideas out.

> **Form a study group with friends**. Join two or three friends and fix times when you'll go through key topics. Do timed questions together, then mark them. Make lists of things you don't understand to ask your teacher.

> **Working together at home**. Message or video with friends and test each other. Go through past exam questions together.

> **Know your key words**. Make lists of key words that you need to know from the specification.

> **Test each other**. Make flash cards of key words and have revision quizzes.

"We prefer to call this test 'multiple choice,' not 'multiple guess.'"

Figure 2 *The dangers of not revising!*

Revising in class

You'll have lessons to revise topics that you're not clear about. Use the time well!

> **Get to know question styles**. Know command words, practise timed answers and plan longer extended answers.

> **Get to know how exam questions are marked**. Know which questions are point marked (one correct point = 1 mark) and those marked using Levels. Know what qualities are required for the highest marks. Look at past papers and mark schemes on AQA's website and AQA GCSE 9–1 Geography Exam Practice books (ISBN 9781382029056 and 9781382029070).

> **Look at past answers**. Some exam boards publish model answers or have marking exercises as part of their training for teachers. Go through these, so that you know how examiners mark.

> **Extra lessons**. Make lists of questions about topics you don't understand, then ask your teacher about them.

> **Ask your teacher for revision help**. Your teacher can give you questions on particular topics you are less confident about.

Revising alone

At some stage, you'll have to revise alone. Don't sit in front of the TV trying to read notes that you're not sure about! Try these variations.

> **Check key ideas**. Make a checklist of key ideas and themes you are not sure about, like the checklists in the section introductions in this book.

> **Work on past exam papers**. The more papers you try, the more familiar you'll be with examiners' style.

> **Watch video clips from YouTube, BBC Bitesize or other websites**. Allow no more than 15 minutes, which is as long as most people can concentrate.

Know your key words!

In your GCSE course, you've been learning to *think* like a geographer – for example, by explaining processes that affect the Earth's surface, and how people affect the natural environment. Now, you must learn to *write* like a geographer, which means knowing key geographical words.

Key words help you to:

- understand a question (e.g. explaining how a process occurs)
- identify features in diagrams or photos, like Figure **3**.
- use key words in your answers. Answers that use key words earn more marks than those that don't.

Beach • Finer beach material
Larger sediment particles • Evidence of slumping
• Cliff face

Figure 3 *A coastline in Cornwall – which of these key terms can you recognise?*

Many words used in geography are also used in day-to-day life, like 'population' or 'beaches'. But you only ever meet some key words in certain topics (e.g. precipitation). Many are key to the subject – like the words in Figure **4**.

Do you know these key words?

In the left-hand column are definitions of terms you should know. Write them in the right-hand column 1 to 5, then check the answers on page 10.

Figure 4 *Which key words are these?*

Description	Geographical term
The rock type of an area, or the study of rocks	1
People coming to live in a country from overseas	2
Gases which warm the atmosphere	3
Specialist service and technical industries	4
The total value of goods and services in a country in a year	5

Mmmm ... mnemonics!

Learning key words and processes can be hard. Even something like spit formation has ten steps to remember (see below). However, **mnemonics** can help – it's a way of developing a system to help your memory.

How mnemonics work

1 Try this way of learning processes that form a coastal spit.

  a) Winds blow at an **angle**

  b) Waves break – **swash**

  c) Sand is moved **up** the beach

  d) Water moves down the beach – **backwash**

  e) Sand moves down the beach – in a **zigzag**

  f) This is called **longshore** drift

  g) Sand reaches an **estuary**

  h) Sand forms a **spit** across the estuary

  i) River currents form a **hook**

  j) **Mudflats** form behind the spit

2 Look at the words in bold – then take the first letter – **A**ngle, **S**wash, **U**p, **B**ackwash, **Z**igzag, **L**ongshore, **E**stuary, **S**pit, **H**ook, and **M**udflats.

3 Write the letters in a list, then create a sentence from the first letters to help you remember – it can be as daft as you like!

4 Learn the sentence!

Over to you

Try making mnemonics for these.

a) Erosion processes along coasts (10.3), rivers (11.2) or glaciers (12.1)

b) Key words in any **one** other topic that you've revised.

Hazards is one of the most popular topics in geography. Hazard events, such as the Haiti earthquake of 2010 (Figure **5**), are among the many examples and case studies that you need to revise for the exam.

- You can use this approach for any hazard (e.g. flood, volcanic eruption).
- You can adapt this approach to revise **any** example or case study.

Figure 5 *The Haiti earthquake in 2010*

1

Build up a factfile

Revising case studies can be hard because there's a lot of detail. Start by building up a basic **factfile**, such as:

- Location – where is it? Can you locate it in an atlas?
- What kind of hazard was it?
- When did it occur? Date and time?
- Was it a single event or one of several?
- Describe what happened. For example, for an earthquake – what date, what time of day, how strong was it, where was the epicentre?
- What were its causes? Is it on a destructive plate margin?

2

Know its impacts

The impacts, or effects, of many hazard events can be significant. What were its primary and secondary impacts? Be clear that you know what these terms mean.

- Primary – caused directly by the event (e.g. falling buildings in an earthquake)
- Secondary – the result of the event (e.g. homelessness or fires).

Next, classify these into economic, social or environmental impacts.

- Economic impacts (related to money, e.g. jobs, businesses, trade, costs).
- Social impacts (about people, health, and housing)
- Environmental impacts (about changes to the surrounding landscape).

You can now list these impacts and classify them, using the grid in Figure **6**.

Impact	Primary impacts	Secondary impacts
Economic		
Social		
Environmental		

Figure 6 *A table for classifying the impacts of a hazard event*

 Over to you

Think how you could adapt a) the factfile b) the table of impacts, to other topics. Consider these possibilities:

1 A study of a country (an LIC or an NEE). What sort of factfile would you produce?

2 A study of a megacity in an LIC or an NEE? How would you build up notes on reasons for its growth, or problems that it is trying to solve?

3 A study of a city in the UK (e.g. Bristol)? How would you build up notes on ways in which it is trying to become more sustainable?

Answers to Fig 4 Page 9

1 Geology
2 Immigration (or immigrants)
3 Greenhouse gases
4 Quaternary industries
5 GDP

How to get the best marks possible in your exams? To reach your best standard of writing on longer answers, follow the advice below.

1

Plan your answer

It helps to organise your thoughts if you plan your answer. You don't need a long plan – just something that takes you 30 seconds to jot down. Some people plan using a spider diagram, others just make a short list. It helps you to get the order of the answer right and makes sure you don't forget what to write. One example of a plan is given in Figure **7**.

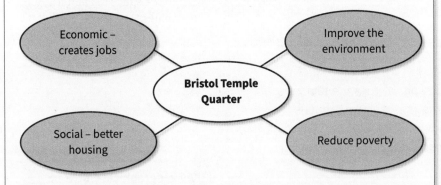

Figure 7 *An example of a plan to a 6-mark question:* Explain the impacts of regeneration on one named major UK city. (6 marks)'
Hint: This refers to pages 202–5 in the Student Book. You could add more details to this.

 Over to you

In the box below, draw a plan like the one in Figure **7** for the question:

Explain the ways in which one named major city in an emerging or low income country has tried to improve access to health and education. (9 marks)

Hint: Use pages 176–177 in the Student Book to help you.

2 Use key words

Below are two exam answers where candidates A and B were supposed to use key words.

- Candidate A gained only 2 marks out of 4
- Candidate B gained only 3 marks out of 6

In each case, the candidate knew the general idea, but there were no key words.

 Over to you

1 Below are two candidate answers from an exam. To the right of each answer are key geographical words. Replace each word in bold in the answer with one of the key geographical words.

2 Write the improved answer in the space to get full marks.

Candidate A answer

Explain two ways in which human activity can lead to climate change. (4 marks)

People are using more and more cars, and the gases that are **given off** go up into the **air** and **damage** the air we breathe and **make it warmer**. By **cutting down trees**, less oxygen is produced and there is more **of other gases** in the air making the **weather** warmer.

_____

_____

_____

_____

_____

_____

Key geographical words to improve the answer:
atmosphere
carbon dioxide
climate
emitted
deforestation
increase the greenhouse effect
pollute

Candidate B answer

Explain how human actions can increase the risk of flooding. (6 marks)

Human actions can increase flood risk. First, **cutting down trees** so there is **grass for cattle to feed on** and fuel means that there are no more trees to **break the fall of rain** so it gets to the soil straight away. More rain gets to the river by **flowing over the land** and the river **fills up** very quickly and **overflows**. Tree roots also bind the soil together and, if **the trees are cut down**, the soil **wears away**. This soil then gets into the river and gets **carried along** and **dropped** on the **bottom of the river** which raises it and reduces **how much water the river can hold**.

_____

_____

_____

_____

_____

_____

_____

_____

Key geographical words to improve the answer:
capacity
deforestation
deforested
deposited
erodes
floods
grazing
intercept
reaches capacity
river bed
surface runoff
transported

Top tips for exam success

You'll often hear students say 'Good luck' to each other as they enter the exam room. If you have done certain things, you won't need luck! Exam success comes from following a few rules. Students who perform well almost always follow these rules:

They revise. Lack of revision always catches up with you. GCSEs are tougher now than in previous years and it's important to know your stuff!

They know which **topics** will be in each exam – for example, which exam tests physical or human geography, and which of their topics, such as hot deserts or cold environments, are on which exam paper.

They look at the **marks**, and know what sort of questions carry the highest marks.

They **practise** answers, often under timed conditions, for example, allowing 4 minutes for a 4-mark question.

They get **timing** right. GCSE 9–1 Geography AQA Exam Practice have marks that are similar to the length of the exam. For example, Paper 1 is 88 marks in 90 minutes. So, if a question has 6 marks, take 6 minutes. Don't get carried away on one question.

They **answer all the questions** that should be answered, and leave no blanks. Even if unsure, they write something. Leaving a 6-mark answer blank could mean giving up a whole grade.

They write in **full sentences**. Single words or phrases are fine for questions of 1–2 marks, but 4-mark answers written out in 'bullet points' rarely score well.

They learn **specific details** about case studies or examples. They take time to learn one or two statistics, names of places, and schemes. They don't just say 'in Africa'! Use specific place knowledge – you need this to earn the highest marks.

Get to know the **mark scheme** and how questions are marked. Longer answers are marked in **levels** based on quality. Examiners use three words to describe answers: Level 1, basic (no named places or examples); Level 2, general (some key points); and Level 3 detailed (facts, data, and examples). Make sure you are in Level 3!

Finally, make sure you have a **timetable** that tells you exactly which day and times every exam is on! Check, and double-check it!

Section A
The challenge of natural hazards

Your exam

Section A The challenge of natural hazards is part of Paper 1: Living with the physical environment.

Paper 1 is a one-and-a-half hour written exam and makes up 35 per cent of your GCSE. The whole paper carries 88 marks (including 3 marks for SPaG) – questions on Section A carries 33 marks.

You need to study all the topics in Section A – in your final exam you will have to answer questions on all of them.

Tick these boxes to build a record of your revision

Your revision checklist

Spec key idea	Theme	1	2	3
1 Natural hazards				
Natural hazards pose major risks to people and property	1.1 What are natural hazards?			
2 Tectonic hazards				
Earthquakes and volcanic eruptions are the result of physical processes	2.1 Plate tectonics theory			
	2.2 Distribution of earthquakes and volcanoes			
	2.3 Physical processes at plate margins			
The effects of, and responses to, tectonic hazards vary between areas of contrasting levels of wealth	2.4 The effects of earthquakes			
	2.5 Responses to earthquakes			
Management can reduce the effects of tectonic hazards	2.6 Living with the risks from tectonic hazards			
	2.7 Reducing the risks from tectonic hazards			
Geographical skills	2.8 Skills Focus: Dispersion graphs			
3 Weather hazards				
Global atmospheric circulation helps to determine patterns of weather and climate	3.1 Global atmospheric circulation			
Tropical storms develop as a result of particular physical conditions	3.2 Where are tropical storms formed?			
	3.3 The formation and structure of tropical storms			
	3.4 How might climate change affect tropical storms?			
Tropical storms have significant effects on people and the environment	3.5 Cyclone Idai – a tropical storm			
	3.6 Reducing the effects of tropical storms			
The UK is affected by a number of weather hazards	3.7 Weather hazards in the UK			
	3.8 Extreme weather in the UK			
Extreme weather events in the UK have impacts on human activity	3.9 The Somerset Level Floods, 2014			
Geographical skills	3.10 Skills Focus: OS map (1:25000) and photo skills			
4 Climate change				
Climate change is the result of natural and human factors, and has a range of effects	4.1 What is the evidence for climate change?			
	4.2 What are the natural causes of climate change?			
	4.3 What are the human causes of climate change?			
Managing climate change involves both mitigation (reducing causes) and adaptation (responding to change)	4.4 Managing climate change – mitigation			
	4.5 Managing climate change – adaptation			
Geographical skills	4.6 Skills Focus: Graphs and charts			

Student Book
See pages 10–11

- what is meant by 'natural hazard'
- different types of natural hazard
- risks from natural hazards and factors affecting these.

What is a natural hazard?

Natural hazards are sudden, severe events which make the natural environment difficult to manage. They disrupt human life, and have huge **economic** and **social impacts**. They fall into three main groups (Figure **1**).

These events do not pose a threat to people if they occur in unpopulated regions. But where they cause high levels of death, injury, damage or disruption they become *disasters*.

The most deadly natural hazards are:

- *floods* – the most frequent and deadly, damaging most property
- *tropical storms* – the next most frequent, almost as dangerous
- *earthquakes*
- *droughts*.

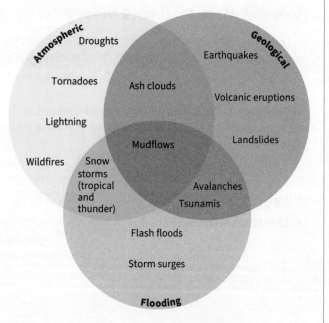

Figure 1 *Venn diagram showing different types of natural hazard and how they interconnect*

What is 'hazard risk'?

Hazard risk means the chance of being affected by a natural hazard. For example, those living near the sea at risk of flooding caused by tropical storms or tsunami. People live in risky areas because they:

- accept the risk, after weighing up advantages and disadvantages
- have no knowledge of the dangers
- have little choice of where to live.

 Big Idea

Just as not all hazards are disasters, not all hazards have to be feared (see 2.6).

What factors affect risk?

As populations grow, more people are exposed to natural hazards. Four factors increase the risk.

- *Urbanisation* – densely-populated urban areas concentrate those at risk.
- *Poverty* – shortage of housing leads to building on risky ground.
- *Farming* – the attraction of fertile silt on floodplains puts people at risk.
- *Climate change* – global warming raises sea levels and generates more extreme weather.

Six Second Summary

- Natural hazards are environmental events threatening people.
- The most deadly natural hazards are floods, storms, earthquakes and droughts.
- As populations grow, so does hazard risk.

Over to you

The number of earthquakes or volcanic eruptions is not changing – so why are more people at risk from natural hazards?

Student Book
See pages
12–13

You need to know:

- what is meant by 'plate tectonics theory'
- how plate tectonics theory developed
- what mechanisms drive plate movements.

How did plate tectonics theory develop?

Early world mapping of continents, mountain ranges and **volcanoes**, as well as fossil evidence, led Alfred Wegener to suggest, in 1912, that the continents were once joined together and had gradually floated apart. Twentieth century seabed mapping provided more evidence for Wegener's *continental drift* and the development of modern plate tectonic theory.

What mechanisms drive plate movements?

Tectonic plates move between 2.5 cm to 16 cm a year, driven by convection currents and gravitational sliding (Figure **2**):

- Spreading convection currents explain the presence of rising magma at constructive (divergent) margins.
- Sinking convection currents coincide with destructive (convergent) margins where one plate subducts below another.
- Gravitational sliding is more important. *Ridge push*, at divergent margins, is caused by rising magma 'pushing' the older part of the plate sideways. *Slab pull*, at convergent margins, is caused by gravity pulling the thick, dense plate downwards.

What is plate tectonic theory?

- The Earth's crust is divided into solid **tectonic plates** up to 100 km thick.
- There are two types of tectonic plate – relatively recently formed, dense, thin, basaltic *oceanic crust*, and older, less dense, thicker, granitic *continental crust*.
- Plates separate (diverge) at **constructive margins**, collide (converge) at **destructive margins** and slide by each other at **conservative margins**.

It is the movement of the plates relative to each other that explains the major features of the Earth's surface (mountain chains, ocean trenches) and the formation of **earthquakes** and volcanoes (see 2.3).

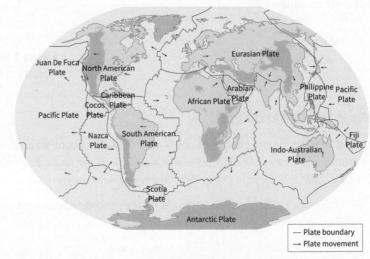

Figure 1 *The Earth's major tectonic plates*

Key
→ Convection currents
→ Direction of plate movement

The hot rock rises towards the solid surface, is forced sideways, cools, becomes denser, and sinks

Deep ocean trench — Mid-ocean ridge — Deep ocean trench

Ridge push — Lithosphere

Subduction zone — Subduction zone

Slab pull — Mantle

Radioactive decay within the Earth's core heats the mantle rocks above

Reheating allows the rock to rise again – completing the convection cycle

Figure 2 *The mechanisms that drive plate movement*

⏱ Six Second Summary

- Plate tectonic theory explains and develops Wegener's theory of continental drift.
- Tectonic plate movement is driven by convection currents and gravitational sliding.
- Plates *separate* at constructive margins, *collide* at destructive margins and *slide by* at conservative margins.

✏ Over to you

- Make a list of the terms introduced in this spread. Add a sentence to explain **each** one.

Student Book
See pages 14–15

You need to know:

- the global pattern of earthquakes and volcanoes
- their links to plate tectonics.

The pattern of earthquakes

An **earthquake** is a sudden, violent period of ground-shaking. Most occur at the margins of slowly moving tectonic plates. Friction and sticking between plates create enormous pressures and stresses which build to breaking point.

Compare Figure **1** with Figure **1** on page 16. Note how:

- the majority of earthquakes are in linear belts that correspond with plate margins
- sparsely distributed earthquakes correspond with constructive plate margins (e.g. the Mid-Atlantic Ridge)
- denser, broader earthquake zones correspond with destructive plate margins (e.g. the 'Pacific Ring of Fire').

Isolated earthquakes occur away from plate margins. Many are triggered by human activities such as mining, oil extraction or reservoir construction.

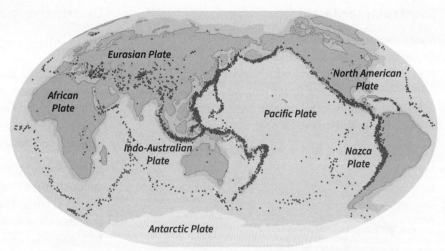

Figure 1 *Global distribution of earthquakes*

The pattern of volcanoes

Volcanoes are large, often cone-shaped landforms, formed over long periods by several eruptions. They are fed by molten rock (magma) deep within the Earth's mantle. Like earthquakes, most volcanoes occur in belts along plate margins (e.g. the 'Pacific Ring of Fire' and the Mid-Atlantic Ridge). But some occur at *hot spots* where the crust is thin, and magma breaks through the surface (e.g. Hawaiian Islands – Figure **2**).

Figure 2 *Eruption of Kilauea volcano, Hawaii, 2018*

Six Second Summary

- Plate movement and tectonic activity at plate margins cause earthquakes and volcanoes.

Over to you

- Name **three** plate boundaries where earthquakes occur.
- Give **one** reason why more earthquakes occur than volcanic eruptions.
- Explain why earthquakes and volcanoes occur at plate boundaries.

Student Book
See pages
16–17

You need to know:

• the physical processes at constructive, destructive and conservative plate margins.

What happens at tectonic plate margins?

Constructive margin

Where two plates move apart, magma forces its way to the surface. As it breaks the crust, it causes mild earthquakes. The magma is very hot and fluid allowing the lava to flow a long way before cooling. This results in typically broad and flat *shield volcanoes* (e.g. Mid-Atlantic Ridge).

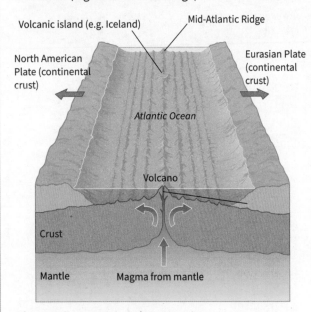

Figure 1 *Constructive plate margin*

Conservative margin

Where two plates move past each other at different rates (e.g. San Andreas Fault, California), friction between them builds stresses and triggers earthquakes when they slip. There are no volcanoes because there is no magma.

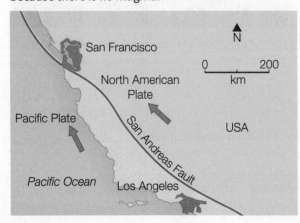

Figure 3 *Conservative plate margin*

Destructive margin

Where two plates move towards each other (e.g. west coast of South America, Figure **2**), dense oceanic plate is *subducted* beneath the less dense continental plate. Friction between them causes strong earthquakes. The sinking oceanic plate creates sticky, gas-rich magma. This results in steep-sided *composite volcanoes* which erupt violently.

Where two continental plates meet, there is no subduction, so there is no magma to form volcanoes. The crust crumples and lifts to form fold mountains (e.g. Himalayas). Powerful earthquakes can be triggered.

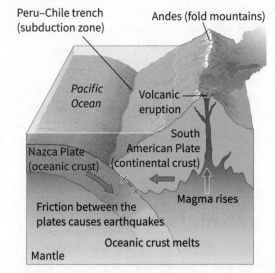

Figure 2 *Destructive plate margin*

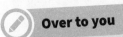

Six Second Summary

• Plates *separate* at constructive margins causing mild earthquakes and volcanic eruptions.
• Plates *collide* at destructive margins causing strong earthquakes and violent volcanic eruptions.
• Plates *slide by* at conservative margins causing powerful earthquakes.

Over to you

Summarise in a table the physical processes that happen at **each** type of plate margin.

Student Book
See pages
18–19

You need to know:

- the primary and secondary effects of earthquakes in two areas with contrasting levels of wealth – Japan and Nepal.

The earthquakes in Japan and Nepal

Earthquakes can have devastating social effects:

- **Primary effects** (caused by ground shaking) destroy buildings and infrastructure, and kill and injure.
- **Secondary effects** (resulting from the shaking) include fires, landslides and deadly tsunami.

Figure 1 *Location of Japan and Nepal*

Figure 2 *Comparison of Japan and Nepal earthquakes*

	Japan, March 2011	Nepal, April 2015
Wealth (GNI) and development (HDI) indicators	• GNI 24th out of 192 countries • HDI 19th out of 189 countries	• GNI 163rd out of 192 countries • HDI 142nd out of 189 countries
Cause	• Sudden slippage between the North American Plate and the subducting Pacific Plate	• Indo-Australian Plate colliding with the Eurasian Plate
Size	• Magnitude 9.0, shallow focus (30 km)	• Magnitude 7.9, very shallow focus (15 km)
Primary effects	• Violent ground shaking caused many injuries and some deaths as buildings collapsed • Thousands of homes destroyed • Power, water, sanitation, and communications disrupted	• 9000 killed, 20 000 injured and 3 million homeless • Widespread destruction of buildings and infrastructure – 3 million people left homeless • Power, water, sanitation and communications cut • US$5 billion damage
Secondary effects	• 10 m-high tsunami waves flooded 560 km^2, caused 18 000 deaths, and left 500 000 homeless • Significant destruction of port facilities, infrastructure, and homes, especially in Sendai • Explosions at Fukushima nuclear power plant led to evacuation of 100 000 people • US$235 billion damage	• Communities cut off by landslides and avalanches – hampering relief efforts • Avalanches on Mount Everest killed at least 19 people • An avalanche in the Langtang region left 250 people missing • Flooding threatened following a landslide blocking the Kali Gandaki River – many people evacuated

Six Second Summary

- Both earthquakes had primary and secondary effects.
- Both earthquakes had devastating effects on people's lives and activities.
- Marked contrasts in wealth and development affected the impacts.

Over to you

Study information in the table.

- Name **three** indicators (figures) which show that Nepal is poorer than Japan.
- Highlight **five** main similarities and **five** main differences between the two earthquakes.

Student Book
See pages 20–1

You need to know:

- the immediate and long-term responses to earthquakes in two areas with contrasting levels of wealth – Japan and Nepal.

Comparing immediate and long-term responses

Earthquakes and associated tsunami are common in Japan. Both government and local communities are prepared, drilled, experienced and wealthy enough for rapid and effective response.

Earthquakes in Nepal are not uncommon. Scientists are familiar with the risks, but poverty prevents widespread adoption of new building regulations or effective preparation.

Figure 1 *Immediate and long-term responses to Japan and Nepal earthquakes*

	Japan, March 2011	Nepal, April 2015
Immediate responses – search, rescue and short-term aid, keeping survivors alive by providing medical care, food, water and shelter	• 500 000 people evacuated to higher ground before tsunami struck • Japanese and international search and rescue teams worked for days – although there were few survivors • Key roads and railways repaired within weeks • Power soon restored but supply intermittent due to the explosions at the Fukushima nuclear power plant	• International search and rescue teams rescued 16 survivors (Figure **3**) • World Vision International provided emergency food kits for 8000 people • Aid included helicopters for search, rescue and supply drops in remote areas, such as Mount Everest • 300 000 people migrated from Kathmandu to seek shelter and support from family and friends
Long-term responses – rebuilding and reconstruction, to restore 'normal' life and reduce future risk	• Long-term plan (2012–2022) identifying zones for reconstruction with simpler planning procedures • Upgraded tsunami warning system launched (2013) • Seawalls and embankments constructed • Most debris cleared and new housing constructed by 2015 • 30 000 new houses replaced temporary homes by 2020 (Figure **2**)	• New National Disaster Risk Reduction Policy (2018) to increase future resilience • Most roads repaired and landslides cleared by late 2015 • 212 000 new homes constructed by September 2020 • UNESCO is working with the government to restore 700 damaged temples, palaces, and museums

Figure 2 *Temporary housing units at Otsuchicho for those made homeless by the earthquake and tsunami*

Rubble to be shifted | Rescue dogs | Listening for survivors | Local knowledge

Lifting equipment | Weak buildings – danger of collapse | Video cameras to see inside collapsed buildings

Figure 3 *Searching for survivors in Kathmandu, Nepal*

 Six Second Summary

- Japan was prepared, experienced and wealthy enough for a rapid and effective response.
- Nepal's response was hindered by poverty, and depended on overseas aid.

Over to you

Practise describing **three** immediate and **three** long-term responses to **each** of the disasters in Japan and Nepal.

Student Book
See pages
22–3

You need to know:

- why people continue to live in areas at risk from earthquakes and volcanoes
- how tectonic activity in Iceland brings huge benefits.

Living at risk from tectonic hazards

The majority of **tectonic hazards** occur at plate margins, some of which run through densely populated regions such as Japan, parts of China and southern Europe.

Poor people have no choice – money, food and family are seen as more important

Plate margins often coincide with favourable areas for settlement and trade, e.g. flat, coastal areas

Earthquakes and volcanic eruptions are rare, so not seen as a great threat

Some people have no experience or knowledge of the risks

Why people live at risk from tectonic hazards

Earthquake-resistant building designs reduce risk

Volcanoes can bring benefits such as fertile soils, rich mineral deposits and hot water

Effective monitoring of volcanoes and tsunami waves allow evacuation warnings to be given

Earthquake fault lines can allow water to reach the surface – important in arid regions

Figure 1 Why people live at risk from tectonic hazards

Living on a plate margin: Iceland

Iceland straddles the Mid-Atlantic Ridge with volcanic eruptions on average every five years. But awareness and monitoring reduces the threat to low risk. Indeed, tectonic activity brings huge benefits, such as the Hellisheidi combined heat and power (CHP) plant which serves Reykjavik.

Figure 2 The Hellisheidi CHP plant is the third-largest geothermal power plant in the world

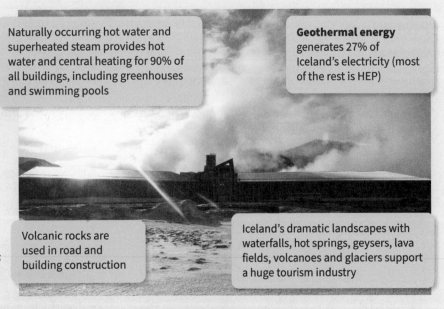

Naturally occurring hot water and superheated steam provides hot water and central heating for 90% of all buildings, including greenhouses and swimming pools

Geothermal energy generates 27% of Iceland's electricity (most of the rest is HEP)

Volcanic rocks are used in road and building construction

Iceland's dramatic landscapes with waterfalls, hot springs, geysers, lava fields, volcanoes and glaciers support a huge tourism industry

Six Second Summary

- Plate margins run through densely populated regions such as Japan and southern Europe.
- Effective monitoring, prediction and protection reduce the risks.
- Iceland benefits from tectonic activity with geothermal power and tourism.

Over to you

List **three** key reasons to explain **each** of the following:

- why people live at risk from tectonic hazards
- how the people of Iceland benefit from living on a plate margin.

Student Book
**See pages
24–5**

You need to know:

- how risks from tectonic hazards can be reduced by monitoring, prediction, protection and planning.

How can risks from tectonic hazards be reduced?

There are four main **management strategies** for reducing the risk from tectonic hazards.

1 Monitoring

Volcanoes

All active volcanoes are now monitored using hi-tech scientific equipment including:

- *seismometers (seismographs)* to detect and record microquakes
- *tiltmeters* to monitor ground deformation as magma rises
- *instruments* to monitor gas emissions and changes in water chemistry.

Earthquakes

Earthquakes generally occur without warning. But a network of seismometers monitor and record them.

Tsunami monitoring systems in the Pacific and Indian Oceans use floating buoys to detect early tsunami waves following an earthquake. Warnings are then issued using sirens, TV and media alerts.

2 Prediction

Volcanoes

Monitoring is now allowing accurate prediction and effective evacuation (e.g. Eyjafjallajökull, Iceland, 2010).

Earthquakes

Accurate predictions are impossible due to a lack of clear warning signs. But historical records can help identify locations at probable risk (e.g. Istanbul on the North Anatolian Fault, Turkey).

3 Protection

Volcanoes

Earth embankments have been used to successfully divert lava flows (e.g. Mount Etna, Italy). In Japan, *weirs* and *small dams* control lahars (mudflows of ash and water).

Earthquakes

Earthquake-resistant engineering of infrastructure and buildings is the best way to reduce risk (Figure **1**). *Seawalls* provide tsunami protection.

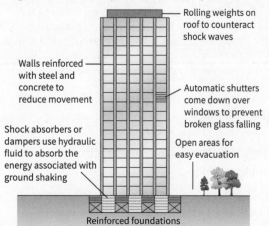

Rolling weights on roof to counteract shock waves

Walls reinforced with steel and concrete to reduce movement

Automatic shutters come down over windows to prevent broken glass falling

Shock absorbers or dampers use hydraulic fluid to absorb the energy associated with ground shaking

Open areas for easy evacuation

Reinforced foundations

Figure 1 *Features of an earthquake resistant building*

4 Planning

Volcanoes

Hazard mapping is used to identify areas to control development in at risk areas, and plan evacuation routes (e.g. Mount Merapi, Indonesia).

Earthquakes

Shakemaps (of past impacts) are used to identify lower-risk areas to locate high-value buildings (e.g hospitals and power stations).

 Six Second Summary

- The risk from tectonic hazards can be reduced by monitoring, prediction, protection and planning.
- Buildings can be constructed to be earthquake-resistant.

 Over to you

Write **three** questions about the material on this page (with answers) to test a friend.

Student Book
See pages
26–7

You need to be able to:

- construct and interpret dispersion graphs.

Dispersion graphs

Dispersion graphs (Figure **1**) are used to show how far data are dispersed or clustered (e.g. the depth of earthquake foci at different types of tectonic plate margins). With a completed dispersion graph, it is possible to apply statistical skills to find the following:

- the *range* (span of all the data)
- the *median* (middle value splitting the data into two halves)
- the *quartiles* (splitting each half into two)
- the *inter-quartile* range (measuring the central range).

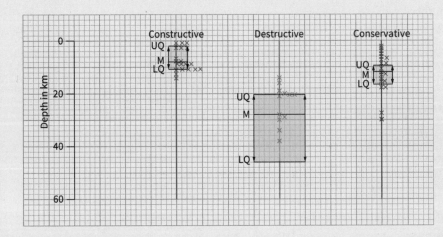

Figure 1 *The top part of a dispersion graph showing the depth (foci) of earthquakes at constructive, destructive and conservative plate boundaries*

Destructive margin (number)	Depth in km
16	46
17	10
18	12
19	46
20	22

Figure 2

Plate margin	Median	Mean	Range
Constructive	7.85	6.75	13.1
Destructive		49.13	
Conservative	10.65	10.65	26.3

Figure 3

Skills

1 Study Figure **1**.

  a Use Figure **2** to plot the earthquake depth values (for locations 16–20) on Figure **1**.

  b Add the destructive plate margin *median* value to Figure **3**.

  c If the whole graph was shown, further destructive plate margin earthquake depths plotted would be at 90 km, 108 km, 155 km and 222 km. Use this information to calculate the *range*, and so complete Figure **3**.

Analysis

1 Use the completed Figure **1** and the completed Figure **3** to compare the depth of earthquakes at the three different plate margins.

2 Suggest why the earthquakes extend far deeper at destructive margins than at constructive and conservative margins.

Evaluation

Study Figure **3**. Do you think the median or mean is the most valid measure of central tendency (average)? Give reasons for your answer.

You need to know:

- how global atmospheric circulation works to affect global weather and climate
- examples of the effects in the UK, deserts and at the Equator.

What is global atmospheric circulation?

The atmosphere is the air above our heads (Figure **1**) on which we depend for life.

Atmospheric circulation involves a number of interconnected circular air movements called cells (Figure **2**).

- Sinking cold air creates high pressure, and rising warm air creates low pressure.
- Surface winds move from high to low pressure, transferring heat and moisture from one area to another.
- These winds curve due to the Earth's rotation and change seasonally as the tilt and rotation of the Earth causes relative changes in the position of the overhead sun.

Add a WOW! factor

In the exam, use an annotated sketch or diagram if it makes your answer clearer. But remember that the marks are in your annotation, not in the quality of the drawing.

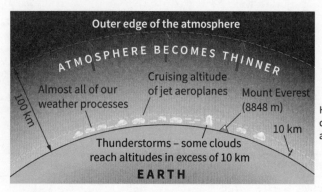

Figure 1 The atmosphere

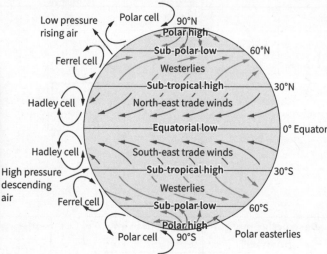

Figure 2 Global atmospheric circulation

How does global circulation affect the world's weather?

Global atmospheric circulation drives the world's weather:

- *Cloudy and wet in the UK* because 50–60 °N is close to where cold polar air from the north meets warm subtropical air from the south. These surface winds from the south-west usually bring warm and wet weather, because rising air cools and condenses forming clouds and rain.

- *Hot and dry in the desert* because most deserts are found at about 30 °N and S and south where sinking air means high pressure, little rain, hot daytime temperatures and very cold nights.
- *Hot and sweaty at the Equator* because low pressure marks where the sun is directly overhead. Hot, humid air rises, cools and condenses, causing heavy rain – hence the tropical rainforests.

Six Second Summary

- Atmospheric circulation involves interconnected cells of air.
- Atmospheric circulation drives the world's weather.

Over to you

Practise drawing an annotated sketch of atmospheric circulation to explain the global location of **both** tropical rainforests and deserts.

Where and how are tropical storms formed?

3.2

Student Book See pages 30–1

You need to know:

- what is a tropical storm
- where they form
- how global atmospheric circulation affects them.

What are tropical storms and where do they form?

Tropical storms are huge storms called **hurricanes**, **cyclones** and **typhoons** in different parts of the world (Figures **1** and **2**). Most form 5–15° north and south of the Equator, in summer and autumn, where:

- ocean temperatures are highest (above 27 °C)
- the spinning (Coriolis) effect of the Earth's rotation is very high
- intense heat and humidity make the air unstable, causing it to rise rapidly.

Big Idea

Hurricanes, cyclones and typhoons are deadly natural hazards.

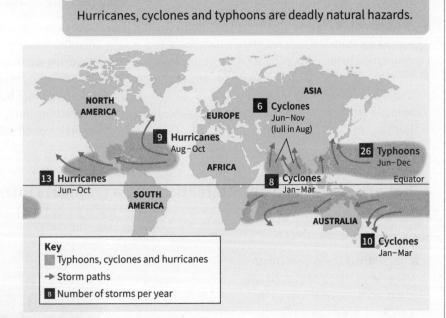

Figure 1 The distribution of tropical storms

Figure 2 Satellite image of `super-typhoon' Haiyan approaching the Philippines from the east in 2013

How does global atmospheric circulation affect tropical storms?

Look again at 3.1 Figure **2**. Global atmospheric circulation affects tropical storms in two ways:

- Unstable rising air in the equatorial regions (where the two Hadley cells converge) encourages air to rise, condense and form storm clouds.
- Winds blow from high-pressure belts (sub-tropical) to low (equatorial). These trade winds are responsible for the predominantly east–west storm paths.

Six Second Summary

- Tropical storms are huge storms, which are known as hurricanes, cyclones and typhoons in different parts of the world.
- Tropical storms form 5–15° north and south of the Equator, in summer and autumn, when ocean temperatures are highest.
- Tropical storm formation and movement is affected by global atmospheric circulation.

Over to you

Make sure you can locate and name tropical storms associated with different parts of the world.

Chapter 3 – Weather hazards 25

You need to know:

- how tropical storms form
- the structure and features of tropical storms.

Student Book
**See pages
32–3**

How do tropical storms form?

It is not certain how tropical storms are formed, but this sequence is always involved:

- Rising air draws huge quantities of evaporated water vapour up from the ocean surface which cools and condenses to form towering thunderstorm clouds.
- Condensation releases heat which powers the storm and draws up yet more water vapour.
- Multiple localised thunderstorms join (coalesce) to form a giant rotating storm.

- Coriolis forces spin the storm at over 120 km/h (75 mph) creating a vast cloud spiral.
- Prevailing winds drift the storm over the ocean surface like a spinning top, gathering strength as it picks up more and more heat energy.
- On reaching land, the energy supply (evaporated water) is cut off and the storm weakens.

What are the structure and features of a tropical storm?

Figure **1** is a cross-section through the centre of a tropical storm.

- The centre is the *eye* – a column of rapidly sinking cool air where conditions are relatively calm and there are no clouds.
- At the outer edge of the eye is the *eye wall* – the most severe conditions with very strong winds (including tornadoes) and torrential rainfall.
- Cumulonimbus clouds swirling around beyond the eye wall bring additional bands of rain.

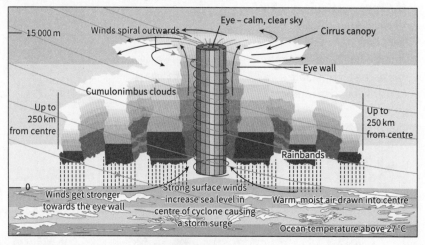

Figure 1 *The structure and features of a tropical storm*

Tropical storms are associated with extremely strong winds – often gusting in excess of 300 km/h (186 mph). But tropical storms move over the ocean slowly, which accounts for the very high rainfall totals that can exceed 400 mm in a day (causing flooding and landslides). Low-lying coastal areas can be inundated by storm surges up to 3 m high, driven onshore by the strong winds.

 Six Second Summary

- Tropical storms are triggered by the upward movement of evaporated air and moisture.
- They cover vast areas but move slowly over the ocean.
- Extremely strong winds, torrential rainfall and storm surges cause widespread destruction.

Over to you

Practise drawing a simplified, labelled sketch of Figure **1**. Important labels would include 'cloud spiral', 'eye' and 'eye wall'. The horizontal and vertical scales are also crucial.

Student Book
See pages
34–5

You need to know:

- how climate change might affect the distribution, frequency and intensity of tropical storms.

Will climate change affect tropical storms?

In the tropics, where tropical storms develop, average temperatures have increased by 0.7–0.8 °C in the last hundred years. In a warmer world, tropical storms may be affected by climate change.

Distribution

Over recent decades, sea surface temperatures have increased by 0.25–0.5 °C. In 2020, scientists concluded that climate change has changed the global distribution (frequency of occurrence) of tropical cyclones over the last 40 years, but the annual changes are small (Figure **1**). Scientists believe that greenhouse gas emissions (see 4.3) and aerosols (tiny particles and droplets such as pollutants from vehicle exhausts and burning fossil fuels) are largely responsible.

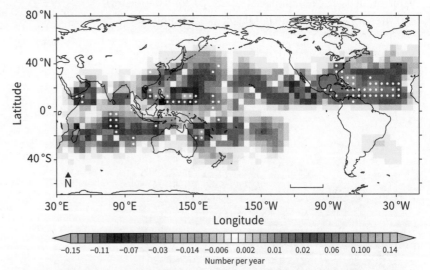

Red to yellow indicates an increase in the number of cyclones per year, while purple to green indicates a decrease.

Figure 1 *Distribution (frequency) of tropical storms, 1980–2018*

Frequency

There is little evidence that the number of storms is increasing. Increases in some regions seem to be balanced by decreases in others (Figure **1**). Indeed, the Intergovernmental Panel for Climate Change (IPCC) cautiously concludes that the frequency of tropical storms will decrease in future but there is expected to be an increase in the number of very intense storms.

Intensity

There is increasing evidence that the intensity of tropical storms has increased in recent years and that this is a result of climate change. Warmer, moist rising air provides extra energy for tropical storm formation. However, some scientists are cautious in identifying a causal relationship until more data is available.

 Six Second Summary

- There is strong scientific evidence of global warming, including increasing sea surface temperatures.
- The IPCC cautiously concludes that the frequency of tropical storms will decrease in future.
- There is increasing evidence that the intensity of tropical storms has increased in recent years.
- More data is needed to allow confident conclusions about how climate change might affect tropical storms.

 Over to you

Think carefully about how your assumptions about this topic may have changed before summarising this page in **five** bullet points.

You need to know:

- the effects of Cyclone Idai
- the responses to Cyclone Idai.

Student Book
See pages 36–7

What happened?

- Cyclone Idai is Africa's deadliest tropical cyclone on record.
- The Category 2 storm made landfall in Mozambique in March 2019 (Figure **1**).
- Strong winds, torrential rainfall and powerful storm surges brought widespread destruction in Mozambique (Figure **2**), Zimbabwe and Malawi.

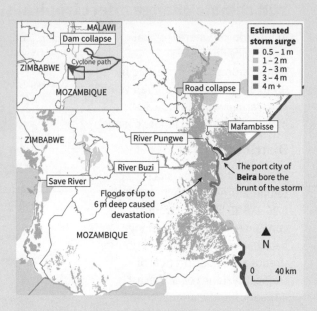

Figure 1 *The effects of Cyclone Idai*

Figure 2 *Devastation caused by strong winds and flooding in Mozambique*

Figure 3 *Effects of and responses to Cyclone Idai*

Primary effects (direct impacts of strong winds, heavy rain and storm surge)	Secondary effects (longer-term indirect impacts resulting from primary effects)
• 1300 killed – mostly drowned • Over 3 million people affected – many homeless • 90% of Beira destroyed by strong winds and storm surge • 600 houses destroyed in Zimbabwe • Agricultural fields and houses flooded in Malawi – leaving people without food and shelter	• 3000 km² flooded by overflowing rivers in Mozambique and Zimbabwe – 700 000 ha of crops destroyed, and roads and bridges washed away • Mudslides hampered rescue efforts in Zimbabwe • Dams collapsed and two HEP plants damaged in Malawi • Lack of sanitation and clean water caused 4000 cases of cholera in Beira
Immediate responses	**Long-term responses**
• Boats and helicopters used to rescue stranded people and drop food • International charities, including the Red Cross, supplied emergency provisions • The UK government provided food, water and shelter kits • The WHO provided 900 000 cholera vaccinations and anti-mosquito nets • 140 evacuation centres set up in Mozambique	• Dutch engineers helped restore water supplies in Beira • CAFOD rebuilt schools and supported local farmers • 90 000 survivors were relocated to 66 safer settlements in Mozambique • Early warning system improved

 Six Second Summary

- Category 2 Cyclone Idai is Africa's deadliest tropical cyclone on record.
- Strong winds, torrential rainfall and powerful storm surges brought widespread destruction in Mozambique, Zimbabwe and Malawi.
- The UN, international governments and charities responded with immediate aid and longer-term help.

 Over to you

Study Figure **3**. Learn **three** bullet points in **each** of four segments of the table.

Student Book
See pages 38–9

You need to know:

- how the effects of tropical storms can be reduced by monitoring, prediction, protection and planning.

Monitoring and prediction

Tropical storms cannot be prevented, but they can be monitored, and their tracks predicted.

Developments in technology, including satellite tracking and radar, provide data for computer programs to analyse, and therefore predict, the track of the storm and its likely impacts. Local authorities and emergency services issue warnings and evacuate people if necessary. In the North Atlantic there are two levels of warning:

- *Hurricane Watch* – advice issued across a wide area.
- *Hurricane Warning* – advice targeted on a specific area and expecting immediate action (e.g. evacuation to higher ground).

Figure **1** shows the predicted track of Cyclone Idai before making landfall. The prediction was fairly accurate and warnings were issued. However, poor communication systems, and limited awareness of the flood threat, contributed to the high death toll.

Big Idea

40 years of monitoring, prediction, protection and planning has decreased tropical cyclone deaths in Bangladesh 100-fold!

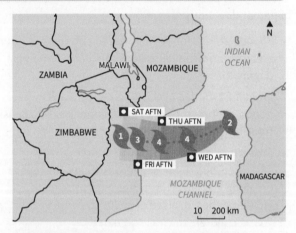

Figure 1 The predicted track of Cyclone Idai

Protection

Methods of protection usually involve anticipation in design – everything from reinforced walls, roofs and window shutters, to storm drains and sea walls. Cyclone shelters in Bangladesh are used as community centres, schools or medical centres for most of the time (Figure **2**).

Constructed of strong concrete

Bicycles used to give warnings to remote communities

Stairs to take people to the safety of the first floor

Shutters over windows

Built on stilts in case of floods

Built on raised ground

Figure 2 Cyclone shelter in Bangladesh

Planning

'Preparedness' is all about contingency planning for the inevitable. It is unrealistic to stop tens of millions of people living in coastal areas at risk from tropical storms, but they can be made safer. Planning mostly means education and media campaigns raising individual and community awareness in order that people understand the dangers, and are able to respond.

Six Second Summary

- Tropical storms can be monitored, their tracks predicted, and warnings issued.
- Buildings can be protected and cyclone shelters built.
- Contingency planning raises awareness allowing people to respond.

Over to you

Summarise what can, and what cannot be done in terms of monitoring, predicting and protecting from tropical cyclones.

Student Book
**See pages
40–1**

You need to know:

- how the UK is affected by weather hazards.

What are the UK's weather hazards?

Despite its moderate climate, the UK does experience weather hazards – occasional **extreme weather** events linked with its 'roundabout' location (Figure **1**) at the meeting point of different types of weather from different directions:

- *Thunderstorms* follow hot weather, bringing lightning and torrential rainfall linked with 'flash' flooding (Figure **2**).

- *Prolonged rainfall* over a long period leads to river floods, such as the very wet winter of 2019/20 causing **flooding** across northern England and the Midlands.

- *Drought and extreme heat* cause rivers to dry up and reservoirs to run dangerously low. The record-breaking 2003 heatwave over much of Europe, including the UK, killed over 20 000 people – mostly young children, the frail and elderly.

- *Heavy snow and extreme cold* are less common nowadays, but can cause great hardship to people in the north of the UK.

- *Strong winds*, such as in February 2014, cause disruption to power supplies, damage from fallen trees and coastal battering from large waves.

Figure 2 *Boscastle, Cornwall, flash flood, August 2004*

Big Idea

Weather describes the day-to-day conditions of the atmosphere – temperature, rain and so on. Climate describes the average weather over a 30-year period.

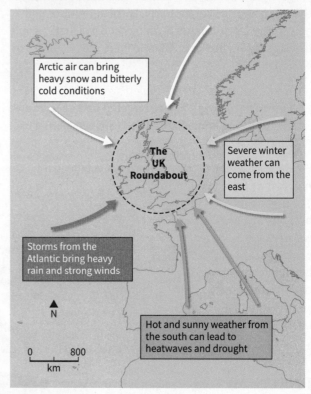

Arctic air can bring heavy snow and bitterly cold conditions

The UK Roundabout

Severe winter weather can come from the east

Storms from the Atlantic bring heavy rain and strong winds

Hot and sunny weather from the south can lead to heatwaves and drought

N

0   800
    km

Figure 1 *The UK's weather roundabout*

Six Second Summary

- Weather describes day-to-day atmospheric conditions; climate is average weather over a 30-year period.
- Weather hazards are extreme weather events.
- The UK climate is moderate overall, but has changeable and occasionally extreme weather.

Over to you

- Make a mnemonic (see page 9) of the **five** weather hazards experienced in the UK. (Remember, the most memorable mnemonics relate to the topic.)
- List **three** impacts of a) strong winds and b) high temperatures in the UK.

Student Book
See pages 42–3

You need to know:

- if the UK's weather is becoming more extreme.

Evidence that UK weather is becoming more extreme

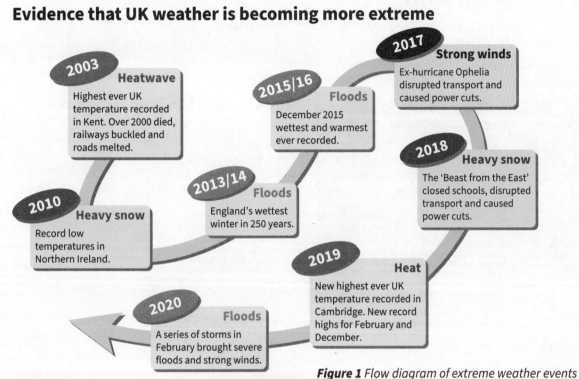

2003 Heatwave
Highest ever UK temperature recorded in Kent. Over 2000 died, railways buckled and roads melted.

2015/16 Floods
December 2015 wettest and warmest ever recorded.

2017 Strong winds
Ex-hurricane Ophelia disrupted transport and caused power cuts.

2013/14 Floods
England's wettest winter in 250 years.

2018 Heavy snow
The 'Beast from the East' closed schools, disrupted transport and caused power cuts.

2010 Heavy snow
Record low temperatures in Northern Ireland.

2019 Heat
New highest ever UK temperature recorded in Cambridge. New record highs for February and December.

2020 Floods
A series of storms in February brought severe floods and strong winds.

Figure 1 Flow diagram of extreme weather events

Figure 2 The 'Beast from the East' brings heavy snow to Crickhowell, Wales, 2018

Six Second Summary

- The UK has experienced an increase in the number of extreme weather events in recent years.
- Scientists believe that the global increase in extreme weather events may be linked to climate change and increasing temperatures.
- The jet stream driving UK weather systems may be getting 'stuck' due to climate change.

Over to you

- Describe **three** points about each of **two** examples of extreme weather in the UK.
- TV, social media and newspapers may report individual weather events as evidence of climate change. Why might this be misleading?

Why might extreme weather events be on the increase?

Recent extreme weather events have also occurred elsewhere in the world – such as the bush fires and floods in Australia in 2020. Whilst no single weather event can be blamed on climate change, trends over many years could be linked to global warming, which:

- lead to more energy in the atmosphere, which could in turn lead to more intense storms
- possibly affect atmospheric circulation, bringing floods to normally dry areas and heatwaves to normally cooler areas.

Could our weather patterns be getting stuck?

UK weather systems, driven by winds from the *jet stream*, usually cross from west to east. The jet stream moves north and south but can 'stick' in one position resulting in prolonged periods of the same type of weather, such as heatwaves.

These 'stuck' periods have become more frequent and could be due to climate change.

EXAMPLE

Student Book
**See pages
44–5**

You need to know:

- the causes, impacts and responses to flooding on the Somerset Levels in 2014.

Where are the Somerset Levels?

The Somerset Levels are an extensive area of low-lying land in south-west England.
They have a long history of flooding (Figures **1** and **2**).

Figure 1 *The village of Burrowbridge almost cut off by the floods*

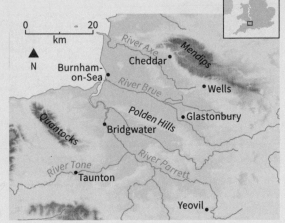

Figure 2 *Location of the Somerset Levels*

The 2014 floods

Figure 3 *Causes, impacts and responses of the Somerset Levels floods, 2014*

Causes	Immediate responses
• A sequence of south-westerly depressions brought record rainfall in January and February. • High tides and storm surges swept water up the rivers from the Bristol Channel preventing normal flow. • Rivers had not been dredged for 20 years.	• Huge media interest was generated. • Cut-off villagers used boats for transport. • Community groups and volunteers gave invaluable support.
Social, economic and environmental impacts	**Longer-term responses**
• Over 600 houses flooded and 16 farms evacuated. • Villages cut off – disrupting work, schools and shopping. • Total cost of flood damage and responses approached £147.5 million. • 14 000 ha of farmland flooded and 1000 livestock evacuated. • Power supply, roads and railway cut off. • Floodwaters contaminated with sewage, oil and chemicals. • Massive debris clearance required.	• Somerset Rivers Authority was launched in 2015 to implement protection and resilience strategies identified in Somerset's £100 million Flood Action Plan. • 8 km of Rivers Tone and Parrett dredged. • Road levels raised in lowest dips. • Old diesel pumping stations replaced with electric pumps. • River banks repaired and raised. • Tidal barrier at Bridgwater planned for completion in 2024.

Six Second Summary

- Exceptional flooding caused by record rainfall, high tides and storm surges.
- Severe impacts included villages isolated and farmland flooded.
- Somerset's £100 million Flood Action Plan will reduce future risk.

 Over to you

Learn **three** causes and **two** of each of the social, economic and environmental impacts of the 2014 floods.

Student Book
See pages
46–7

You need to be able to:

- interpret a 1:25 000 map and aerial photograph.

SKILLS FOCUS

Practising map and photograph interpretation

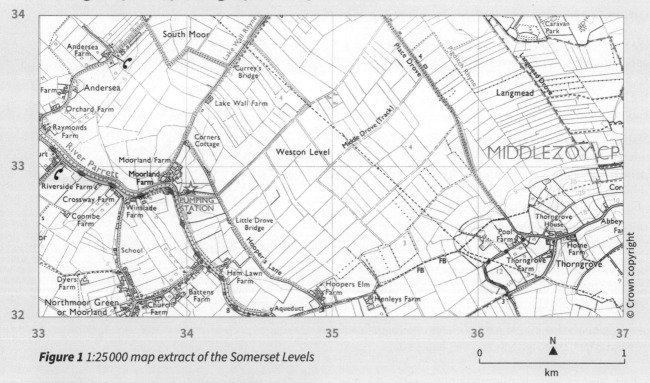

Figure 1 *1:25 000 map extract of the Somerset Levels*

© Crown copyright

Figure 2 *Flooding in Moorland, Somerset, 2014*

Skills

1 Use the map (Figure **1**) to answer the following questions (the key for OS maps can be found on page 208).

   (a) What is the evidence from the map that this area is very flat and low-lying?

   (b) Why does the area have so many drainage ditches?

   (c) What is the evidence that most of this area is farmland?

   (d) Name the feature at GR 341328.

2 Study the aerial photograph (Figure **2**). The photograph shows part of the flooded village of Moorland (named as Northmoor Green or Moorland on the map extract at GR 337321). The church is shown by the cross at the road junction in the centre of the village.

   (a) In what direction is the photograph looking?

   (b) What is the name of the farm at the top left of the photograph?

   (c) What has been done to stop this property from flooding?

   (d) Describe the extent of flooding in the photograph.

Analysis

Suggest the likely social, economic and environmental impacts of flooding on the residents of Moorland.

Student Book
See pages
48–9

You need to know:

- the evidence for climate change from the beginning of the Quaternary period to the present day.

What is the evidence for climate change?

We know that climates have changed throughout geological time. For example, scientists using fossil records have found fluctuations in temperature for the last 5.5 million years, and, interestingly, a gradual cooling trend!

Marked fluctuations throughout the last 2.6 million years (the **Quaternary period**) explain *glacial periods* and warmer *inter-glacial periods*. Oxygen trapped in layers of ocean sediments, and water molecules in Antarctic snow, can be analysed to calculate temperature because reliable thermometer records only go back around 100 years.

But these direct measurements indicate a clear warming trend, with most of the increase since the mid-1970s (Figure **1**).

This is 'global warming', which has already had significant effects on global ecosystems and on people's lives.

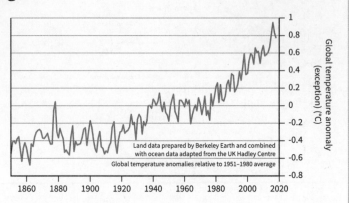

Land data prepared by Berkeley Earth and combined with ocean data adapted from the UK Hadley Centre
Global temperature anomalies relative to 1951–1980 average

Figure 1 *Average global temperature, 1850–2018*

Global effects of climate change

Figure 2 shows the summer minimum of arctic sea ice in 2020.
The median extent between 1981 and 2020 is shown by the orange line.

Shrinking glaciers and melting ice
- Some glaciers may disappear by 2035.
- Arctic sea ice has thinned by 65% since 1975.

Recent evidence for climate change?

Rising sea level
- Global mean sea level is rising and accelerating due to glacier and ice cap melting adding fresh water and thermal expansion – warm ocean waters expand in volume.
- Low-lying islands such as the Maldives and Tuvala are vulnerable.

Seasonal changes
- Tree flowering and bird migration is advancing.
- Bird nesting is earlier than in the 1970s.

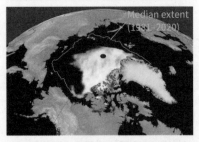

Median extent (1981–2020)

Figure 2 *Arctic sea ice extent, September 2020*

 Six Second Summary

- Global temperatures have been cooling gradually over 5.5 million years, but increasing in recent decades.
- Melting glaciers, rising sea levels, changing seasons and direct temperature measures give evidence of climate change.
- Climate change is having a significant effect on global ecosystems and on people's lives.

Over to you

Study Figure **1**.

- Describe the trend of the average temperature throughout the period of the graph.
- Comment on **how far** this is strong evidence for global warming.
  (Don't forget you'd need to justify your answer with evidence.)

Student Book
See pages
50–1

You need to know:

- the natural causes of climate change – orbital changes, solar activity and volcanic activity.

Natural causes of climate change

1

Orbital changes – the Milankovitch cycles

Three distinct cycles increase (cooling) or decrease (warming) the distance from the Sun:

- *Eccentricity* – every 100 000 years or so the orbit changes from almost circular, to mildly elliptical (oval) and back again.
- *Axial tilt* – every 41 000 years the tilt of the Earth's axis moves back and forth between 21.5° and 24.5°.
- *Precession (or wobble like a spinning top)* – over a period of around 26 000 years the axis wobbles from one extreme to the other.

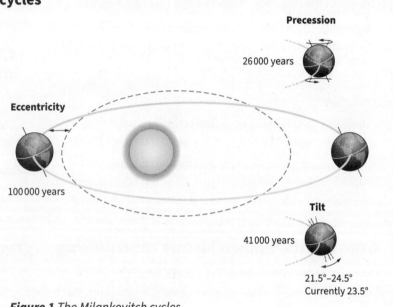

Figure 1 *The Milankovitch cycles*

2

Solar activity

The surface of the Sun has dark patches called *sunspots* which mark short-term regions of reduced surface temperature. They are usually accompanied by explosive, high-energy solar flares increasing heat output.

Over a period of around 11 years, sunspots increase from a minimum to a maximum, and back again.

3

Volcanic activity

Volcanic ash can block out the Sun, reducing temperatures on the Earth. This is a short-term impact.

Sulphur dioxide is also blasted out which converts to droplets of sulphuric acid, and acts like mirrors to reflect solar radiation back into space. This longer-term impact (over many years) also reduces temperatures.

 Six Second Summary

- Milankovitch cycles (orbital changes) constantly change the Earth's distance from the Sun.
- Solar activity varies with the number of sunspots and high-energy solar flares.
- Volcanic activity produces ash and sulphuric acid droplets which reduce temperature.

 Over to you

'**O**ver **c**enturies **s**olar **a**ctivity **v**aries **a**lways' is a mnemonic of the **three** natural ways in which climate can change.

- **Either** make your own mnemonic(s), mind-map (spider diagram), or topic poster to help learn the details of this 'wordy' topic **Or** use the *Six Second Summary* to make your own flash cards – but adding examples from the Student Book.
- Practise summarising **each** reason why climate can change naturally over time.

Student Book
See pages
52–3

You need to know:

- what the greenhouse effect is
- how human activities can enhance it.

What is the greenhouse effect?

The greenhouse effect keeps the Earth naturally warm enough to support life (Figure **1**). It works like a glass greenhouse by:

- greenhouse gases (e.g. water vapour, carbon dioxide (CO_2), methane (CH_4) and nitrous oxide) trapping heat that would otherwise escape into space
- allowing short-wave radiation (light) from the Sun through to the Earth
- trapping some of the longer wavelength radiation (heat) that would otherwise be radiated back into the atmosphere.

In recent years the amounts of greenhouse gases in the atmosphere have increased (Figure **2**). Scientists believe that this *enhanced greenhouse effect* is due to human activities.

Figure 1 *How the greenhouse effect works*

What are the human factors contributing to greenhouse gases?

There are multiple human sources of greenhouse gases including sewage treatment, emissions from landfill sites, coal mines and natural gas pipelines. But three key sources dominate:

Use of fossil fuels
- Most CO_2 comes from burning **fossil fuels** in industry and power stations. Transport and farming also contribute.
- Since 1960, CO_2 emissions from fossil fuels have increased rapidly (Figure **2**).

Agriculture
- Agriculture accounts for about 30% of global greenhouse gas emissions.
- Livestock (e.g. cattle) burp extraordinary volumes of CH_4.
- Paddy rice cultivation also releases CH_4.
- 75% of all nitrous oxide comes from manure and nitrogen-rich fertilisers.

Key human factors contributing to greenhouse gases

Deforestation
- **Deforestation** involves clearing trees, usually for farming, settlement or industry.
- 70% of deforestation is to create grazing land for commercial livestock.
- Deforestation in tropical regions (e.g. rainforests) accounts for 20% of global greenhouse gas emissions.
- Through photosynthesis, trees naturally convert atmospheric CO_2 into (stored) carbon. But deforestation releases the CO_2 back.

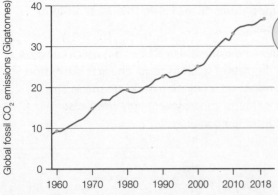

Figure 2 *Increase in CO_2 obtained from direct readings at the Mauna Loa Observatory, Hawaii*

 Six Second Summary

- The natural greenhouse effect keeps the Earth warm enough to support life.
- In recent years greenhouse gases produced by human activities have increased.
- This enhanced greenhouse effect is changing climates, weather patterns and sea levels.

Over to you

- The trend of Figure **2** is identical to that of average global temperatures. So does this support the suggestion that human activities may be contributing to global warming? You must be able to explain your answer.

Student Book
See pages
54–5

You need to know:

- how the causes of climate change can be managed (mitigated).

How can climate change be managed?

Alternative energy sources

The burning of **fossil fuels** accounts for most CO_2 emissions. Alternative sources of energy such as **hydroelectric power (HEP), nuclear power, solar, wind** and *tides* represent **sustainable**, low carbon alternatives.

The UK aims to produce 65 per cent of its energy from **renewable energy sources** by 2030.

Figure 1 *Hornsea One – the world's largest wind farm, 90 km off the east coast of England*

Carbon capture

Carbon *capture and storage (CCS)* uses technology to capture CO_2 that is produced by burning fossil fuels in electricity generation and industrial processes. Once captured, the CO_2 is compressed, piped and injected underground for long-term storage in suitable geological reservoirs, such as depleted oil and gas wells.

Planting trees

Trees act as carbon sinks, removing CO_2 from the atmosphere by the process of *photosynthesis*. They also release moisture, producing more cloud and so reducing incoming solar radiation.

Afforestation (planting trees in new areas) and *reforestation* have huge potential as a land-based carbon sink.

International agreements

Figure **2** stresses why climate change is a global issue requiring global solutions. Governments are negotiating towards a more sustainable future. For example, the Paris Agreement (implemented in 2016) was the first legally binding global climate deal. It aims to limit global temperature increases to 1.5 °C above pre-industrial levels.

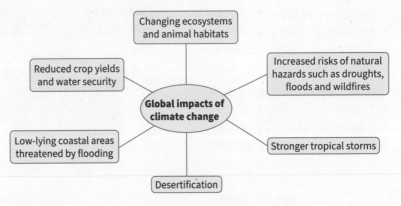

Changing ecosystems and animal habitats

Reduced crop yields and water security

Increased risks of natural hazards such as droughts, floods and wildfires

Global impacts of climate change

Low-lying coastal areas threatened by flooding

Stronger tropical storms

Desertification

Figure 2 *Global impacts of climate change*

Six Second Summary

- Alternative energy sources represent sustainable alternatives to fossil fuels.
- Tree planting is established; widespread CCS is not yet economically viable.
- International agreements seek global solutions to issues of climate change.

Over to you

- Learn two points about **each** way in which climate change could be managed.
- How might you argue the importance of international agreements in helping to solve the problems associated with climate change? Think of **three** things to say.

Student Book
See pages
56–7

You need to know:

- how people can adapt to climate change.

How can we adapt to climate change?

Change in agricultural systems

Scientists believe that climate change will have a huge impact on agricultural systems across the world, particularly in low latitudes. In order to adapt, farmers will need to:

- cope with extreme weather such as floods, heatwaves and drought
- manage water supply by storing water, use efficient irrigation systems, grow drought-resistant crops, and adapt to seasonal changes
- plant trees to shade seedlings
- change crops and livestock to suit the new climatic conditions.

Managing water supply

Climate change is already affecting patterns of rainfall. This is impacting on levels of water supply which may be managed by:

- constructing reservoirs to store water
- transferring water from areas of surplus to areas of deficit
- using grey water (clean waste-water) for irrigation
- constructing desalination plants to convert seawater to freshwater
- improving water conservation to reduce waste.

Reducing risk from sea-level change

Having already risen 21 cm since 1900, average sea level rises of up to 1.1 m by 2100 are possible. This will:

- threaten important agricultural land in countries such as Bangladesh, India and Vietnam
- increase rates of coastal erosion and damage from storm surges
- contaminate freshwater supplies with saltwater.

The low-lying Indian Ocean islands of the Maldives are already tackling this change by adopting practical management strategies (Figure **1**).

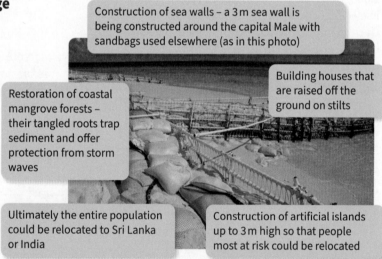

Construction of sea walls – a 3 m sea wall is being constructed around the capital Male with sandbags used elsewhere (as in this photo)

Restoration of coastal mangrove forests – their tangled roots trap sediment and offer protection from storm waves

Building houses that are raised off the ground on stilts

Ultimately the entire population could be relocated to Sri Lanka or India

Construction of artificial islands up to 3 m high so that people most at risk could be relocated

Figure 1 *How can the Maldives manage sea-level rise?*

Six Second Summary

- Climate change will have a huge impact on agricultural systems, particularly in low latitudes.
- Farmers will have to adapt by changing crops, livestock and techniques, and manage water supplies.
- Sea-level rise will require management of coastal areas.

Over to you

- Learn **three** threats to farmers posed by climate change.
- Which of the sea-level rise management strategies adopted in the Maldives are immediately relevant, and which are longer-term?

You need to be able to:

- construct and interpret line graphs.

Line graphs

Is Arctic sea ice decreasing?

The second smallest ever concentration (extent) of Arctic sea ice was recorded in September 2020 (see page 34). But is this following any trend and/or valid evidence of climate change? Graphing annual data of the minimum extent of Arctic sea ice may help answer these questions (Figure **1**).

Add a *WOW!* factor

Manipulate the data when describing, explaining and analysing graphs (e.g. go further than simply stating highs, lows, trends and anomalies – quote percentage or proportional rises, falls and so on).

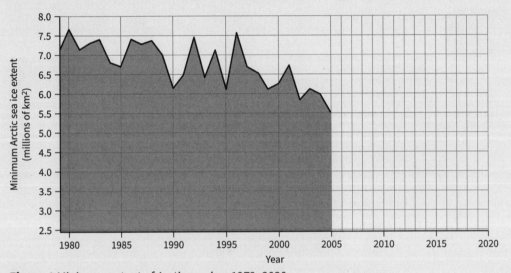

Figure 1 *Minimum extent of Arctic sea ice, 1979–2020*

Figure 2 *Minimum Arctic sea ice extent, 2006–2020*

Year	Minimum Arctic sea ice extent (millions km²)
2006	5.9
2007	4.3
2008	4.7
2009	5.3
2010	4.9
2011	4.6
2012	3.6
2013	5.2
2014	5.2
2015	4.6
2016	4.5
2017	4.8
2018	4.8
2019	4.4
2020	3.9

Skills

1 Study Figure **1**.

    a Use Figure **2** to complete the line graph on Figure **1**. (Use a pencil to plot each value with a cross. Join the crosses to complete your graph.)

    b Trends may be easier to spot if you 'lift' the line graph 'off the page' by shading underneath the plotted points. Use a (coloured) pencil to complete the shading on Figure **1**.

    c Whether straight lines or smooth curves, *trend lines* may be drawn approximately through the middle of the points, with roughly the same number of points on either side. Use a different (contrasting) coloured pencil to draw a smooth curving trend line on Figure **1**.

    d Describe the pattern of minimum Arctic sea ice extent from 1979 to 2020.

Analysis

Analyse the trend of Arctic sea ice shrinkage between 1979 and 2020.

Evaluation

Evaluate the validity of using minimum Arctic sea ice as an indicator of climate change. Does the completed graph and trend line (Figure **1**) provide sufficient evidence to show, or even prove, climate change?

Section B
The living world

Your exam

Section B The living world is a part of Paper 1: Living with the physical environment.

Paper 1 is a one-and-a-half hour written exam and makes up 35 per cent of your GCSE. The whole paper carries 88 marks (including 3 marks for SPaG) – questions on Section B will carry 25 marks.

You have to study ecosystems and tropical rainforests in Section B. You will then study *either* hot deserts *or* cold environments – in your final exam you will have to answer questions on the three topics you have studied.

Tick these boxes to build a record of your revision

Your revision checklist

Spec key idea	Theme	1	2	3
5 Ecosystems				
Ecosystems exist at a range of scales and involve the interaction between living and non-living components	5.1 A small-scale UK ecosystem – freshwater pond			
	5.2 How does change affect ecosystems?			
	5.3 Introducing global ecosystems			
6 Tropical rainforests				
Tropical rainforests have distinctive environmental characteristics	6.1 Physical characteristics of rainforests			
	6.2 Adaption and biodiversity in rainforests			
Deforestation has economic and environmental impacts	6.3 Causes of deforestation in Malaysia			
	6.4 Impacts of deforestation in Malaysia			
Tropical rainforests need to be managed to be sustainable	6.5 The value of tropical rainforests			
	6.6 Sustainable management of tropical rainforests			
Geographical skills	6.7 Skills Focus: Graphs			
7 Hot deserts				
Hot desert ecosystems have distinctive environmental characteristics	7.1 Physical characteristics of hot deserts			
	7.2 Adapting to hot desert environments			
Geographical skills	7.2 Skills Focus: Climate graphs			
Development of hot desert environments creates opportunities and challenges	7.3 Opportunities for development in hot deserts			
	7.4 Challenges of developing hot deserts			
Areas on the fringe of hot deserts are at risk of desertification	7.5 Causes of desertification in hot deserts			
	7.6 Reducing the risk of desertification in hot deserts			
8 Cold environments				
Cold environments (polar and tundra) have distinctive characteristics	8.1 Physical characteristics of cold environments			
	8.2 Adapting to cold environments			
Geographical skills	8.2 Skills Focus: Climate graphs			
Development of cold environments creates opportunities and challenges	8.3 Opportunities for development in cold environments			
	8.4 Challenges of development in cold environments			
Cold environments are at risk from economic development	8.5 Value of cold environments as wilderness areas			
	8.6 Managing cold environments			

Student Book
**See pages
60–1**

You need to know:

- what is meant by an ecosystem
- the components of a small-scale ecosystem
- details of a small-scale ecosystem in the UK.

What is an ecosystem?

An **ecosystem** is a complex natural system made up of plants, animals and the environment. They occur at different scales from small (e.g. pond, woodland) to global (e.g. tropical rainforest). **Global ecosystems** are called *biomes* – ecosystems at a bigger scale.

Within an ecosystem there are often complex interrelationships (links) between the **biotic** (living) features (e.g. plants, animals and fish) and the **abiotic** (non-living) environmental factors (e.g. climate, soil and light).

- **Producers** (e.g. plants) convert energy from the Sun by *photosynthesis* into carbohydrates (e.g. sugars) for growth.
- **Consumers** get their energy from eating producers, creating direct links within ecosystems (**food chains**) and more complex **food webs**.
- Finally, dead plant and animal material is broken down by **decomposers** (e.g. bacteria and fungi) to add to nutrients within the soil.
- These nutrients are then used by plants in a process called **nutrient cycling**.

A freshwater pond ecosystem

Freshwater ponds provide a variety of habitats (homes) for plants, insects and animals (Figure 1). You need to learn an example of a producer and a consumer, and also an example of a food chain and of a food web.

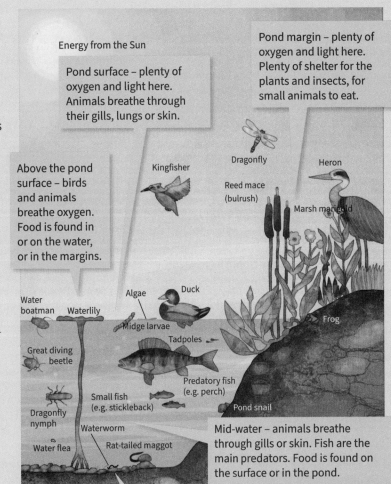

Energy from the Sun

Pond surface – plenty of oxygen and light here. Animals breathe through their gills, lungs or skin.

Pond margin – plenty of oxygen and light here. Plenty of shelter for the plants and insects, for small animals to eat.

Above the pond surface – birds and animals breathe oxygen. Food is found in or on the water, or in the margins.

Kingfisher

Dragonfly

Heron

Reed mace (bulrush)

Marsh marigold

Water boatman   Waterlily

Algae   Duck

Great diving beetle

Midge larvae

Tadpoles

Frog

Dragonfly nymph

Small fish (e.g. stickleback)

Predatory fish (e.g. perch)

Pond snail

Waterworm

Water flea   Rat-tailed maggot

Mid-water – animals breathe through gills or skin. Fish are the main predators. Food is found on the surface or in the pond.

Pond bottom – little oxygen or light. Plenty of shelter (rotting plants and stones) and food. Decomposers and scavengers live here.

Figure 1 *A freshwater pond ecosystem*

Six Second Summary

- An ecosystem is a complex system made up of plants, animals and the environment.
- Ecosystems occur at different scales from small (e.g. pond) to global (biomes).
- There are complex interrelationships between *biotic* (living) and *abiotic* (non living) components of ecosystems.
- Within each ecosystem are producers, consumers, a food chain, a food web, decomposers and a nutrient cycle.

Over to you

List the terms that appear **bold** on this page.

Define each term and illustrate it, where relevant, using examples from a freshwater pond ecosystem.

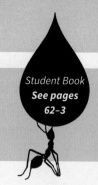
Student Book
See pages
62–3

You need to know:

- how changes to the ecosystem affect the balance between its components.

What are the impacts of change on an ecosystem?

Ecosystems can take thousands of years to develop a sustainable balance. Yet global-scale changes (e.g. climate change) and local-scale changes (e.g. hedgerow removal) can upset this balance very quickly.

Natural changes

Slow natural changes have few harmful effects, but rapid changes have serious impacts. For example, extreme weather events like droughts can be devastating to freshwater ponds - killing fish, plants and the birds that are dependent upon them.

Changes due to human activities

Human activities can have many impacts on ecosystems (Figure 1). However, many farmers are trying to keep ecosystems in balance by using less fertiliser. Some have planted hedgerows and grass margins to protect wildlife such as bees, insects and wildflowers.

Figure 1 The impact of human changes on small-scale ecosystems

Agricultural fertilisers can lead to eutrophication: nitrates increase growth of algae, which will deplete oxygen and fish may die.

Woods cut down, destroying habitats for birds and affecting the nutrient cycle.

Ponds may be drained to use for farming. Aquatic plants will die, as will fish and other pond life.

Hedgerows removed to increase size of fields. Habitats will be destroyed, altering the plant/animal balance.

Managing Stow Bedon, Breckland, Norfolk

Surveys of these ancient Breckland ponds showed a limited diversity of wetland plants and animals due to excessive growth of willow scrub out-competing other species, such as water vole, great crested newt and tabular water-dropwort.

Since 2018 the removal of willow scrub has opened up the pond margins, encouraging moss to establish. Pond mud snails have become more abundant, increasing species diversity, and improving the balance between components of the ecosystem (Figure 2). Plans to return grazing animals to the area will ensure that the ponds remain clear of marginal vegetation and stay in balance.

Figure 2 Water voles are under threat because of habitat loss

 Six Second Summary

- Changes to one component can seriously affect the balance of an ecosystem.
- Changes to ecosystems can take place at all scales from local to global.
- Changes to ecosystems can be due to natural causes or human activities.

Over to you

- In **one** sentence state a) a short-term change and b) a long-term change to ecosystems.
- Practise writing a brief account of Stow Bedon's pond restoration to illustrate positive changes.

Student Book
**See pages
64–5**

You need to know:

- the distribution and characteristics of large-scale global ecosystems (known as biomes).

The distribution and characteristics of large-scale global ecosystems (biomes)

Biomes are mainly defined by one dominant type of vegetation. They form broad belts usually parallel to lines of latitude (Figure **1**). This is because the climate and characteristics of ecosystems are determined by global atmospheric circulation (see 3.1).

Variations occur in these west-to-east belts of vegetation because of factors such as ocean currents, winds, altitude and the distribution of land and sea. These create small changes in temperature and moisture which, in turn, affect the ecosystems.

Tundra – mainly located between the Arctic Circle to about 60°–70° North.

Cold, windy and dry conditions support low-growing plants easily damaged by developments, e.g. oil exploitation and tourism.

Deciduous and coniferous forests – located roughly 50°–60° North. Deciduous trees shed their leaves in winter, but cone-bearing coniferous evergreens are better suited to colder climates and so dominate further north.

Temperate grassland – located 30°–40° north and south of the Equator, and always inland.

Warm, dry summers and cold winters support grasses for grazing animals.

Key
- Tundra
- Coniferous forest
- Temperate deciduous forest
- Temperate grassland
- Mediterranean
- Desert
- Tropical rainforest
- Tropical grassland (savanna)
- Other biomes (e.g. polar, ice, mountains)

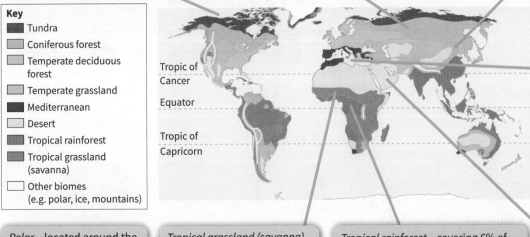

Tropic of Cancer

Equator

Tropic of Capricorn

Mediterranean – (also isolated locations south of the Equator).

Hot, sunny, dry summers and mild winters support olive groves and citrus fruits.

Polar – located around the North and South Poles. Low temperatures (below −50 °C) and dry conditions prohibit most plant and animal life.

Tropical grassland (savanna) – located between 15°–30° north and south of the Equator.

Distinct wet and dry seasons support large herds of grazing animals and their predators.

Tropical rainforest – covering 6% of the Earth's land surface mainly close to the Equator.

High temperatures and heavy rainfall create ideal conditions for vegetation.

More than half of all plant and animal species, and a quarter of all medicines originate here.

Desert – covering one-fifth of the Earth's land surface.

High daytime temperatures, low night-time temperatures and very low rainfall restrict plants and animals to highly specialised species.

Figure 1 *Characteristics of global ecosystems (biomes)*

Six Second Summary

- Large-scale global ecosystems are known as biomes.
- Biomes are defined mainly by the dominant type of vegetation growing there.
- Biomes are distributed in broad belts across the world from west to east, parallel to lines of latitude.
- The climate and characteristics of biomes are determined by global atmospheric circulation.

Over to you

Make sure that you can explain:
a) why most biomes form broad latitudinal belts across the world
b) why minor variations can occur within them.

Student Book **See pages** 66–7

You need to know:

- where tropical rainforests are found
- their characteristic climates, soils and nutrient cycling.

Where are tropical rainforests found?

Tropical rainforests are located mostly a few degrees either side of the Equator between the Tropics of Cancer and Capricorn (see 5.3, Figure **1**).

What is the climate like?

Tropical rainforests thrive in *equatorial* climates where:

- temperatures are high throughout the year (averaging 27 °C) because the Sun is mostly overhead
- rainfall is high (over 2000 mm a year) because global atmospheric circulation causes an area of low pressure to form at the Equator. The rising air creates clouds and triggers heavy rain.
- variation in rainfall is due to months where the equatorial low pressure area is directly overhead, causing a distinct wet season of intense rainfall.

What are rainforest soils like?

Tropical rainforest soils (*latosols*) are typically old, deep, iron-rich and so red in colour (Figure **1**). Despite supporting lush vegetation, they are surprisingly infertile because they are prone to rapid *leaching* where minerals are lost in solution, and **nutrient cycling** is so rapid (Figure **2**).

Figure 1 *Thick, iron-rich soils beneath tropical rainforest, South America*

Nutrient cycling

Figure **2** shows the three major nutrient stores (biomass, soil and litter) and the transfer processes responsible for nutrient cycling. The size of the circles and arrows indicates their relative significance. Note how:

- the majority of nutrients are stored in the biomass – the lush vegetation
- few nutrients are stored as litter, due to rapid decomposition by fungi and bacteria
- few nutrients are stored in the soil, due to the rapid uptake by plants and significant leaching.

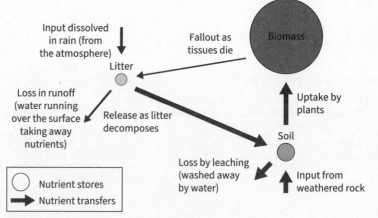

Figure 2 *Nutrient cycling in a tropical rainforest*

 Six Second Summary

- Tropical rainforests are found in a broad band near the Equator.
- The equatorial climate has high temperatures and high rainfall all year.
- Soils (called latosols) in tropical rainforests are surprisingly infertile – they are leached by heavy rainfall.

Over to you

Draw a spider diagram with the phrase 'physical characteristics of rainforests' at the centre. Add legs to show 'climate', 'soils' and 'nutrient cycling'. Develop detail out from each of these.

Student Book
See pages
68–9

You need to know:

- about plant and animal adaptations in tropical rainforests
- about biodiversity in tropical rainforests.

Plants and animals in tropical rainforests

Tropical rainforests cover only 7 per cent of the Earth's surface yet support more than 50 per cent of all living organisms – a remarkable **biodiversity** of plants, micro-organisms, fungi, insects, birds and animals.

How have plants adapted to living in the rainforest?

Through *stratification*, tropical rainforest vegetation has adapted to cope with the challenges associated with competition for sunlight, and shortages of available nutrients (Figure **1**).

Lower tree canopy (10–20 m) Shaded, less substantial trees waiting to take advantage of the next available light space. Interlocking spindly branches and climbing woody creepers (*lianas*) form green corridors along which lightweight animals can travel.

Top canopy (35–50 m) Hardy exposed *emergent* trees with straight branchless trunks receive the most light.

Middle canopy (20–35 m) The most productive layer as each mushroom-shaped crown has an enormous photosynthetic surface of dark, leathery leaves. *Drip tips* help them shed water quickly and efficiently.

Figure 1 Stratification, vegetation and soil adaptations in a tropical rainforest

Shrub and ground layer (0–10 m) Limited to ferns, woody plants and younger trees because of lack of light. Bacteria and fungi rapidly rot the fallen leaves, dead plants and animals. Thick *buttress* roots help to spread the weight of the towering trees above.

Soils (*latosols*) cycle nutrients rapidly to support new growth. But if the rainforest is cleared they become exposed to excessive leaching and are quickly exhausted of stored nutrients.

How have animals adapted to living in the rainforest?

Animal survival adaptations include:

- *camouflage*, enabling creatures to blend into the natural environment, concealing themselves from potential prey (e.g. green-eyed frogs looking like tree bark)
- *mimicry*, by pretending to be something else (e.g. grasshoppers looking and behaving like stinging wasps)
- *limiting diets* (e.g. toucans only consuming fruits that other birds and animals cannot access)
- *habitat adaptation* (e.g. sloths, with long arms and claws, living in treetops).

Biodiversity under threat?

Despite huge biodiversity, tropical rainforests are very fragile and highly interdependent ecosystems. Threats include:

- *deforestation* – replacing rainforest trees with pasture, commercial plantations or settlements
- *water pollution* – gold and other mining, which poisons rivers, reducing aquatic life and killing wildlife
- *climate change* – deforestation reducing evapotranspiration causing *climatic drying*.

Six Second Summary

- Tropical rainforest vegetation is stratified (layered) in competition for sunlight.
- Tropical rainforest animals live successfully by adapting (e.g. camouflage and mimicry).
- Tropical rainforest biodiversity is huge, but vulnerable to deforestation, water pollution and climate change.

Over to you

Write **four** questions about the key themes of this page to test a friend. Make sure you are able to write the answers as well!

Student Book
See pages
70–1

You need to know:

- the causes of deforestation in Malaysia.

CASE STUDY

Deforestation in Malaysia

In 2019, the Tropics lost nearly 12 million hectares of tree cover, one-third of which was primary rainforest – untouched, and in its original condition. Malaysia (Figure **1**) currently has one of the highest rates of **deforestation** in the world – clearing the equivalent of a football pitch every four minutes! Despite a recent reduction in deforestation rates, Malaysia lost almost 16 per cent of its primary forest between 2002 and 2018.

Figure 1 *The location of Malaysia*

What are the causes of deforestation in Malaysia?

- *Logging* – since the 1980s, Malaysia has been one of the world's largest exporter of highly valued tropical wood. But destructive *clear felling* has now largely been replaced by **selective logging** of mature trees only.
- *Road building* – roads are constructed to provide access to logging and mining areas, new settlements and energy projects (Figure **2**).
- *Energy development* – **Hydro-electric power** projects boost Malaysia's electricity supplies (Figure **3**).
- *Mineral extraction* – tin mining is established and drilling for oil and gas has recently started.
- *Settlement and population growth* – poor people from urban areas have been encouraged to move into the countryside from rapidly growing cities. This *transmigration* has set up new settlements.
- *Commercial farming* – Malaysia is one of the largest exporters of palm oil in the world. Ten-year tax incentives encourage more deforestation for more plantations.
- *Subsistence farming* – traditional short-term clearance is small scale and sustainable, but 'slash and burn' fires can grow out of control destroying large areas of forest.

Figure 2 *Road construction in Sabah, in the north of Malaysian Borneo*

Figure 3 *Bakun HEP Dam in Sarawak, in the Malaysian Borneo*

 Six Second Summary

- Malaysia currently has one of the highest rates of deforestation in the world.
- Deforestation in Malaysia is caused by logging, energy development, mineral extraction, transmigration, and commercial and subsistence farming.

 Over to you

Make a mnemonic (see page 9) to help you remember the list of reasons why deforestation in Malaysia is taking place. Add **one** cause for **each** reason you have listed.

You need to know:

- the impacts of deforestation in Malaysia – loss of biodiversity, soil erosion, contribution to climate change and economic gains and losses.

CASE STUDY

Impacts of deforestation in Malaysia

Deforestation destroys the ecosystem and the many habitats that exist on the ground and in the trees (Figure **1**). Stripping away vegetation:

- *reduces biodiversity* with incalculable losses of undiscovered plant species and their medicinal potential
- *exposes the ground* (previously shaded, and with soil bound together by the roots of trees and plants) to **soil erosion** by wind and rain
- *contributes to climate change* by reducing photosynthesis, transpiration and the cooling effect of evaporation. Consequently, there is less moisture to condense into clouds, and higher temperatures. So, the 'double negative' of fewer trees absorbing CO_2 and the burning of the wood, increases CO_2 emissions and, therefore, the effectiveness of the greenhouse effect.

Figure 1 *Deforestation in Malaysia*

Economic development

Most deforestation is driven by profit. But are these just short-term economic gains?

Economic gains	Economic losses
Job creation – directly in construction and operations, and indirectly in supply and support industries.	Water pollution in an increasingly dry climate may limit supplies.
Tax revenue used to supply public services (e.g. education).	Fires pollute and destroy vast areas of valuable forest.
Improved transport **infrastructure** benefits industrial development and tourism.	Rising temperatures could devastate established farming.
Plantation products (e.g. palm oil and rubber) support processing industries.	Plants that could form the basis of hugely profitable medicines may become extinct.
HEP is cheap and plentiful.	Climate change could have economic costs (see 4.4 and 4.5).
Minerals (e.g. gold and tin) are valuable for export.	Rainforest tourism could decrease.

 Six Second Summary

- Deforestation leads to loss of biodiversity, soil erosion and climate change.
- There may be short-term economic gains, but long-term economic losses.

 Over to you

Construct a spider diagram to summarise the impacts of deforestation in Malaysia.

You need to know:

- the value of tropical rainforests to people and the environment.

Student Book
See pages
74–5

Why are tropical rainforests valuable to people?

Indigenous people living sustainably

There are around 50 million indigenous people living in the world's tropical rainforests. Most have lived where they do for thousands of years, relying on rainforests for food, water and shelter. Traditionally, many indigenous peoples live nomadically as hunter gatherers – a sustainable lifestyle that does not harm the rainforest. Even those who are forced to settle permanently (e.g. the Achuar people in the Peruvian Amazon) continue to adopt a sustainable lifestyle.

Resources

Tropical rainforests provide:

- valuable hardwoods, such as mahogany and teak
- nuts, fruit and rubber
- rich mineral resources, such as gold, tin, oil and gas (see 6.3).

The rainforest's medicine cabinet

The Amazon rainforest is known as the 'world's largest medicine cabinet'. Around 25 per cent of all drugs used today are derived from rainforest plants and animals (Figure **1**). For example:

- quinine, used to treat malaria
- extracts from the bark of lianas, used to treat Parkinson's disease
- wild yams, used in birth control pills
- vampire bat saliva helping prevent heart attacks.

Figure 1 *Madagascan periwinkle, used to treat cancer, is an endangered rainforest species*

Why are tropical rainforests valuable to the environment?

Biodiversity
Tropical rainforests contain about half of all the plants and animals in the world – and how many species still to be discovered?

Climate change
Rainforests absorb and store CO_2

Water
Rainforests are important sources of clean water

Climate
Rainforests prevent the climate from becoming too hot and dry – and produce 20% of the world's oxygen!

Six Second Summary

- Around 50 million indigenous people live sustainably in the world's tropical rainforests.
- Around 25 per cent of all drugs used today are derived from rainforest plants and animals.
- Tropical rainforests provide hardwoods, nuts, fruit, rubber and rich mineral resources.
- Tropical rainforests have extraordinary biodiversity, moderate the climate and provide clean water.

Over to you

Make sure that you can explain:

a) **five** reasons why tropical rainforests are valuable
b) why they should be protected.

Student Book
See pages
76–7

You need to know:

- different strategies for managing tropical rainforests sustainably.

How can rainforests be managed sustainably?

Rainforests need to be managed sustainably in order to:

- ensure that they remain a lasting resource for future generations
- harness valuable resources without causing long-term damage to the environment.

Indigenous tribes like the Peruvian Achuar (see 6.5) manage rainforests sustainably, but support relatively few people. It is the wealthy landowners, large companies and illegal loggers, in their drive for profits that do the damage.

Sustainable commercial management

- *Selective logging and replanting* – introduced in Malaysia (Figure **1**) – avoids the completely destructive *clear felling*.
- *Conservation and education* encourages preservation of rainforests in national parks and nature reserves for scientific research (e.g. the Caura Basin, Venezuela).
- ***Ecotourism***, such as in Costa Rica and Malaysia, introduces people to the natural world and provides long-term income to local people and governments (Figure **2**).
- *International agreements* recognise the global importance of rainforests in combating climate change. They include 'debt-for-nature-swapping' agreements whereby some donor countries and organisations reduce their debt repayment demands in return for calling a halt to deforestation.

The Forest Stewardship Council (FSC) promotes sustainably managed forestry through education programmes and its FSC-labelled products.

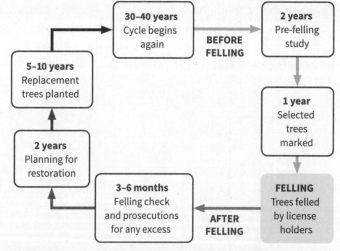

Figure 1 *Malaysia's Selective Management System*

Figure 2 *Tourist accommodation in an eco-lodge*

Six Second Summary

- Rainforests need to be managed sustainably in order to preserve them for the future and to make use of their resources without damaging the environment.
- Rainforests can be managed sustainably by selective logging, replanting, conservation, education, ecotourism and international agreements.

Over to you

Take four cards and label each one 'Selective logging and replanting', 'Conservation and education', 'Ecotourism' and 'International agreements'. On each card, outline how and why it contributes to sustainable management of rainforests. Then arrange the cards in order of importance.

SKILLS FOCUS

> **You need to be able to:**
> - use data to construct bar graphs and pie charts.

Student Book
See pages
78–9

Bar graphs and pie charts

Rates and impacts of deforestation

Deforestation of primary forest leads to soil erosion, climate change and loss of biodiversity. But how can we judge the scale of deforestation, or visualise an impact? Using bar graphs and pie charts may help answer these questions (see Figures **1** and **2**).

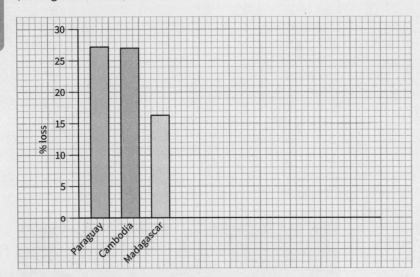

Figure 1 Rates of primary rainforest loss, 2001–18

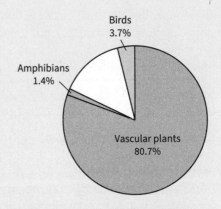

Figure 2 Biodiversity in Malaysia's rainforests, 2018

Country	Loss of primary forest (%) (2001–18)
Brazil	6.7
Indonesia	9.8
DR Congo	4.2
Malaysia	15.7
Bolivia	6.0
Peru	2.6
Colombia	2.5

Figure 3 Rates of primary rainforest loss, 2001–18

Animal/plant group	Species count	%	Degrees for pie chart
Birds	718	3.7	13
Amphibians	269	1.4	5
Reptiles	486		
Fishes	1938		
Mammals	336		
Vascular plants	15500	80.7	291
Total	19247	100	360

Figure 4 Biodiversity in Malaysia's rainforests, 2018

Skills and analysis

1 Study Figure **1**.

  a Use Figure **3** to complete the bar graph on Figure **1**. (Arrange the bars in order, from the highest on the left to the lowest on the right.)

  b In 2018 Malaysia had 13430905 hectares of primary rainforest. Assuming a constant yearly (annual) rate of deforestation of 145000 hectares (the rate in 2018), suggest a date when all primary rainforest might disappear. Comment on the likelihood of your answer.

2 Study Figure **4**.

  a Calculate the percentage values for reptiles, fishes and mammals. Express your answers to one decimal place.

  b Convert these percentage values into degrees by multiplying the percentage value by 3.6.

3 **a** Complete the pie chart (Figure **2**), including shading and labelling the missing segments.

  b Using Figure **2**, describe biodiversity in Malaysia's rainforests.

Student Book
See pages
80–1

You need to know:

- the locations of hot deserts, their physical characteristics and interdependence.

What are deserts like?

Deserts are dry (arid) areas. They are both hot (e.g. the Sahara) and cold (e.g. Antarctica), but all receive less than 250 mm of rainfall per year.

Where are hot deserts found?

Hot deserts are mostly found in a belt between approximately 30°N and 30°S (Figure **1**). This is largely explained by global atmospheric circulation (see 3.1). Most occupy dry continental interiors, but coastal deserts also exist (e.g. the Atacama Desert in South America).

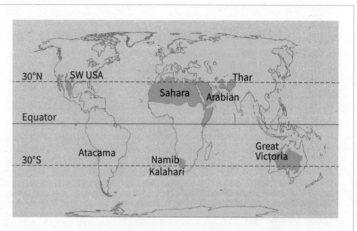

Figure 1 *Location of the world's hot deserts*

Climate, soils, plants and animals

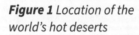

Like rainforests, hot desert climates are explained by the global atmospheric circulation (see 3.1). At these latitudes, air that has risen from the Equator descends (sinks), forming a persistent belt of high pressure. This explains both the lack of cloud and rain, and the extreme temperature range – very hot days and very cold nights.

Hot desert soils tend to be sandy or stony. Limited leafy vegetation means little organic matter and fertility. Evaporation of moisture draws salts to the surface.

Hot deserts are home to a surprising biodiversity of plants, animals and birds. In all but the driest areas they find ways (adaptations) to survive (see 7.2).

Interdependence in hot deserts

Extreme climatic conditions in hot deserts are very challenging for plants, animals and people. Survival depends on high levels of interdependence between the biotic (e.g. plants) and abiotic (e.g. climate) components of the ecosystem (see 5.1). For example:

- animals adapt to store water, lose heat and seek shelter from the sun (e.g. rodents burrowing into the loose, sandy soil for shade)
- plant seeds remain dormant for years, bursting into life when infrequent rainstorms finally arrive
- traditional people are *pastoralists*, sustainably migrating with their animals to fresh pastures watered by seasonal rainfall, thus avoiding **overgrazing**.

Six Second Summary

- Hot deserts are located in a belt between 30°N and 30°S.
- The climate has very low rainfall and an extreme temperature range.
- Soils are dry and infertile with little organic matter.
- A wide diversity of plants, animals and birds have adapted to the hostile environment.
- Survival for plants, animals and people depends on high levels of interdependence.

Over to you

Make sure that you can:
- locate and name examples of hot deserts
- explain their aridity and extreme temperatures
- explain interdependence in hot deserts.

Adapting to hot desert environments

Student Book
See pages
82–3

You need to know:

- how plants and animals have adapted to hot deserts.

How have plants and animals adapted?

Plants, animals and birds find ways to survive. Vegetation has several adaptations:

- small leaves, spines and waxy surfaces reduce transpiration
- succulents (e.g. cacti) store water in their roots, stems, leaves or fruit
- seeds, dormant for years, germinate quickly when it rains
- long taproots reach groundwater.

Animals have also found ways to adapt:

- nocturnal rodents live in burrows underground
- snakes and lizards retain water beneath waterproof skins which retain water
- camels can withstand days without water.

Six Second Summary

- A wide diversity of plants, animals and birds have adapted to the hostile desert environment.
- This biodiversity is threatened by climate change, wildfires, overgrazing, over-cultivation, and desert tourism.

Threats to biodiversity

Hot desert environments are very biodiverse. However, this biodiversity is threatened by:

- *climate change* – changing patterns of rainfall and droughts
- *wildfires* – replacing slow-growing shrubs with faster-growing grasses
- **overgrazing** *and* **over-cultivation** – exposing soil to erosion and leading to **desertification**
- *desert tourism* – damaging vegetation and disturbing wildlife.

Climate graphs

You need to be able to:

- construct and interpret a climate graph.

SKILLS FOCUS

Constructing a climate graph: Death Valley, USA

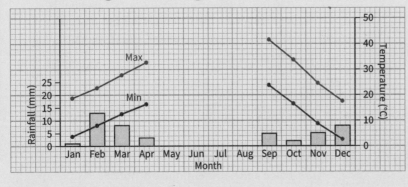

Figure 1 Climate graph for Death Valley, USA

Annual average ...	May	June	July	August
Max temp (°C)	38	43	47	46
Min temp (°C)	23	27	31	30
Rainfall (mm)	1	1	2	3

Figure 2 Climate data for Death Valley, USA

Skills

1 Use Figure **2** to complete the climate graph (Figure **1**). (Use a sharp pencil to draw the missing vertical bars for rainfall. Plot temperature points midway in each month, and complete the maximum and minimum lines.)
2 Describe the main characteristics of the climate.

Analysis

1 Which month experiences the greatest temperature range?
2 Which months experience the lowest average rainfall?

Student Book
See pages
84–5

CASE STUDY

You need to know:

- how people use hot desert environments
- what development opportunities exist in the Thar Desert.

Where is the Thar Desert?

The Thar Desert is the most densely populated desert in the world! It stretches across north-west India and into Pakistan.

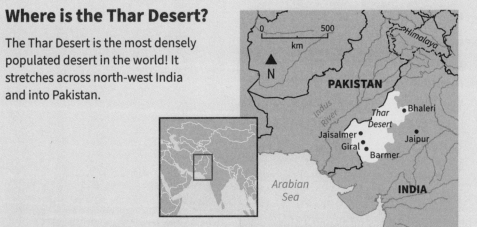

Figure 1 *Location of the Thar Desert*

 Big Idea

Hot deserts are so much more than empty, useless wastelands!

What are the opportunities for development?

- *Mineral extraction* – valuable reserves of gypsum, feldspar, phosphorite and kaolin are used domestically and for export. Limestone and marble are also extracted.
- *Tourism* – desert safaris on camels exploit the beautiful landscapes.
- *Energy* – includes coal, oil, solar and wind (Figure **2**).
- *Farming* – subsistence grazing of animals in grassy areas, vegetable and fruit cultivation, and commercial farming of pulses, sesame, mustard, maize, cotton and wheat (Figure **3**).
- **Irrigation** from the Indira Gandhi Canal (see 7.3) has made what was once scrubby desert productive.

Figure 3 *Growing wheat on irrigated land in the desert*

Figure 2 *The Jaisalmer Wind Park – India's largest wind farm*

 Six Second Summary

- The Thar Desert offers opportunities for economic development, including mineral extraction, tourism, and wind and solar energy.
- Improvements in irrigation have led to the growth of commercial farming.

Over to you

Summarise this page in **five** bullet points that disprove the assumption that hot deserts are empty, useless wastelands.

Student Book
See pages
86–7

CASE STUDY

You need to know:

- the challenges of developing Thar Desert.

Extreme temperatures

The Thar Desert suffers from extremely high temperatures which:

- makes physical work hard, especially for those who work outside, such as farmers
- limits tourism to the cooler months of the year
- causes high rates of evaporation leading to water shortages
- leads to dehydration of animals and plants.

Water supply

Water in the Thar Desert is a scarce resource because:

- annual rainfall is low, and high temperatures and strong winds cause high rates of evaporation
- as population has increased, farming and industry have developed, increasing the demand for the limited water supply.

There are several sources:

- traditional storage ponds – human-made *johads* and natural *tobas* (Figure **1**)
- a few intermittent rivers and streams
- underground aquifers requiring wells, though often the water is saline (salty).

This is why the Indira Gandhi Canal is so important (Figure **2**). Constructed in 1958 with a length of 650 km, it has helped to transform an extensive area of desert and revolutioned farming.

Figure 1 *Collecting water in the desert*

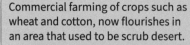
Commercial farming of crops such as wheat and cotton, now flourishes in an area that used to be scrub desert.

The canal provides drinking water to many people in the desert.

Two of the main areas to benefit from the canal are centred on the cities of Jodhpur and Jaisalmer where over 3500 km² of land is under irrigation.

Figure 2 *The Indira Gandhi Canal*

Inaccessibility

Vast barren areas and very extreme weather limit the road network, as tarmac can melt during the day and strong winds blow sand over the roads. Many places are accessible only by camel.

Six Second Summary

- Extreme temperatures, water shortages and poor accessibility present challenges of developing the Thar Desert.
- The Indira Gandhi Canal is the main source of irrigation, and has revolutionised farming.

Over to you

Why might many people argue that the very high temperatures and a limited road network present the greatest challenges of developing the Thar Desert?

Student Book
See pages
88–9

You need to know:

- the causes of desertification in hot deserts.

What is desertification?

Desertification is where land is gradually turned into desert. It occurs mostly on the ecologically fragile borders of existing deserts (Figure **1**). Desertification:

- is a result of both natural (e.g. droughts) and human (e.g. mismanagement) events
- affects both poor and rich countries
- threatens one billion people in areas at risk.

Slight changes in temperature and rainfall (associated with climate change) make these areas even more prone to **over-cultivation, overgrazing** or the stripping of vegetation for fuelwood.

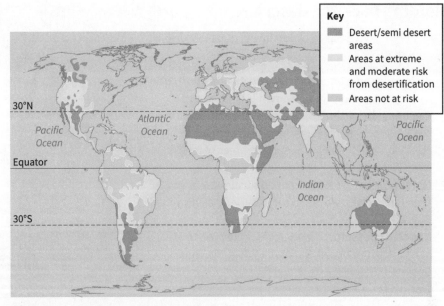

Key
- Desert/semi desert areas
- Areas at extreme and moderate risk from desertification
- Areas not at risk

Figure 1 *Areas at risk of desertification*

Causes of desertification

Climate change is resulting in drier conditions and unreliable rainfall in some regions (e.g. the Sahel on the southern margins of the Sahara).

Overgrazing Population pressure results in the limited vegetation supporting too many animals (e.g. nomadic Bedouin herding more sheep, goats and camels in the Badia, eastern Jordan).

Soil erosion Where vegetation is destroyed, exposing soil which cracks and breaks up, making it vulnerable to erosion by wind and rain.

Over-cultivation More people need more food, which exhausts the soil turning it to dust.

Fuelwood Population growth increases demand. Trees that are stripped of branches eventually die.

Salinisation Rapid evaporation of poorly practised irrigation leads to surface salts building-up, which kill the plants (see 7.6, Figure **1**).

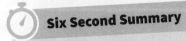

Six Second Summary

- Desertification is the process of deserts spreading.
- It is the result of both natural events and human mismanagement.
- The ecologically fragile borders of existing deserts are most at risk.

Over to you

- List the causes of desertification using headings 'Natural causes' and 'Human mismanagement'.
- Decide which of these is more important in explaining desertification, with reasons.

Student Book
**See pages
90–1**

You need to know:

- how desertification can be reduced.

Holding back the desert

Land at risk from desertification needs to be managed sustainably.

- *Water and soil management* – irrigation needs to be managed carefully if salinisation is to be avoided. Too much **irrigation** and/or badly drained schemes build-up toxic salts on the surface (Figure **1**).
- *Ponding banks* – low walls enclose areas of land to store water.
- *Contour traps* – embankments built along slopes prevent soil being washed away during heavy rainfall (e.g. Australia).
- *National park status* – gives legal protection to areas at risk (e.g. the Desert National Park in the Thar Desert, India).
- *Tree planting* – reduces soil erosion because the roots bind the soil together, and the leaves and branches provide shade, grazing for animals and fuelwood (e.g. in the Thar Desert, a community-led project has planted one million trees to form a 'green wall' at Bikaner in Western Rajasthan).

Appropriate technology

Practical and sustainable approaches to farming address the needs of poor people who are unable to afford expensive machinery.

For example, stone bunds in Burkina Faso, West Africa have reduced desertification and increased crop yields by up to 50 per cent by trapping water and soil (Figure **2**).

Figure 2 Walls of stone bunds in Burkina Faso

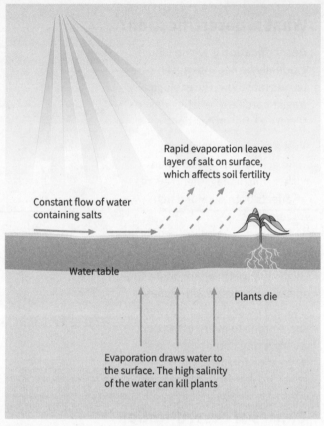

Rapid evaporation leaves layer of salt on surface, which affects soil fertility

Constant flow of water containing salts

Water table

Plants die

Evaporation draws water to the surface. The high salinity of the water can kill plants

Figure 1 *The process of salinisation*

Six Second Summary

- Areas at risk from desertification need to be managed sustainably.
- Sustainable management includes effective water and soil management, national park protection, tree planting and the use of appropriate technology.

Over to you

- List **four** ways of sustainable management to help stop desertification.
- Make sure that you understand the meaning and importance of appropriate technology, and can quote examples.

Student Book
See pages
92–3

You need to know:

- the location of cold environments
- the physical characteristics and interdependence of cold environments.

Big Idea

Cold environments cover around one-third of the world's land surface. They are ecologically fragile and present demanding development and conservation challenges.

What are cold environments?

Cold environments experience temperatures of 0°C or below for long periods. They include ice sheets, **polar** and **tundra** regions, and less extreme high mountain Alpine areas (Figure **1**).

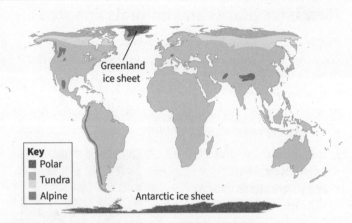

Key
- Polar
- Tundra
- Alpine

Greenland ice sheet

Antarctic ice sheet

Figure 1 *Location of the world's cold environments*

Figure 2 *Characteristics of cold environments*

	Polar	Tundra
Climate	Extreme – winter temperatures can fall below –50°C, strong winds, low snow totals	Less extreme – winter temperatures may drop to –20°C, warm brief summers, snow highest in coastal regions
Soils	**Permafrost** covered by ice	Summer surface permafrost melting (of the *active layer*) causing waterlogging
Plants	Mosses and lichens on the fringes of the ice	Low-growing flowering plants with special adaptations (see 8.2)
Animals	Polar bears well adapted with thick fur and foot pads; Antarctic penguins	Several species due to more food options and less extreme climate (e.g. Arctic fox, summer birds and insects)

Interdependence in cold environments

Cold environments are very fragile, with extreme climatic conditions that are challenging for plants, animals and people. Their survival depends on high levels of interdependence (see 5.1). For example:

- plants and animals adapt (see 8.2)
- permafrost restricts plant root growth and animal burrowing. Summer surface melting causes waterlogging, which supports breeding insects
- traditional Sámi reindeer herders in northern Scandinavia sustainably migrate between summer and winter pastures.

The impact of climate change

Significant impacts include:

- extensive melting of permafrost creating huge lakes and exposing topsoil to erosion
- earlier seasonal plant growth
- indigenous species threatened (e.g. Arctic fox by red fox moving northwards)
- increasing human access (e.g. Arctic tourism) threatening delicate ecological balance.

Six Second Summary

- Cold environments have extreme climatic conditions including very low temperatures.
- Survival for plants, animals and people depends on adaptation and high levels of interdependence.
- Climate change is having significant impacts on the Arctic's 'web of life'.

Over to you

Make sure that you can:

a locate and name examples of cold environments
b describe their key characteristics especially relating to climate change
c explain interdependence in cold environments.

Student Book
See pages 94–5

You need to know:

- how plants and animals adapt to cold environments

How have plants and animals adapted?

Plants and animals have adapted in different ways to cope with the significant challenges of cold environments. Animals typically have thick fur to keep them warm, small ears to reduce heat loss and wide foot pads to enable them to walk on snow. Plants, such as the abundant bearberry (Figure **1**), have several adaptations:

- Low-growing, so protected from strong winds.
- Thick bark stems improve stability.
- Small leathery leaves retain moisture.
- Hairy stems insulate the plant.
- Bright red berries attract birds to help spread the seeds.

Figure 1 *The bearberry plant*

Threats to biodiversity

Cold environments are very biodiverse. This biodiversity is threatened by:

- *climate change* – associated with global warming (see 4.1)
- *wildfires* – as climates become warmer and drier
- *Increasing human activity* – oil exploration, industrial fishing and tourism.

Six Second Summary

- Plants and animals adapt to the hostile conditions of cold environments.
- Biodiversity is threatened by climate change, wildfires and increasing human activities.

Climate graphs

You need to be able to:

- construct and compare climate graphs.

SKILLS FOCUS

Comparing climate graphs

	J	F	M	A	M	J	J	A	S	O	N	D
Annual average maximum temperature (°C)	−7	−7	−9	−5	−1	4	7	6	3	−1	−3	−6
Annual average minimum temperature (°C)	−11	−14	−15	−12	−5	1	4	3	0	−5	−8	−10
Annual average precipitation (mm)	26	25	24	15	20	19	25	40	36	39	37	31

Figure 2 *Climate data for Spitsbergen, Svalbard*

Skills

1 Use Figure **2** to construct a climate graph for Spitsbergen.
2 Describe the main characteristics of the climate.

Analysis

1 Which two months experience the greatest temperature range?
2 Which month experiences the lowest average precipitation?

Evaluation

1 Evaluate the usefulness of comparing climate graphs against those recording your own experience (e.g. a region in England).
2 How would you advise a friend to avoid potential problems when comparing climate graphs?

If necessary, refer to 7.2 for help with construction of climate graphs.

CASE STUDY

You need to know:

- about development opportunities in Svalbard.

Where is Svalbard?

Norway's Svalbard is close to the Mid-Atlantic Ridge and is the world's most northerly inhabited territory (Figure **1**).

Svalbard has five major islands, and 60 per cent of the land area is covered in glaciers and the rest is tundra. There are no trees – it is too cold!

Most of its population of around 2700 live in the main town of Longyearbyen on Spitzbergen, the largest of the islands.

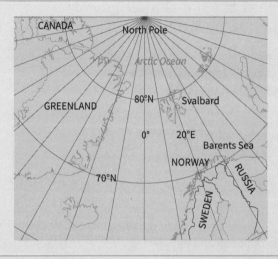

Figure 1 *Location of the Norwegian territory of Svalbard*

Opportunities for development

- *Mineral extraction* – rich reserves of coal, which is the main economic activity but environmentally controversial.
- *Energy developments* – the Longyearbyen coal-fired power station supplies all of Svalbard's energy needs (Figure **2**). **Geothermal energy** is a likely future source of energy,
- *Fishing* – the Arctic waters of the Barents Sea are rich fishing grounds with 150 species, including cod, herring and haddock. Fishing is carefully controlled and monitored to ensure **sustainability** of the ecosystem.
- *Tourism* – now provides as many jobs as mining. Increasingly popular in recent years as tourists seek the Northern Lights and explore more extreme natural environments.
  - Cruise passengers land at Longyearbyen seeking glaciers, fjords and wildlife – especially polar bears
  - Adventure tourists seeking hiking, kayaking and snowmobile safaris (Figure **3**).

Figure 2 *The coal-fired power station at Longyearbyen*

Figure 3 *Adventure tourism in Svalbard*

 Six Second Summary

- Svalbard is a group of islands in the Arctic Ocean, close to the Mid-Atlantic Ridge.
- Development opportunities include coal mining, geothermal energy, fishing and tourism.

Over to you

- Define the phrase 'environmentally controversial'.
- Learn **two** points to explain why coal is controversial; then **two** more explaining why fishing and tourism are also controversial.

Student Book
See pages
98–9

You need to know:

- the challenges of developing Svalbard.

What are the challenges for development?

Living and working in such an extreme environment poses extraordinary challenges, not least throughout the four months of winter darkness.

Extreme temperatures

- Even in Longyearbyen, winter temperatures can fall below −30°C.
- Given the risk of frostbite, several layers of thick clothes, gloves, socks and boots are essential.
- Protected like this, outside work can be slow, difficult and dangerous.

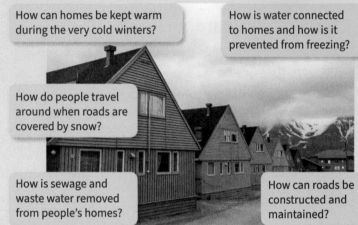

How can homes be kept warm during the very cold winters?

How is water connected to homes and how is it prevented from freezing?

How do people travel around when roads are covered by snow?

How is sewage and waste water removed from people's homes?

How can roads be constructed and maintained?

Figure 1 *Challenges of living and working in Svalbard*

Construction

- Most building, construction and maintenance happen during the brief summer.
- The frozen ground surface (permafrost) has to be protected from melting, or buildings would collapse.
- Most dirt and gravel roads are raised above the ground surface.

Services

- Most power, water and sanitation pipes have to be heated, insulated and raised above ground (Figure **2**).
- This allows easy maintenance and prevents thawing of the permafrost.

Figure 2 *Overground service pipes*

Accessibility

- Svalbard can only be reached by sea or air.
- There are no roads outside Longyearbyen.
- International flights link to mainland Norway and Russia, with smaller aircraft connecting to other islands.
- Most people use snowmobiles, particularly in winter (Figure **3**).

Figure 3 *Snowmobiles parked in Longyearbyen*

 Six Second Summary

- Living and working in the extreme environment of Svalbard poses development challenges.
- These include inaccessibility, four months of darkness, extreme cold, difficulties with construction and service provision on permafrost.

Over to you

- Describe **four** challenges of development in Svalbard.
- Explain **one** way in which **each** challenge is overcome.

Student Book
**See pages
100–1**

You need to know:

- about cold environments as wilderness areas
- why they need protecting.

CASE STUDY

What is a wilderness area?

A **wilderness area** is a wild, unspoiled area unaffected by human activity (e.g. rainforests, deserts or cold environments).

Why are cold environments fragile?

Tundra vegetation takes a very long time to become established. Tundra is a delicate ecosystem which is easily disturbed by human activities. For example, off-road driving in summer leaves deep tyre tracks scaring the swampy, thawed, surface permafrost. Recovery can take decades!

Why are cold environments at risk?

In Alaska (USA) and Siberia (Russia), rich reserves of oil and gas remain in high demand, but their exploitation requires the construction of:

- access roads through forests and across tundra vegetation
- supply bases and settlements for workers
- drilling equipment and pipelines.

The potential for long-lasting or even permanent damage to such **fragile environments** is great, especially from pollution incidents (Figure **1**).

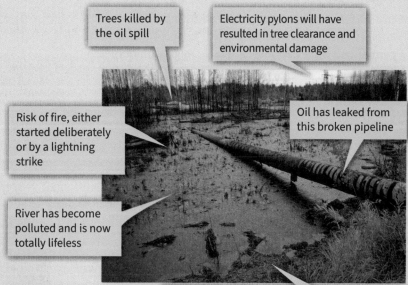

Trees killed by the oil spill

Electricity pylons will have resulted in tree clearance and environmental damage

Risk of fire, either started deliberately or by a lightning strike

Oil has leaked from this broken pipeline

River has become polluted and is now totally lifeless

River edge habitats polluted and destroyed – the vegetation may never recover

Figure 1 *Oil-polluted river in Siberia, Russia*

Why should cold environments be protected?

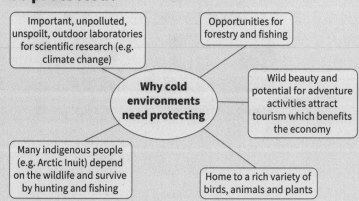

Important, unpolluted, unspoilt, outdoor laboratories for scientific research (e.g. climate change)

Opportunities for forestry and fishing

Why cold environments need protecting

Wild beauty and potential for adventure activities attract tourism which benefits the economy

Many indigenous people (e.g. Arctic Inuit) depend on the wildlife and survive by hunting and fishing

Home to a rich variety of birds, animals and plants

Figure 2 *Why should cold environments be protected?*

Six Second Summary

- A wilderness area is a wild and unspoiled area unaffected by human activity.
- Cold environment ecosystems are easily damaged and can take a very long time to recover.
- Exploitation of oil and gas reserves can cause pollution.
- There are strong arguments for the protection of these fragile environments.

Over to you

Write **three** questions about the key themes of this page to test a friend. Make sure you are able to write the answers as well!

Student Book
See pages
102–3

> **You need to know:**
>
> • strategies to reduce the risks to cold environments.

Balancing economic development and conservation

Cold environments need to be managed sustainably. There are four ways to do this.

1

Using technology – Trans-Alaska pipeline

Discovering oil in Prudhoe Bay, northern Alaska, in 1969 stimulated a technological solution to Arctic Ocean ice preventing tanker movements in winter – a revolutionary 1300 km pipeline. The Trans-Alaska pipeline (Figure **1**):

• crosses two mountain ranges and 800 rivers
• is raised and insulated to prevent the hot oil melting the permafrost, while allowing caribou to migrate underneath (Figure **2**)
• is engineered to slide during earthquakes, but with automatic shut-off systems if there is a leak.

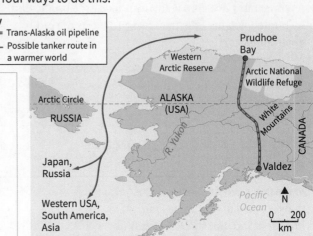

Key
▬▬ Trans-Alaska oil pipeline
← Possible tanker route in a warmer world

Figure 1 *Route of the Trans-Alaska pipeline and protected wilderness areas*

2

Government actions – Alaska, USA

The US government protects **wilderness areas** and their abundant wildlife through various laws and policies that protect Alaska's unique environment, native people and marine habitats.

3

International agreements – the Antarctic Treaty

Such wilderness protection has even been achieved on an international scale. For example, the Antarctic Treaty:

• prevents economic development
• promotes scientific research
• controls tourism to keep disturbance at a minimum (Figure **3**).

Figure 2 *The Trans-Alaska pipeline*

4

The work of conservation groups

Conservation groups such as the World Wide Fund for Nature (WWF, originally World Wildlife Fund) are working with oil companies, Inuit organisations, local communities and government regulators to plan for a sustainable future for the Arctic.

Figure 3 *Antarctica – the world's last great wilderness*

> **Six Second Summary**
>
> • Cold environments need to be managed sustainably.
> • Technology can be used to reduce the impact of development.
> • Action by conservation groups, governments and international agreements help protect cold environments, manage development and raise awareness.

> **Over to you**
>
> Make a list of the arguments **for** and **against** protecting wilderness areas from economic development.

Section C
Physical landscapes in the UK

Your exam

Section C Physical landscapes in the UK is part of Paper 1: Living with the physical environment.

Paper 1 is a one-and-a-half hour written exam and makes up 35 per cent of your GCSE. The whole paper carries 88 marks (including 3 marks for SPaG) – questions on Section C will carry 30 marks.

You have to study the introduction to UK physical landscapes. You must also study two of the other three types of landscapes – in your final exam you will have to answer any two questions from a choice of three.

Your revision checklist

Tick these boxes to build a record of your revision

Spec key idea	Theme	1	2	3
9 UK landscapes				
The UK has a range of diverse landscapes	9.1 Skills Focus: The UK's diverse landscapes			
10 Coastal landscapes				
The coast is shaped by a number of physical processes	10.1 Wave types and their characteristics			
	10.2 Weathering and mass movement			
	10.3 Coastal processes			
Distinctive coastal landforms are the result of rock type, structure and physical processes	10.4 Coastal erosion landforms			
	10.5 Coastal deposition landforms			
	10.6 Coastal landforms at Swanage			
Geographical skills	10.7 Skills Focus: Photos and OS maps			
Different management strategies can be used to protect coastlines from the effects of physical processes	10.8 Managing coasts – hard engineering			
	10.9 Managing coasts – soft engineering			
	10.10 Managing coasts – managed retreat			
	10.11 Coastal management at Lyme Regis			
11 River landscapes				
The shape of river valleys changes as rivers flow downstream	11.1 Changes in rivers and their valleys			
	11.2 Fluvial (river) processes			
Distinctive fluvial (river) landforms result from different physical processes	11.3 River erosion landforms			
	11.4 River erosion and deposition landforms			
	11.5 River landforms on the River Tees			
Geographical skills	11.6 Skills Focus: Photos and OS maps			
Different management strategies can be used to protect river landscapes from the effects of flooding	11.7 Physical and human factors affecting flood risk			
	11.8 Managing floods – hard engineering			
	11.9 Managing floods – soft engineering			
	11.10 Managing floods at Banbury			
12 Glacial landscapes				
Ice was a powerful force in shaping the physical landscape of the UK	12.1 The role of ice in shaping the UK's landscapes			
Distinctive glacial landforms result from different physical processes	12.2 Glacial erosion landforms			
	12.3 Glacial transportation and deposition landforms			
Geographical skills	12.4 Skills Focus: Photos and OS maps			
Glaciated upland areas provide opportunities for different economic activities, and management strategies can be used to reduce land use conflicts	12.5 Economic opportunities in glaciated upland areas			
	12.6 Conflicts in glaciated upland areas			
	12.7 Managing tourism in the Lake District			

Student Book
See pages 104–5

You need to be able to:

- interpret an atlas map of the UK
- use an atlas map to calculate height differences.

SKILLS FOCUS

Using an atlas map of the UK

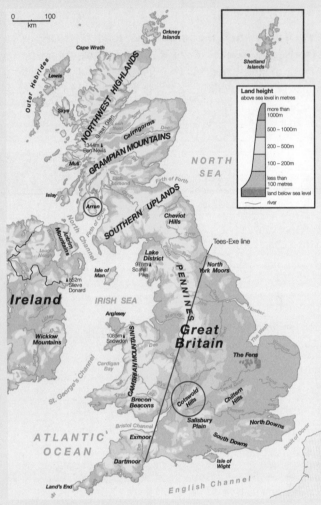

Figure 1 *Atlas map of the UK*

Figure 2 *Dramatic mountains in Arran, Scotland*

Figure 3 *The Cotswold Hills*

Skills

Using Figures **1, 2** and **3**, answer the following questions.

1 a The highest mountain in each of the four countries of the United Kingdom are shown on Figure **1**. What is the name and height of the highest mountain in Wales? In what mountain range is it located?

b Locate your home area and describe the relief.

c Compare the relief of Arran and the Cotswold Hills shown in Figures **2** and **3**.

2 Describe the pattern of lowland areas (below 100 m) in the UK.

3 a In which UK countries would you find these rivers: Teifi, Wensum, Clyde? (Hint – they are all in different countries.)

b On Figure **1**, locate the river that is closest to your home, and describe its course.

Analysis

The Tees–Exe line on Figure **1** joins the River Tees in north-east England with the River Exe in the south-west. More resistant rocks are found north and west of the line, and less resistant rocks to the south and east.

Use the information above to explain the difference in landscapes shown in Figures **2** and **3**.

Evaluation

Discuss whether Figure **1** provides enough detail to accurately describe the relief of the UK.

Student Book
See pages
106–7

You need to know:

- how waves form
- what happens when they reach the coast
- about different types of waves.

How do waves form?

- By wind blowing over the sea.
- Friction with the surface of the water causes ripples that develop into waves.
- *Tsunamis* form when earthquakes or volcanic eruptions shake the seabed.

The distance that wave-generating winds blow across the water is called the *fetch*.
Remember: The longer the fetch, the bigger and more powerful the wave.

What happens when waves reach the coast?

In the open sea there is little horizontal movement of water. Figure **1** shows what happens as waves approach the shore.

Figure 1 *Waves approaching the coast*

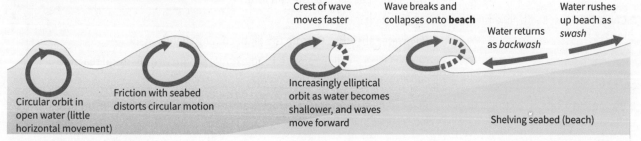

Two types of wave

1

Constructive waves

Formed by storms often hundreds of kilometres away. Common in summer.

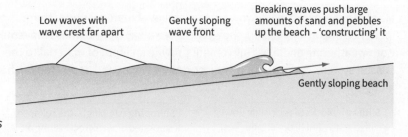

Figure 2 *Constructive waves*

2

Destructive waves

Formed by local storms close to the coast. Common in winter.

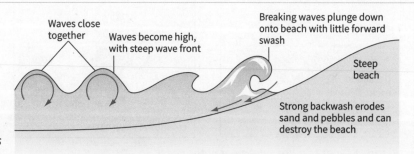

Figure 3 *Destructive waves*

 Six Second Summary

- Most waves are caused by the friction of the wind on the sea.
- There are two types of wave – constructive and destructive.

Over to you

Draw **two** spider diagrams – one for constructive and one for destructive waves. Add legs for their different characteristics: wave height; swash; backwash; building/destroying the beach; and anything else you can think of.

Student Book
See pages
108–9

You need to know:

- how the processes of weathering and mass movement combine with the action of the waves in shaping the coast.

What are the processes of weathering?

Weathering is the decay or disintegration of rock. It is mostly caused by the action of weather, but also by plants and animals.

Type of weathering	Example and description
1 Mechanical (physical) – the disintegration of rock	*Freeze-thaw* Water collects in cracks in rock. At night, water freezes and expands, making cracks larger. As temperature rises, ice thaws and water seeps deeper into rock. Repeated freezing and thawing makes rock fragments break off. They collect as scree at the cliff foot.
2 Chemical – caused by chemical changes	*Carbonation* Rainwater absorbs CO_2 from the air becoming slightly acidic. Contact with alkaline rocks, e.g. limestone, produces a chemical reaction causing rocks to slowly dissolve.
3 Biological – caused by the actions of flora and fauna	Plant roots grow in cracks in rocks, and animals (e.g. rabbits) burrow into weak rocks and sands.

What are the processes of mass movement?

Mass movement is the downward movement of material under the influence of gravity. Figure **1** shows the three main types of mass movement. Both weathering and mass movement provide an input of material to the coastal system. Much of this is transported by waves and deposited further along the coast.

1 Sliding – blocks of rock slide down a cliff (due to rainfall or earthquakes)

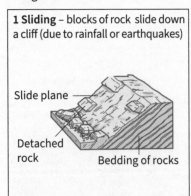

2 Slumping (slipping) – the collapse of saturated or weak rocks along a curved surface

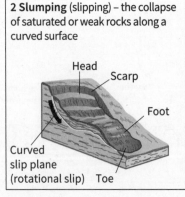

3 Rockfalls – rock breaks away often due to freeze-thaw weathering

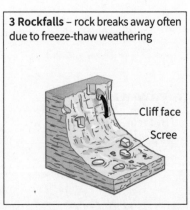

Figure 1 *Types of mass movement at the coast*

Six Second Summary

- Weathering is the decay and disintegration of rock. **Three** main types are mechanical (physical), chemical and biological.
- Mass movement is the downward movement of material. **Three** main examples are sliding, slumping and rock falls.

Over to you

From memory, draw a diagram to show the process of freeze-thaw weathering. Add detailed labels.

Student Book
See pages
110–11

You need to know:

- how the processes of erosion, transportation and deposition combine with the action of the waves to shape the coast.

Coastal erosion

Erosion means wearing away the landscape. The processes of coastal erosion are shown in the table.

1 Hydraulic power	The power of the waves as they hit a cliff. Trapped air is forced into cracks in the rock eventually causing it to break up.
2 Abrasion	The 'sandpapering' effect of pebbles being dragged over a rocky platform. The term *corrasion* involves fragments of rock picked up by the sea and hurled at a cliff.
3 Attrition	Rock fragments carried by the sea knock against each other becoming smaller/more rounded. This process is not responsible for eroding landforms.

Figure 1 Processes of coastal erosion

Coastal deposition

Deposition happens when water slows down and waves lose their energy.

- Beaches are formed of sediment deposited in bays.
- Mudflats and saltmarshes are often found in sheltered estuaries behind spits.

Six Second Summary

- There are **three** processes of coastal erosion.
- There are **four** ways sediment is transported along the coast.
- Longshore drift moves sediment along the coast.
- Deposition happens when waves lose their energy.

Over to you

From memory, draw a diagram to show the **three** processes of coastal erosion. Add annotations to explain the processes.

Coastal transportation

Eroded material (sediment) is transported in four different ways (Figure **2**).

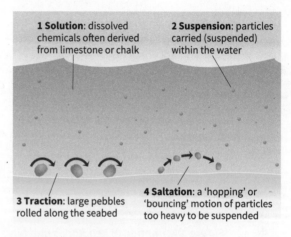

Figure 2 Types of coastal transportation

Longshore drift

The movement of sediment depends on the direction that waves approach the coast, as a result of the prevailing wind direction.

1 Where waves approach 'head on' sediment moves up and down the beach.

2 Where waves approach at an angle, sediment moves along the beach in a zigzag pattern. This is called **longshore drift**.

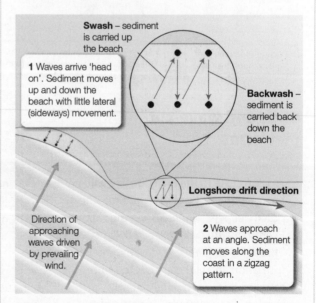

Figure 3 Longshore drift

Student Book
See pages
112–13

You need to know:

- about the role of geology in influencing coastal landforms
- about the characteristics and formation of coastal landforms that result from erosion.

The role of geological structure and rock type

1 *Geological structure* – refers to the arrangement of rocks, and features associated with folding and faulting.

2 *Rock type* (lithology) – some rocks (e.g. granite, limestone) are tougher and more resistant to erosion than others, such as sands and clays.

Landforms resulting from erosion

Headlands and bays

- Tougher, resistant bands of rock are eroded slowly to form **headlands**.
- Weaker rock erodes more easily to form **bays**. Bays are sheltered, deposition occurs, and a beach forms.

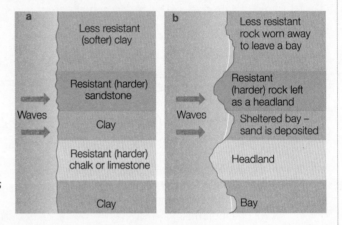

***Figure 1** Formation of headlands and bays*

Caves, arches and stacks

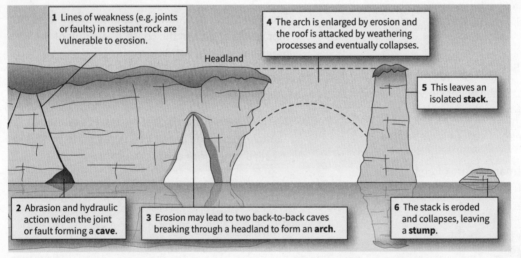

1 Lines of weakness (e.g. joints or faults) in resistant rock are vulnerable to erosion.

4 The arch is enlarged by erosion and the roof is attacked by weathering processes and eventually collapses.

5 This leaves an isolated **stack**.

2 Abrasion and hydraulic action widen the joint or fault forming a **cave**.

3 Erosion may lead to two back-to-back caves breaking through a headland to form an **arch**.

6 The stack is eroded and collapses, leaving a **stump**.

***Figure 2** Formation of caves, stacks and arches*

Cliffs and wave-cut platforms

- When waves break against a **cliff**, erosion close to the high tide line will form a **wave-cut notch**. Over time, the notch deepens, undercutting the cliff. Eventually the overlying cliff collapses.
- Through a sequence of wave-cut notch formation and cliff collapse, the cliff retreats. It leaves behind a gently sloping rocky platform – **a wave-cut platform**.

Six Second Summary

- Coastal landforms are influenced by geological structure and rock type.
- Different types of rock erode at different rates.
- Coastal erosion produces distinctive landforms.

Over to you

- Close your book and name **five** coastal erosion landforms.
- Sketch an annotated diagram to show how **two** of them form.

Student Book
**See pages
114–15**

You need to know:

- about the characteristics and formation of landforms resulting from coastal deposition.

Beaches

Beaches are deposits of sand and shingle.

- Sandy beaches are mainly found in sheltered bays and are created by constructive waves.
- Along high-energy coasts (e.g. England's southern coast) sand is washed away leaving behind a pebble beach.
- The diagram shows the profile of a typical sandy beach, including **sand dunes**.

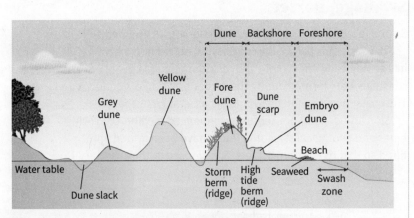

Figure 1 *Cross-section though beach and sand dunes*

Sand dunes

At the back of the beach, sand blown inland can build up to form *dunes*.

Embryo dunes form around obstacles (e.g. rocks).

↓

Dunes develop and are stabilised by vegetation (e.g. marram grass) to form fore dunes and tall yellow dunes.

↓

Decomposing vegetation makes sand more fertile and a wider range of plants colonise the back dunes.

↓

Ponds (dune slacks) can form in depressions.

Figure 2 *Development of sand dunes*

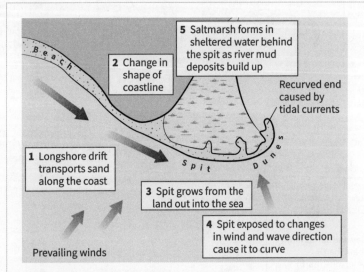

1 Longshore drift transports sand along the coast

2 Change in shape of coastline

3 Spit grows from the land out into the sea

4 Spit exposed to changes in wind and wave direction cause it to curve

5 Saltmarsh forms in sheltered water behind the spit as river mud deposits build up

Recurved end caused by tidal currents

Prevailing winds

Figure 3 *Formation of a spit*

Spits and bars

- A **spit** is a long finger of sand or shingle jutting out into the sea.
- **Bars** form when longshore drift causes spits to grow across a bay.
- *Offshore bars* form further out to sea where waves approaching a gently sloping coast deposit sediment (due to friction with the sea bed).
- In the UK, some offshore bars have been driven on shore by rising sea levels.
- These are called *barrier beaches*, e.g. Chesil Beach (Dorset).

Six Second Summary

- Coastal deposition creates landforms such as beaches, sand dunes, spits and bars.

Over to you

Create a word cloud of words to do with coastal deposition processes and landforms.

EXAMPLE

Student Book
**See pages
116–17**

You need to know:

- an example of a coastline in the UK
- how to identify if its landforms are caused by erosion and deposition.

Swanage, Dorset

Swanage sits on the Jurassic Coast in Dorset, on England's south coast. This part of the coast is named Jurassic because it is geologically important – the rocks on this 154 km of coastline were formed during the Jurassic geological period. The coastline surrounding Swanage has a range of coastal erosion and deposition landforms influenced by different rock types and geological structure. Rocks have been folded and tilted so that different rock types are exposed at the coast.

Poole Harbour – one of the UK's largest natural harbours. Two spits have formed at the mouth.

Old Harry stack, cliffs and arches

Ballard Point

Swanage

N

0 ————— 10
km

Key
▨ Clay and sands (soft)
▨ Chalk (hard)
▨ Limestone (hard)

Concordant coastline forms where different rock types run parallel to the coast, so the coast is mainly formed of one type.

Figure 1 *Geology of the Swanage coast*

Studland Bay – there are lagoons, saltmarshes, sand dunes and beaches

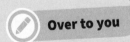

Discordant coastline forms where there are alternating bands of harder (more resistant) and softer (less resistant) rocks. This creates headlands and bays.

Swanage Bay is sheltered with a broad, sandy beach

Six Second Summary

Different rock types and geological structure are important factors in the formation of erosional and depositional landforms around the coast near Swanage.

Over to you

Learn this example!

- Where is Swanage?
- What factors affect the formation of the features on this coastline?
- What are concordant/discordant coasts? Which of these applies to Swanage?
- What coastal features can you identify and name?
- How have they formed?

You need to be able to:

- use photos and OS maps to study coastal landforms.

Using an OS map with a photo

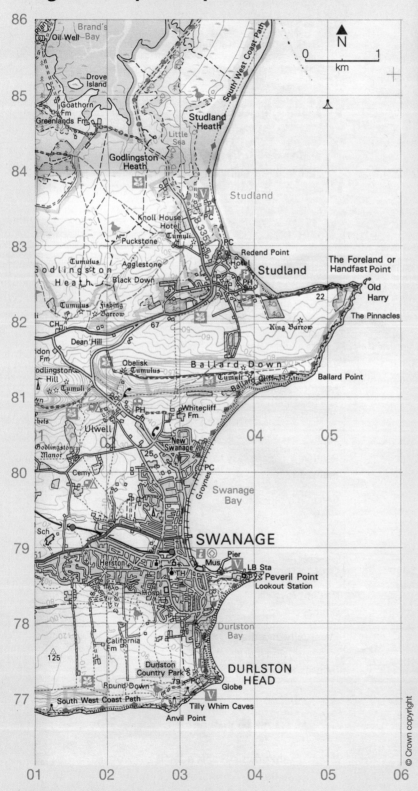

Figure 1 *1:50 000 OS map extract of Swanage coast*

© Crown copyright

Figure 2 *Aerial view of the coastline between Ballard Point and the Foreland*

Skills

1 a What type of coastal landform is the Foreland?

b Give the four-figure grid references for the three squares that include the coastline from Ballard Point to The Foreland.

2 a What map evidence is there that deposition is happening in Swanage Bay?

b How does this deposition help to explain the growth of Swanage as a tourist resort?

3 a Identify one of each of the following on Figure 1: a bay, a beach and a stack.

b Give the six-figure grid reference for an example of each feature.

c State whether the feature is created by erosion or deposition.

Analysis

1 a Using evidence from the map, describe the natural environment found around Studland Heath.

b Why does this environment need to be managed sustainably?

2 Explain how different rock types and geological structure have influenced the formation of erosional and depositional landforms on the coast from Durlston Head to Studland Bay.

Evaluation

Which is better for studying coastal landforms – OS maps, photos or both? Explain your answer.

Student Book
**See pages
120–1**

You need to know:

- about the costs and benefits of hard engineering methods to protect the coast.

Managing coasts

Coasts are managed to protect people from erosion and flooding. But coastal defences are expensive, and in some cases increasing costs might outweigh the benefits. In future, some coastlines could be left undefended.

 Big Idea

The options for managing the coast are:

1 **Hard engineering** – uses artificial structures to control natural processes.

2 **Soft engineering** – involves methods that work with natural processes.

3 **Managed retreat** – controlled retreat of the coast (e.g. by allowing the sea to flood low-lying land).

Hard engineering

Method	Cost	Advantages	Disadvantages
Sea walls – concrete or rock barrier at the foot of cliffs or top of beach. Curved to reflect waves out to sea.	£5000–£10 000 per metre	Effective at stopping the sea Often creates a walkway.	Can look obtrusive and unnatural Very expensive with high maintenance costs
Groynes – rock or timber structures built at right angles to beach. They trap sediment moved by longshore drift and enlarge the beach. Wider beach reduces wave damage.	Timber groynes £150 000 each (every 200 metres)	Create a wider beach – good for tourism Not too expensive	Interrupting longshore drift can lead to increased erosion elsewhere Unnatural and rock groynes are unattractive
Rock armour – piles of large boulders at foot of cliff. Rocks absorb wave energy to protect the cliff.	£200 000 per 100 metres	Relatively cheap; easy to maintain Can add interest to the coast	Rocks are often from elsewhere and don't fit in with local geology Expensive to transport rock Can be obtrusive
Gabions – rock-filled wire cages that support a cliff and provide a buffer against the sea.	Up to £50 000 per 100 metres	Cheap to produce Can improve cliff drainage Eventually become vegetated and merge into landscape	Unattractive initially Cages rust within 5–10 years

 Six Second Summary

- There are **three** options for protecting the coast from the sea.
- Hard engineering methods include the use of sea walls, groynes, rock armour and gabions.

 Over to you

Exam practice! This question is worth 6 marks – so you've 6 minutes to complete it.

Assess the advantages and disadvantages of hard engineering at the coast.

Student Book
See pages 122–3

You need to know:

- about the costs and benefits of soft engineering methods to protect the coast.

Soft engineering

Soft engineering schemes are generally cheaper than hard engineering, though they may need more maintenance (e.g. beaches need more sand/shingle every few years). But they are more sustainable and are the preferred option for coastal management.

Method	Cost	Advantages	Disadvantages
Beach nourishment – sand or shingle is dredged offshore and transported to the coast by barge. It is dumped on the beach and shaped by bulldozers creating a wider, higher beach (known as **re-profiling**). Beach protects land and property (Figure **1**).	Up to £500 000 per 100 metres	Blends in with existing beach Bigger beach increases tourist potential	Needs constant maintenance Expensive
Dune regeneration – marram grass is planted to stabilise dunes and help them develop, which makes them effective buffers to the sea. Fences keep people off newly planted areas (Figure **2**).	£200–£2000 per 100 metres	Maintains a natural environment – good for wildlife Relatively cheap	Time-consuming to plant grass and construct fencing Can be damaged by storms
Dune fencing – fences are constructed along the seaward side of existing dunes to encourage new dune formation. New dunes help to protect existing dunes.	£400–£2000 per 100 metres	Little impact on natural systems Controlling access protects other ecosystems	Can be unsightly Needs regular maintenance

Figure 1 *Beach nourishment at Eastbourne, East Sussex*

Figure 2 *Dune regeneration at Calgary Bay, Mull, Scotland*

Six Second Summary

- Soft engineering is a more sustainable way of managing the coast as it works with natural processes.
- Soft engineering methods include beach nourishment and re-profiling, dune regeneration and dune fencing.

Over to you

Check you know what *sustainability* means.

Then explain why soft engineering methods are generally more sustainable than hard engineering methods as a way of protecting the coast.

You need to know:

- about coastal management and adaptation
- how managed retreat and coastal realignment works.

Student Book
See pages 124–5

Coastal management and adaptation

In England and Wales, Shoreline Management Plans (SMPs) identify the most sustainable way to manage flood and coastal erosion risks in the short, medium and long term. SMPs take account of the likely changes associated with climate change (e.g. rising sea levels).

Increasingly, coastal management is determined by costs and benefits. Only areas of high value land (e.g. a mainline railway) will be protected by expensive schemes. A 'do nothing' approach is likely for relatively low value land (e.g. farmland), and people have to adapt, by moving inland, for example.

There are four possible approaches to coastal management. These are:

- *No active intervention / do nothing* – there are no plans to build defences
- *Hold the line* – maintain current defences
- *Advance the line* – increase defences to extend the coastline
- *Managed retreat/realignment* – allow the sea to flood or erode low-value land, so the coastline retreats inland

Medmerry managed retreat

The flat, low-lying land at Medmerry, near Chichester in southern England, is mainly used for farming and caravan parks. In the past, it was protected by a low sea wall.

The land is of relatively low value, so the sea was allowed to breach the sea wall in 2013 and flood some of the farmland ('A' in Figure 1).

Costing £28 million, this managed retreat scheme will:

- create a large natural saltmarsh (a natural buffer to the sea)
- help to protect surrounding farmland and caravan parks from flooding
- establish a wildlife habitat and encourage visitors to the area.

Embankments have been built inland to protect farmland, roads and settlement ('B' in Figure 1). Alteration of the coastline like this is called *coastal realignment*.

Big Idea

Managed retreat allows the sea to flood or erode an area of relatively low-value.

Figure 1 *Managed retreat at Medmerry, West Sussex*

Six Second Summary

- There are **four** approaches to coastal management.
- Managed retreat is a form of soft engineering, which is used to manage the coast where land is of relatively low value.
- People living or working where the coast is not protected, or is allowed to retreat, must adapt or move.

Over to you

1 List the opinions that any **six** different groups might have about managed retreat, e.g., farmers, caravan park owners.

2 Which of your groups might be in favour of managed retreat and who might be against?

3 Where might conflict arise?

Student Book
See pages
126–7

You need to know:

- why a coastal management scheme was needed at Lyme Regis
- the features of the scheme, and the outcomes.

EXAMPLE

Where is Lyme Regis?

Lyme Regis is a small coastal town in Dorset, on England's south coast, and is popular with tourists.

Reasons for management

- Unstable cliffs.
- Powerful waves from the south-west cause rapid erosion.
- Foreshore erosion has damaged many properties.
- Sea walls have been breached many times.

How has the coastline been managed?

The Lyme Regis Environmental Improvement Scheme was set up in the early 1990s to provide long-term coastal protection and reduce the threat of landslips. Engineering works were completed in 2014.

Key features of the scheme

Phases 1 and 2:

- New sea walls and promenades
- Cliffs stabilised
- Creation of wide beach to absorb wave energy
- Extension of rock armour to absorb wave energy and retain beach

Phase 4:

- New sea wall for extra protection
- Cliffs stabilised to protect homes

Total cost: £43 million

A planned **Phase 3** didn't go ahead – costs outweighed benefits. **Phase 5** will upgrade The Cobb and improve lighting and signage.

How successful has it been?

Positive outcomes
• New beaches have increased visitor numbers and seafront businesses are doing well.
• New defences have withstood stormy winters.
• Harbour is better protected.

Negative outcomes
• Increased visitor numbers has caused conflict due to traffic congestion and litter.
• Some think the new defences spoil the landscape.
• The new sea wall might interfere with natural processes and cause problems elsewhere.

Big Idea

The Lyme Regis scheme used **both** hard and soft engineering.

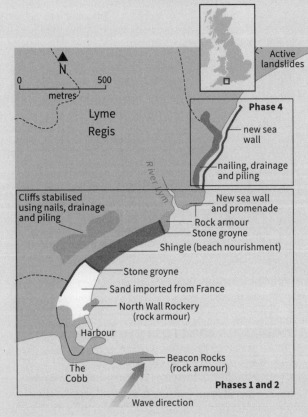

Figure 1 *Coastal management at Lyme Regis*

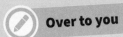

Six Second Summary

- Lyme Regis is built on cliffs that are being rapidly eroded.
- The management scheme aimed to protect the town and reduce the threat of landslips.
- The scheme was completed in phases over a period of more than 20 years.

Over to you

Learn this example! Make sure you know:

- *where* Lyme Regis is
- *what* the coastal management issues were
- *how* the coastline has been *managed* – note the *key features*
- *how successful* it has been.

Student Book
See pages
128–9

You need to know:

- what is meant by the term 'drainage basin'
- how river channels and their valleys change shape downstream.

What is a drainage basin?

A *drainage basin* is the area of land drained by a river and its tributaries.

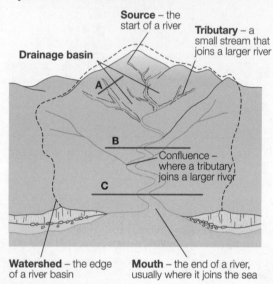

Figure 1 *Drainage basin*

How does a river's long profile change?

Figure **2** shows a river's **long profile** and how its gradient changes downstream. Put simply – it's steep in upland areas (the river's upper course), and gentle in the lowlands (the river's lower course).

In reality it varies, for example, a waterfall creates a step in the long profile.

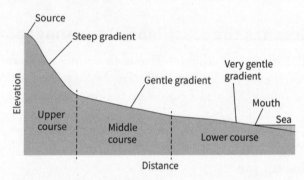

Figure 2 *Long profile of a river*

How does the cross profile change?

Figure **3** shows the **cross profile** – the shape of the valley from one side across to the other as the river flows downstream. Letters **A**, **B** and **C** refer to the position of each cross profile on Figure **1**. Changes are due to the amount of water flowing in the river. As tributaries add more water (and energy) to the river, it erodes its channel, making it wider and deeper.

Changes to the valley cross profile are mainly due to channel erosion, broadening and flattening the base of the valley. Together with weathering and mass movement, these processes make the sides of the valley less steep.

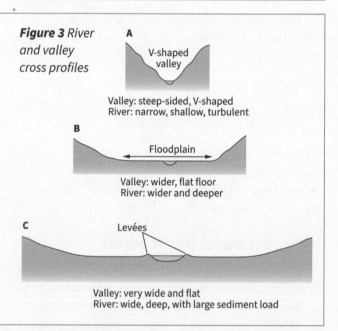

Figure 3 *River and valley cross profiles*

Six Second Summary

- A drainage basin is the area drained by a river and its tributaries.
- A long profile shows how the gradient of a river changes downstream.
- A cross profile is a cross-section of a river valley.

Over to you

Make some 'key term' flashcards for: drainage basin, source, tributary, confluence, mouth, watershed, long profile, cross profile.

Now write a *geographical* definition for each term. Test yourself with a friend!

Student Book
See pages
130–1

You need to know:

- different processes of erosion
- how a river's load is transported
- when deposition happens.

What are the processes of erosion?

There are two types of erosion:

- **vertical** (downwards)
- **lateral** (sideways).

These combine to change the river channel and the river valley as the river flows downstream – see 11.1.

There are four processes of river erosion – see Figure **1**.

1 Hydraulic action	The force of water hitting the river bed and banks. Most effective when water is moving fast and at high volume.
2 Abrasion	The load carried by the river hits the bed or banks, dislodging particles.
3 Attrition	Stones carried by the river knock against each other, becoming smaller/more rounded.
4 Solution	Alkaline rocks, e.g. limestone, are dissolved by slightly acidic river water.

Figure 1 *Processes of river erosion*

What are the processes of transportation?

Material transported by a river is called its *load*. The four main types of river transportation are shown in Figure **2**.

The size and amount of load carried depends on a river's speed, or *velocity*. After heavy rain rivers look muddy – they are fast flowing and transporting large amounts of sediment. At low flow, rivers look clearer and little sediment is transported.

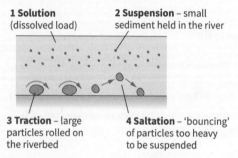

1 Solution (dissolved load)

2 Suspension – small sediment held in the river

3 Traction – large particles rolled on the riverbed

4 Saltation – 'bouncing' of particles too heavy to be suspended

Figure 2 *Types of river transportation*

When does deposition happen?

Figure **3** shows the balance between erosion, transportation and deposition along a river's course.

When a river's velocity decreases, and it no longer has the energy to transport its load, it deposits it.

- Larger rocks transported mainly by **traction** are only carried short distances during periods of *high flow*. They are deposited in a river's upper course.
- Smaller sediment is carried further downstream – mostly in **suspension**. It is deposited on a river's bed and banks where velocity slows due to friction.
- Lots of deposition occurs at a river's mouth where its velocity reduces because of the gentle gradient and also by interaction with tides.

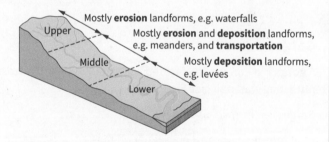

Mostly **erosion** landforms, e.g. waterfalls

Mostly **erosion** and **deposition** landforms, e.g. meanders, and **transportation**

Mostly **deposition** landforms, e.g. levées

Upper

Middle

Lower

Figure 3 *Processes and landforms along a river's course*

Six Second Summary

- Vertical and lateral erosion combine to change a river's channel and valley downstream.
- There are **four** processes of river erosion and **four** types of river transportation.
- Deposition happens when a river's velocity decreases.

Over to you

Make up a mnemonic (a phrase or sentence, with words beginning with the first letter of each process) to help you remember the **four** processes of river erosion (HAAS), and **four** types of transportation (SSTS).

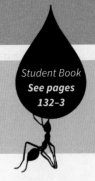

Student Book
See pages
132–3

You need to know:

- the characteristics and formation of these fluvial landforms – interlocking spurs, waterfalls and gorges.

River erosion landforms

1

Interlocking spurs

In Figure **1**, a mountain stream erodes vertically creating a *V-shaped valley*. It winds around areas of resistant rock to create **interlocking spurs** which jut out into the valley.

V-shaped valley

Interlocking spurs

Figure 1 V-shaped valley and interlocking spurs

2

Waterfalls

As a river flows downstream it crosses different rock types. More resistant rocks are less easily eroded than less resistant rocks, forming steps in a river's long profile. The steps form **waterfalls** – see Figure **2**.

Waterfalls can also form:

- when sea level drops causing a river to cut down into its bed creating a step (called a *knick point*)
- in glacial **hanging valleys**.

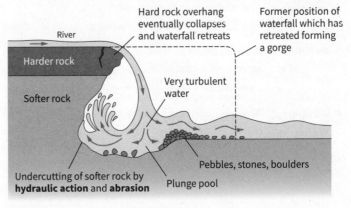

River

Harder rock

Softer rock

Hard rock overhang eventually collapses and waterfall retreats

Former position of waterfall which has retreated forming a gorge

Very turbulent water

Pebbles, stones, boulders

Undercutting of softer rock by **hydraulic action** and **abrasion**

Plunge pool

Figure 2 Formation of a waterfall

3

Gorges

A **gorge** is a narrow, steep-sided valley found downstream of a retreating waterfall (see Figure **2**).

Gorges can form in other ways:

- at the end of the last glacial period masses of water from melting glaciers poured off upland areas forming gorges (e.g. Cheddar Gorge, Somerset)
- on limestone, when large underground caverns can accommodate an entire river.

💡 Big Idea

Erosion is the dominant process in a river's upper course creating **interlocking spurs, waterfalls** and **gorges**.

⏱ Six Second Summary

- Each stage of a river's course (upper, middle, lower) has distinctive landforms.
- The main river erosion landforms in a river's upper course are interlocking spurs (in V-shaped valleys), waterfalls and gorges.

✏ Over to you

Draw a sketch of a river in its upper course to show its V-shaped valley and interlocking spurs. Then draw a diagram to show how waterfalls and gorges form.

Add annotations to explain how the landforms are created.

Student Book
See pages
134–5

You need to know:

- the characteristics and formation of river landforms resulting from erosion and deposition.

Landforms resulting from erosion and deposition

Meanders

- **Meanders** are bends in a river found mainly in lowland areas. They constantly change shape and position.
- Figure **1** shows the main features and processes taking place in a meandering river. The *thalweg* is the line of fastest current. It swings from side to side causing erosion on the outside bend, and deposition on the inside bend. These processes cause meanders to migrate across the valley floor.
- Meandering streams may develop alternating deep sections – *pools* (caused by erosion on the outside bend), and shallow sections – *riffles*. These result from the deposition of coarse sediment and have more turbulent slow-flowing water.

Ox-bow lakes

As meanders migrate across the valley floor they erode towards each other, eventually forming an **ox-bow lake** (Figure **2**).

Landforms resulting from deposition

Floodplains and levées

Floodplains are wide, flat areas on either side of a river in its middle and lower courses. They are created by migrating meanders and floods depositing layers of silt to form alluvium.

Levées form when, in low flow, deposition raises the river bed so the channel can't carry as much water. During flooding, water flows over the sides of the channel. As velocity decreases, coarser sediment is deposited first on the banks – then finer sand and mud, raising the height of the levées.

Estuaries

An **estuary** is where the river meets the sea. They are affected by tides, wave action *and* river processes. As the tide rises, rivers can't flow into the sea, so velocity falls and sediment is deposited forming *mudflats*, which develop into *salt marshes*.

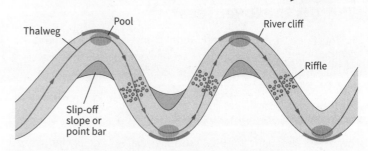

Figure 1 *Meandering river – processes and landforms*

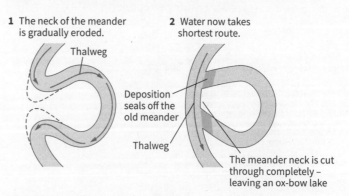

Figure 2 *Formation of an ox-bow lake*

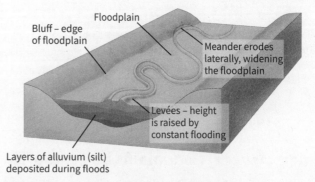

Figure 3 *Formation of floodplains and levées*

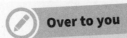

Six Second Summary

- Meanders and ox-bow lakes form as a result of erosion *and* deposition.
- Floodplains and levées are formed by deposition.
- The main process operating in estuaries is deposition.

Over to you

Outline the processes that create the following landforms: meanders, ox-bow lakes, floodplains, levées. Draw labelled diagrams to explain the formation of **two** of these.

EXAMPLE

You need to know:

- what landforms are found along the River Tees.

Student Book
**See pages
136–7**

Where is the River Tees?

The River Tees is in north-east England and its source is in the Pennines Hills. It flows roughly east to reach the North Sea at Middlesbrough.

In its upper course, the River Tees carves a steep-sided valley with interlocking spurs, rapids and small waterfalls.

Cow Green Reservoir (Figure **1**) supplies water to heavy industry on Teeside. It also stores water to reduce the risk of flooding downstream, and releases it during dry periods.

Figure 1 Cow Green Reservoir, Upper Teesdale

High Force waterfall and gorge

High Force (Figure **2**) is in the upper course of the River Tees. The river drops 20 m and continues through a gorge.

A resistant band of igneous rock (dolerite) cuts across the valley. The river can't erode this resistant rock and created a 'step' in its long profile. This forms the waterfall.

Underlying weaker rock (less resistance sandstone and limestone) is eroded to form and overhang.

The overhang collapses, and the waterfall retreats upstream to form a gorge.

Figure 2 High Force on the River Tees

Meanders, levées, floodplains and estuaries

Darlington is about halfway along the course of the Tees. The gradient here is less, and the river widens over a broad and mainly flat valley, with meanders and levées (Figure **3**).

The River Tees flows into the North Sea just north of Middlesbrough and forms a wide tidal estuary. River deposition has created mudflats that have been reclaimed for industrial developments, e.g. chemical works.

Figure 3 Meander on the River Tees near Darlington

 Six Second Summary

The River Tees has good examples of erosion and deposition landforms e.g. High Force (waterfall and gorge), meanders, levées and floodplains.

 Over to you

- List the landforms found along the River Tees.
- Which are formed by erosion? Which are formed by deposition? Which are formed by both erosion *and* deposition?

Student Book
See pages
138–9

You need to be able to:

- use a photo and OS map to study river deposition landforms on the River Tees.

Using photos and an OS map

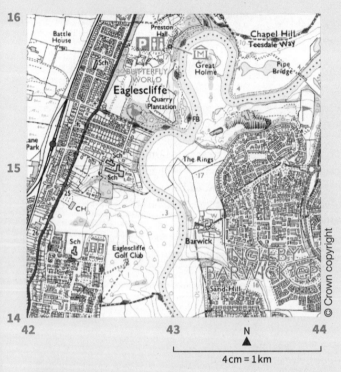

© Crown copyright

Figure 1 *1:25 000 OS map extract of the River Tees near Stockton-on-Tees*

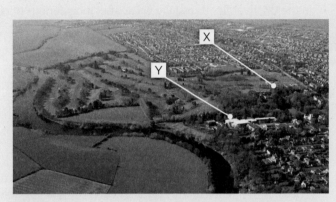

Figure 2 *Aerial photo of the River Tees at Egglescliffe (Eaglescliffe)*

SKILLS FOCUS

Skills

1 Find the spot height in grid square 4214 on Figure **1**. What is the height in metres?

2 Identify a meander on Figure **1**, and give the 4-figure grid reference for the square it is located in.

3 There are broad areas on either side of the river in Figure **1** banded by a 5-metre contour line. What is this area called?

4 Draw a sketch of the area shown in Figure **2**. Compare it with the map extract in Figure **1** and add the following labels:

  a Meander

  b Flood plain

  c Direction of river flow

  d Golf club

  e Main areas of settlement

  f School

Analysis

1 Figure **1** shows a meander but no ox-bow lakes.

  a Identify a grid square where an ox-bow lake might develop.

  b Draw a sequence of diagrams to show how an ox-bow lake forms.

2 Identify a grid square which shows a levée. Describe, with the aid of a diagram, how a levée forms.

3 Look at Figure **2**. Most of the land adjacent to the river is used for farming. Explain why it is not used for housing.

Evaluation

Which is better for studying river landforms – OS maps, photos or both? Explain your answer.

Student Book
See pages
140–1

You need to know:

- what factors affect the risk of flooding
- what a hydrograph is, and what affects its shape.

What causes river flooding?

- In the UK, river floods usually occur after long periods of rain – most frequently during winter or spring.
- Sudden floods, called *flash floods*, tend to occur in summer and are associated with thunderstorms.
- Physical and human factors can each increase flood risk.

 **Big Idea**

A river flood occurs when a river channel can no longer hold the amount of water flowing in it. Water overspills the banks onto the floodplain.

Physical factors	Human factors (land use)
• *Precipitation* – torrential rainstorms and/or prolonged periods of rain can lead to flooding. • *Geology* – impermeable rocks don't allow water to pass through, so it flows overland into river channels. • *Relief* – steep slopes mean water flows quickly into river channels.	• *Urbanisation* – impermeable surfaces, e.g. tarmac roads, mean water flows quickly into drains, sewers and river channels. • *Deforestation* – when trees are removed, much of the water which had been evaporated from leaves, or stored on leaves and branches, flows rapidly into river channels. • *Agriculture* – exposed soil leads to increased surface runoff (especially if ploughing occurs up and down slopes).

What is a hydrograph?

A hydrograph shows how a river reacts to a rainfall event. It shows rainfall and **discharge** – the volume of water flowing in a river measured in m³ per second (cumecs). *Lag time* shows how quickly water is transferred into the river channel. The shorter the lag time, the greater the risk of flooding.

These factors affect the shape of a hydrograph:

- basin size
- drainage density
- rock type and permeability
- land use
- relief
- soil moisture
- rainfall intensity
- antecedent rainfall

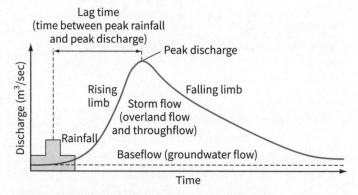

Figure 1 *A flood hydrograph*

 Six Second Summary

- Flooding occurs when a river can't hold the amount of water flowing in it.
- Human and physical factors increase the flood risk.
- A flood hydrograph shows how a river reacts to a rainfall event.
- Different factors affect the shape of a hydrograph.

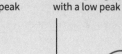 **Over to you**

Draw a larger version of the two hydrographs below. Annotate each one to explain what factors have affected their shape.

1 'Flashy' hydrograph with a short lag time and high peak

2 A flat hydrograph with a low peak

Student Book
See pages
142–3

You need to know:

- what hard engineering is, and some examples of it
- about costs and benefits of hard engineering strategies to manage river flooding.

What is hard engineering?

Hard engineering involves using artificial structures to prevent, or control flooding. It is usually very expensive and the *costs* have to be weighed against *benefits*.

- *Costs* are disadvantages, such as high financial costs and negative impacts on people/the environment.
- *Benefits* are advantages, such as environmental and the financial savings of preventing flooding.

Dams and reservoirs	Channel straightening	Embankments	Flood relief channels
• Widely used to regulate river flow and reduce risk of flooding. • Often multi-purpose, e.g. flood prevention; HEP generation; water supply. • Can be effective in regulating water flow and can store water in reservoir. • Expensive and controversial – reservoirs often flood large areas of land.	• Cutting through meanders creating a straight channel, speeding up water flow. But can increase flood risk downstream. • Straightened channels may be lined with concrete. This can be unattractive and can damage wildlife habitats and reduce biodiversity.	• Raise the level of a river bank allowing the channel to hold more water to help prevent flooding. • Concrete or stone walls are often used in towns, though mud dredged from the river can be used. This is cheaper, more sustainable and looks more natural.	• These can be built to by-pass urban areas. At times of high flow, sluice gates allow excess water to flow into the flood relief channel, reducing the threat of flooding. • They can support biodiverse aquatic ecosystems and provide recreation opportunities, but also involve land use change.

Figure 1 *Hard engineering strategies*

Clywedog reservoir, Llanidloes

The Clywedog reservoir was built in the 1960s to help prevent flooding of the River Severn. The reservoir stretches for nearly 10 km. It fills in the winter and water is released in the summer to maintain a constant flow.

Figure 2 *Clywedog dam and reservoir*

Jubilee River, Maidenhead

The Jubilee River is an 11 km long flood relief channel built to reduce the flood risk on the Thames. It opened in 2002. It has had a positive impact on the environment by creating new wetlands.

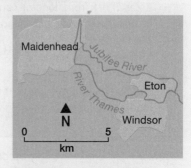

Figure 3 *The Jubilee River*

Six Second Summary

- Hard engineering involves the use of artificial structures to prevent or control flooding.
- Hard engineering schemes have costs and benefits.

Over to you

Use two highlighters to highlight the *costs* and *benefits* of strategies listed in Figure **1**. Summarise each strategy under the following headings:

- What is it?
- How does it work?
- Advantages
- Disadvantages

Student Book
See pages 144–5

You need to know:

- about flood warnings and preparation
- what soft engineering is, and some examples of it
- the costs and benefits of soft engineering strategies to manage river flooding

Flood warnings and preparation

In England and Wales, the Environment Agency issues **flood warnings**. There are three levels:

- *Flood watch* – flooding of low-lying land and roads expected. Be prepared.
- *Flood warning* – a threat to homes and businesses. People should move valuable items upstairs and turn off electricity and water.
- *Severe flood warning* – extreme danger to life and property. People should stay upstairs or leave their home.

The Environment Agency produces flood maps showing areas at risk of flooding. People living in these areas should plan for floods by using sandbags and floodgates to prevent water damaging property.

Local authorities and emergency services use flood maps to plan their responses to floods including installing temporary flood barriers, evacuating people and closing roads. Some places can become blighted by being mapped as 'at risk' from flooding with increased insurance costs and reduced property values.

Soft engineering

Soft engineering involves working *with* natural processes to manage flood risk. It aims to reduce and slow movement of water into a river channel to help prevent flooding. As with hard engineering, there are costs (disadvantages) and benefits (advantages).

Floodplain zoning	Afforestation (planting trees)	River restoration
• This restricts different land uses to certain zones on the floodplain. • Areas at risk from flooding can be used for grazing, parks and playing fields. • Cost effective in reducing exposure to flooding. • Can be difficult to implement on land already developed.	• Trees intercept rainfall, and slow down the transfer of water to river channels. • It is relatively cheap and has environmental benefits. • This strategy is widely used in the UK.	• When a river's course has been changed artificially, it can be restored to its original course. • It uses the natural processes and features of a river, e.g. meanders and wetlands to slow down flow and reduce the likelihood of flooding downstream. • It is relatively cheap, with long-term environmental benefits.

Figure 1 *Soft engineering strategies*

Six Second Summary

- Soft engineering works with natural processes to manage flood risk, and includes the use of floodplain zoning, afforestation and river restoration. floodplain zoning and river restoration.
- The Environment Agency produces flood maps and issues flood warnings.

Over to you

Use two highlighters to highlight the *costs* and *benefits* of strategies listed in Figure **1**. Summarise each strategy under the following headings:

- What is it?
- How does it work?
- Advantages
- Disadvantages

How would you decide whether hard or soft engineering is better if asked in an exam? Give a precise answer – no waffle.

Student Book
See pages
146–7

You need to know:

- why a flood management scheme was needed in Banbury
- what the scheme consists of
- the costs and benefits of the scheme.

Where is Banbury?

- Banbury is about 50 km north of Oxford.
- The population is about 45 000.
- Much of the town is on the floodplain of the River Cherwell (a tributary of the Thames).

Figure 1 *Location of Banbury*

Add a *WOW!* factor

A 200-year flood event is a flood which is expected to happen once every 200 years.

Why was the scheme needed?

Banbury has a history of flooding.

- In 1998 flooding closed the railway station, shut roads and caused £12.5 million of damage.
- In 2007 it was flooded again (along with much of central and western England).

What has been done?

In 2012 the flood defence scheme was completed. Figure **2** shows what was done.

Social	• The raised A361 stays open during a flood avoiding disruption. • Quality of life improved with new footpaths and green areas. • Less anxiety about flooding.
Economic	• The scheme cost £18.5 million, paid for partly by the Environment Agency and Cherwell District Council. • Over 400 houses and 70 businesses protected at a value of over £100 million.
Environmental	• Earth needed to build embankments was extracted locally, creating a small reservoir. • A new habitat has been created with ponds, trees and hedges.

Figure 3 *Costs and benefits*

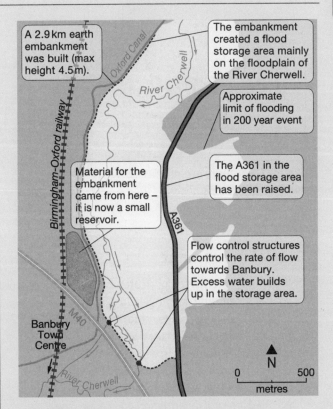

Figure 2 *Features of the Banbury Flood Storage Reservoir. A new pumping station transfers excess water into the river below the town.*

Six Second Summary

- Banbury is on the floodplain of the River Cherwell and at risk from flooding.
- A flood defence scheme has created a flood storage area and allowed the flow of the river to be controlled.
- The scheme has costs and benefits.

Over to you

Create a poster/flashcards/spider diagram to help you learn this example. You need to know:

- *where* is Banbury?
- *why* the scheme was needed
- *what* the flood defence scheme consists of (what has been done)
- the social, economic and environmental *issues*.

You need to know:

- how far ice extended across the UK during the last ice age
- the glacial processes that shaped the landscape.

Student Book
See pages 148–9

The UK under ice

During the last glacial period ice covered much of the UK. Glaciers in the north and west carved deep valleys and troughs. Further south and east land was permanently frozen *(permafrost)*.

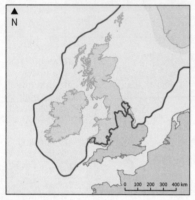

Figure 1 *Maximum extent of ice cover across the UK during the last glacial period (about 27000 years ago)*

Glacial movement

- In summer, meltwater lubricates the glacier so that it can slide downhill – *basal slip*. In hollows high on the valley side, the movement may be more curved – **rotational slip**.
- In winter the glacier is frozen to the rock surface. The weight of the ice and effect of gravity cause ice crystals to change shape. This is called *internal deformation* and causes the glacier to move slowly downhill.

Glacial deposition

- Deposition occurs when ice melts; most occurs at the glacier's *snout* (the front).
- As a glacier melts and retreats, it leaves behind poorly sorted rock fragments called **till** or *boulder clay*.
- In front of the glacier, meltwater transports sediment away. Larger rocks are deposited close to the ice, finer material is carried further away. This sandy and gravel material is called **outwash**.

Weathering processes

The main process in glacial environments is **freeze-thaw** (see 10.2). It's mainly seasonal – water freezes in winter, and thaws in summer. Freeze-thaw:

- helps create a jagged landscape of frost-shattered rock
- weakens rocks so they are more easily eroded
- creates *scree* which acts as a powerful erosion tool when trapped under moving glaciers.

Erosion processes

There are two main types of glacial erosion:

- **abrasion** – a 'sandpaper' effect caused by ice scouring the valley floor. *Striations* (scratches) are caused by large rocks below the ice.
- **plucking** occurs when meltwater beneath a glacier freezes around rock. Loose rock is 'plucked' away as the glacier moves over it.

Glacial transportation

- Sediment carried by a glacier – called **moraine** – can be transported *on, in* or *below* the ice.
- As a glacier moves it pushes loose material ahead of it – it's called **bulldozing**.

 Six Second Summary

- During the last glacial period much of the UK was covered by ice.
- Processes operating in glacial environments include weathering, erosion, movement, transport and deposition.

Over to you

Create a flow diagram to show how the processes of weathering, erosion, glacial movement, transport and deposition are linked in a glacial environment.

Student Book
**See pages
150–1**

You need to know:

- the characteristics and formation of landforms resulting from glacial erosion.

Corries

Also know as *cirques* and *cwms* – **corries** are large depressions found on the upper slopes of glaciated valleys. They have a steep back wall and a raised 'lip' at the front. Figure **1** shows their formation.

 **Big Idea**

Ice is a powerful agent of erosion, creating spectacular landforms in mountainous areas.

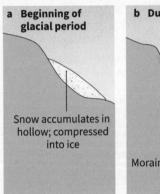

a Beginning of glacial period

Snow accumulates in hollow; compressed into ice

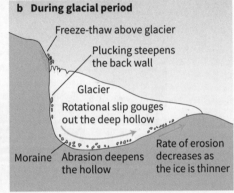

b During glacial period

Freeze-thaw above glacier

Plucking steepens the back wall

Glacier

Rotational slip gouges out the deep hollow

Moraine Abrasion deepens the hollow

Rate of erosion decreases as the ice is thinner

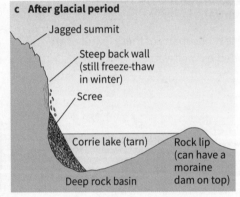

c After glacial period

Jagged summit

Steep back wall (still freeze-thaw in winter)

Scree

Corrie lake (tarn) Rock lip (can have a moraine dam on top)

Deep rock basin

Figure 1 *Formation of a corrie*

Arêtes and pyramidal peaks

- An **arête** is a narrow knife-edged ridge separating two corries.
- Arêtes typically form when erosion occurs in two adjacent corries.
- If three or more corries erode back-to-back a **pyramidal peak** may form.

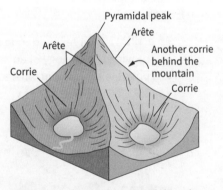

Pyramidal peak

Arête

Arête

Corrie

Another corrie behind the mountain

Corrie

Figure 2 *Arêtes and pyramidal peaks*

Six Second Summary

- Ice is a powerful agent of erosion.
- Corries, arêtes and pyramidal peaks are found on the upland parts of glaciated valleys.
- Glacial valley landforms include glacial troughs, truncated spurs, hanging valleys and ribbon lakes.

Glacial valley landforms

Most glaciers flow along already existing river valleys. They can't flow round obstacles, so carve straight courses.

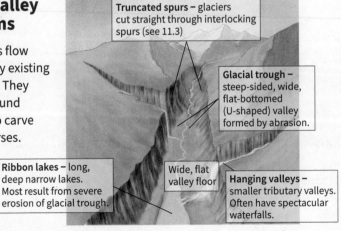

Truncated spurs – glaciers cut straight through interlocking spurs (see 11.3)

Glacial trough – steep-sided, wide, flat-bottomed (U-shaped) valley formed by abrasion.

Ribbon lakes – long, deep narrow lakes. Most result from severe erosion of glacial trough.

Wide, flat valley floor

Hanging valleys – smaller tributary valleys. Often have spectacular waterfalls.

Figure 3 *Glacial valley landforms*

Over to you

What's the difference between an arête and a pyramidal peak; a glacial trough and a hanging valley; a ribbon lake and a corrie lake (tarn)?

Now, draw an annotated diagram to show the formation of **one** glacial erosion landform.

Student Book
**See pages
152–3**

You need to know:

- the characteristics and formation of landforms resulting from glacial transport and deposition.

Moraine

Glaciers act like conveyor belts carrying weathered and eroded rock (**moraine**) from the mountains to the lowlands (see 12.1 on transport and deposition). There are several types of moraine (Figure **1**).

As ice melts many of these features are eroded by meltwater.

Lateral moraine – forms at the edges of the glacier. Mostly consists of scree resulting from freeze-thaw weathering. When ice melts, it forms low ridges on the valley sides.

Medial moraine – forms when a tributary glacier joins the main glacier and two lateral moraines merge. On melting, medial moraine forms a ridge down the centre of the valley.

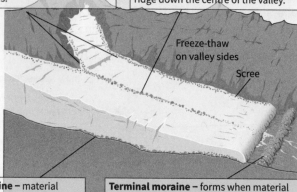

Freeze-thaw on valley sides

Scree

Ground moraine – material transported below a glacier and left behind when it melts. Often forms uneven hilly ground.

Terminal moraine – forms when material piles up at the glacier's snout, and forms a ridge across the valley. Represents the furthest extent of glacier's advance.

Figure 1 Types of moraine

Drumlins

- **Drumlins** are smooth, egg-shaped hills several hundred metres long. They are found in clusters on the floor of a glacial trough.
- They consist of moraine that has been shaped by the moving ice.
- They usually have a blunt end (facing up-valley) and a more pointed end (facing down-valley).

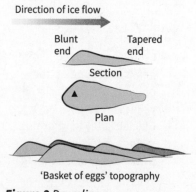

Figure 2 Drumlins

Erratics

- An **erratic** is a large boulder resting on a different type of rock.
- By studying the geology of an area, and the direction of ice flow, it is possible to work out where an erratic came from.

Figure 3 Erratics in the Scottish Highlands

Six Second Summary

- There are **four** types of moraine: ground, lateral, medial and terminal.
- Drumlins are smooth, egg-shaped hills found on the floor of a glacial trough.
- Erratics are large boulders that have been transported by glaciers.

Over to you

What's the difference between lateral and medial moraine; ground and terminal moraine; a drumlin and an erratic?

Now, draw a labelled diagram to show how drumlins form.

Student Book
See pages
154–5

SKILLS FOCUS

EXAMPLE

You need to be able to:

- use photos and OS maps to study glacial landforms.

Using photos and an OS map

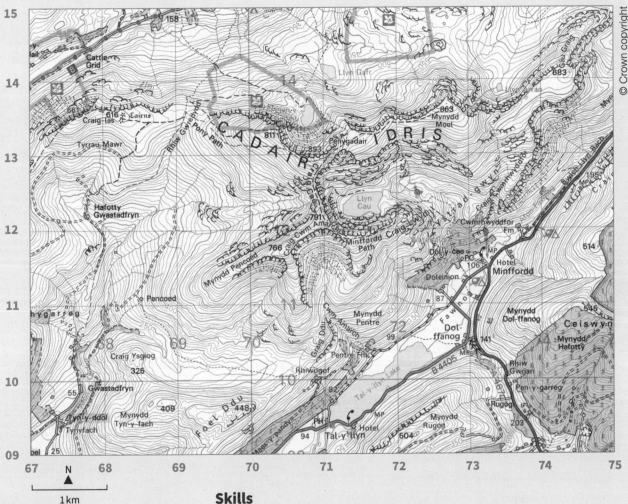

Figure 1 1:50 000 OS map extract of Cadair Idris

Figure 2 Cadair Idris and Lynn Cau

Figure 3 Tal-y-llyn Lake

Skills

1. Find the summit of Cadair Idris in grid square 7113 on Figure **1** (it's marked by a triangulation point). What is the height in metres?

2. **a** Identify an arête on Figure **1** and give the four-figure grid reference for the square it is located in.

   b What is the evidence that shows this is an arête?

   c Draw a diagram to show how an arête forms.

3. Identify the following landforms on Figure **1** and give the six-figure grid reference of each one: pyramidal peak, corrie, tarn, truncated spur.

Analysis

1. **a** Suggest why the landscape shown in Figure **2** is popular with visitors.

   b Describe the characteristics of the glacial features shown in the photograph.

2. **a** Describe the landscape shown in Figure **3**.

   b What type of landforms are shown in Figure **3**?

   c In what direction is the photo looking?

   d At about what height was the photo taken?

Evaluation

Which is better for studying glacial landforms – OS maps, photos or both? Explain your answer.

Student Book
See pages 156–7

You need to know:

- how glaciated upland areas in the UK provide opportunities for farming, forestry, quarrying and tourism.

Farming

- In upland areas, glacial erosion stripped away soil and vegetation. Soils are thin and acidic and mainly used for grazing. Sheep can tolerate the cold, wet and wind, and the poor vegetation.

- In summer, sheep graze the steep valley slopes and mountains. In winter, they are brought down from the high fells to be cared for on the valley floor.

- Soils in valleys are thicker because of deposition. It's easier to use machinery on flat-bottomed glacial troughs, so crops including cereals and potatoes are grown. Land is also used for growing winter feed (hay and silage) for animals.

Forestry

- Coniferous trees are adapted to cope with the acidic soils in glaciated upland areas of the UK and large plantations (mostly of conifers) have been planted.

- Conifers can be left to grow for 20–30 years before being cut down to produce 'soft' wood which is used for timber in the construction industry, or for making paper.

- In Scotland, large areas of the Loch Lomond and Trossachs National Park are used for industrial scale plantation forestry. In the Cairngorms, the focus is on promoting the spread of native woodland.

Quarrying

- Upland glaciated areas consist of hard, resistant rock which can be quarried and crushed for use in the construction industry and for road building.

- In the Cairngorms National Park there is a proposal to extend quarrying at Dalwhinnie. It will provide employment but could damage the environment and have a negative impact on tourism.

- Limestone (found in the Pennine Hills) is used in the chemical industry, for improving soils and for making cement.

Tourism

- The UK's glaciated upland areas attract tourists who enjoy outdoor activities and cultural heritage.

- Tourism provides employment for thousands of people.

- Aviemore (near the Cairngorm Mountains, Scotland) is one of the UK's main mountain activity centres with mountain biking, skiing, walking, climbing, and lots of wildlife.

Six Second Summary

- Glaciated upland areas of the UK provide opportunities for economic activities including tourism, farming, forestry and quarrying.

Over to you

Create a spider diagram of economic opportunities in glaciated areas. Add a leg for each of: tourism, farming, forestry and quarrying. Add as much detail to it as you can.

Student Book
See pages 158–9

You need to know:

- about conflicts between development and conservation in glaciated upland areas in the UK.

Wind farms in the Lake District

Kirkstone Pass is one of the Lake District's most remote valleys. A project to build three 16m wind turbines was completed in 2012, and cost £150000.

The turbines provide power for a pub which had relied on generators for heat and light. There was opposition, but the Friends of the Lake District supported the scheme. The group said that 'green power' was good for the environment, and helped to secure the future of the pub and its employees.

But arguments against wind farms elsewhere in the Lake District include:

- people think they spoil the natural landscape
- fewer tourists stay in the area, affecting the local economy
- house prices might fall if views are spoilt by turbines.

Big Idea

Development in glaciated areas can lead to **land use conflict**:

- *quarrying* can lead to land and river pollution and spoil the landscape
- *tourism* creates problems over access to land, traffic congestion and rising house prices
- building *reservoirs* can create environmental issues.

Zip-wire developments in the Lake District

Zip-wires are popular tourist developments in upland glaciated areas, providing stunning views and a high-adrenalin experience. But they often cause conflict.

In 2014, Windermere-based company, Treetop Trek, proposed constructing parallel one-mile long zip-wires above Glenridding in Patterdale. The plans were dropped because local people were concerned about **conservation**. They feared the development would threaten the area's views, tranquillity and natural environment, and have a negative impact on tourism.

In 2017, Treetop Trek proposed a £1.8m zip-wire development at Thirlmere near Keswick (Figure **1**). It was expected to attract 50000 tourists, boosting the local economy. Thousands opposed it, claiming it would ruin the landscape, threaten natural habitats and increase pollution. This planning application was also dropped.

Figure 1 *Thirlmere reservoir, proposed zip-wire site*

Six Second Summary

- Opportunities for development in glaciated upland areas can lead to conflict.
- Some people are opposed to the construction of wind farms in the Lake District.
- The proposed zip-wire development is a good example of conflict between development and conservation.

Over to you

Create a mind-map of different land *uses* and *developments* in the Lake District.

Add notes to the links to show where conflict might occur.

Student Book
**See pages
160–1**

EXAMPLE

> **You need to know:**
>
> • about the attractions, impacts and management of tourism in the Lake District.

Why do people visit the Lake District?

The Lake District in north-west England is an upland glaciated area and a National Park. It is famous for its scenery (Figure **1**).

Physical attractions	Cultural attractions
• Lakes (e.g. Windermere) provide water sports, cruises and fishing. • Mountains (e.g. Helvellyn) are popular for walking and mountain biking. • Adventure activities include abseiling and rock climbing.	• The landscape has inspired poets (e.g. Wordsworth) and writers (e.g. Beatrix Potter, whose home is a tourist attraction). • Scenic towns and villages (e.g. Ambleside) are popular. • Monuments such as Muncaster Castle at Ravenglass.

Figure 1 *Lake Windermere and Ambleside*

What are the impacts of tourism on the Lake District?

Social	Economic	Environmental
• 20 million visitors in 2018 (there are 40 000 residents!). • 83% of visitors arrive by car which causing congestion. • High house prices – 20% are holiday lets or second homes. • Most tourism jobs are seasonal and poorly paid.	• Tourists spent £3 billion in 2019 supporting hotels, shops, restaurants. • Provides 65 000 jobs. • New businesses, such as adventure tourism, provide jobs for local people. • Congestion slows down business communications.	• Honeypot sites are overcrowded and footpaths are damaged. • Pollution from cars and boats damages ecosystems. • Walkers damage farmland and dogs disturb livestock.

How is tourism managed?

The *Go Lakes Travel programme* is a £6.9 million initiative to encourage sustainable transport options, including:

• building dual-carriageways around the Lake District
• improving public transport and traffic management to reduce congestion
• developing integrated networks for walking and cycling, with wheelchair access
• creating transport hubs (e.g. at Ambleside)
• expanding park-and-ride schemes connecting car parks with popular villages and footpaths.

Footpath erosion

• The Upland Path Landscape Restoration Project and Fix the Fells repair paths and re-plant native plants.
• There are still hundreds of kilometres of footpaths that need on-going maintenance.

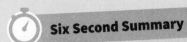

Six Second Summary

• The Lake District has many attractions for visitors.
• Tourism has a range of impacts on the area.
• Different strategies are used to manage tourism.

Over to you

Create a poster, flashcards, spider diagram or whatever works best for you. You need to learn:

• what *attracts* tourists to the Lake District
• the *impacts* of tourism
• how tourism is *managed*.

Section A
Urban issues and challenges

Your exam

Section A Urban issues and challenges is part of Paper 2: Challenges in the human environment.

Paper 2 is a one-and-a-half hour written exam and makes up 35 per cent of your GCSE. The whole paper carries 88 marks (including 3 marks for SPaG) – questions on Section A will carry 33 marks.

You need to study all the topics in Section A – in your final exam you will have to answer questions on all of them.

Tick these boxes to build a record of your revision

Your revision checklist

Spec key idea	Theme	1	2	3
13 The urban world				
A growing percentage of the world's population lives in urban areas	13.1 An increasingly urban world			
	13.2 Factors affecting the rate of urbanisation			
Urban growth creates opportunities and challenges for cities in low income countries and newly emerging economies	13.3 Introducing Rio de Janeiro			
	13.4 Social opportunities in Rio			
	13.5 Economic opportunities in Rio			
	13.6 Managing the challenges of urban growth			
	13.7 Managing water, sanitation and energy			
	13.8 Social challenges – access to health and education			
	13.9 Challenges of social and environmental issues			
	13.10 Planning for Rio's urban poor			
Geographical skills	13.11 Skills Focus: Line chart and satellite image			
14 Urban change in the UK				
Urban change in cities in the UK leads to a variety of social, economic and environmental opportunities and challenges	14.1 Where do people live in the UK?			
	14.2 Introducing Bristol			
	14.3 How can urban change create opportunities? (1)			
	14.4 How can urban change create opportunities? (2)			
	14.5 How can urban change create opportunities? (3)			
	14.6 Urban change – challenges (1)			
Geographical skills	14.7 Skills Focus: Graphs and statistical skills			
	14.8 Urban change – challenges (2)			
	14.9 Urban change – challenges (3)			
	14.10 Urban regeneration in Bristol (1)			
	14.11 Urban regeneration in Bristol (2)			
15 Sustainable urban development				
Urban sustainability requires management of resources and transport	15.1 Planning for urban sustainability			
	15.2 Sustainable traffic management strategies			

You need to know:

- about the global pattern of urban change.

Student Book
See pages
162–3

How is the world's population changing?

The world's population is increasing. Since the 1900s, the bigger the global population has become, the faster it has grown (Figure **1**). The global population is projected to level out in the twenty-second century.

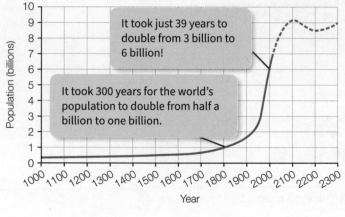

It took just 39 years to double from 3 billion to 6 billion!

It took 300 years for the world's population to double from half a billion to one billion.

Figure 1 *Global population growth since the year 1000*

What is urbanisation?

Urbanisation is the proportion of the world's population who live in cities.
Urbanisation is growing because of natural increase (births minus deaths) and migration.

Urban growth is the increase in the area covered by cities.

The global pattern of urban change

- Urbanisation is slowing in **high income countries (HICs)**.
- The greatest rate of urbanisation is in **low income countries (LICs)** and **newly emerging economies (NEEs)**.
- Of the increase in the world's urban population, 90 per cent is taking place in Africa and Asia, especially India, China and Nigeria.

In south and south-east Asia, and in Africa, around half the population live in towns and cities.

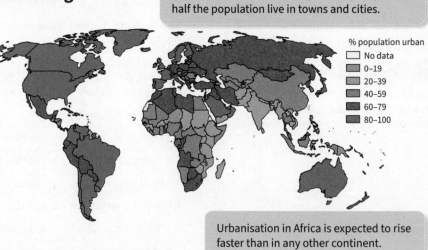

% population urban
- No data
- 0–19
- 20–39
- 40–59
- 60–79
- 80–100

In most (HICs), over 60% of the population live in cities.

Urbanisation in Africa is expected to rise faster than in any other continent.

Figure 2 *Global urban population, 2017*

Six Second Summary

- The global population has grown rapidly since 1950.
- Urbanisation is growing around the world.
- Currently, urbanisation is higher in HICs than in LICs.
- Urban populations are growing more quickly in less developed regions, especially in Africa and Asia.

Over to you

Write a clear definition of urbanisation. Write **five** statements that show how urbanisation varies in different parts of the world.

Student Book
**See pages
164–5**

You need to know:

- the factors that make cities grow.

Why do cities grow?

There are two main reasons why cities are getting bigger: natural increase and rural–urban migration.

1

Natural increase

Natural increase is where the birth rate is higher than the death rate.

Natural increase is higher in LICs and some NEEs because:

- there are lots of young adults aged 18–35
- improvements to health care have significantly lowered the death rate.

What are megacities?

Megacities are cities with a population of over 10 million. Most are in less-developed countries.

The table below shows three types of megacities.

Type	Features	Examples
Slow-growing	No squatter settlements	Tokyo Los Angeles (often in HICs)
Growing	Under 20% in squatter settlements	Beijing Rio de Janeiro (often in NEEs)
Rapid-growing	Over 20% in squatter settlements	Jakarta Mumbai (often in NEEs or LICs)

Figure 1 *Satellite image of Tokyo*

2

Rural–urban migration

Rural–urban migration is the movement of people from the countryside into towns and cities.

This is caused by *push* and *pull factors*.

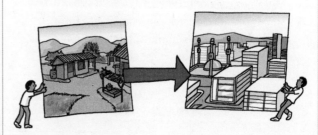

Push factors

Reasons why people want to leave the countryside:

- Farming is hard and poorly paid.
- Farming is often at subsistence level, leaving nothing to sell.
- Rural areas are isolated, often with few services.

Pull factors

Reasons why people are attracted to the city:

- A higher standard of living is possible.
- There are better medical facilities.
- There is a better chance of getting an education.

Six Second Summary

- Cities are growing because of natural increase and rural–urban migration.
- Rural–urban migration is caused by push factors and pull factors.
- Megacities have a population of over 10 million.
- Megacities are growing more quickly in NEEs and LICs.

Over to you

Make a list of **three** push factors and **three** pull factors. Make sure they're not just opposites of each other.

Student Book
**See pages
166–7**

You need to know:

- why the city of Rio de Janeiro is growing so rapidly.

CASE STUDY

The location of Rio and its importance

Rio de Janeiro is situated around Guanabara Bay in the south-east of Brazil. Rio is:

- a 'global city'
- an important industrial and financial centre
- a major regional, national and international centre for many companies
- an international transport hub
- seen as the cultural capital of Brazil
- a UNESCO World Heritage Site.

 **Big Idea**

Rio de Janeiro is major city in an NEE. It is a case study to show how urban growth creates *opportunities* and *challenges* for cities in LICs and NEEs.

Figure 1 *Sugar Loaf Mountain, Rio*

How and why has Rio de Janeiro grown?

Rio has grown rapidly in the last 50 years as a result of **migration** and **natural increase** (Figure **2**).

International migration

This table summarises migration to Rio.

Where from?	When?	Why?
Portugal	Until the late 1800s	Portugal is the former colonial power
Germany and Japan	20th century	Labour for coffee plantations
USA and UK	21st century	Skilled workers attracted by jobs
South Korea, the Philippines and China		New business opportunities
Portugal		Common language

Natural increase

Most migrants to the city are young, leading to a relatively high birth rate and a low death rate. Better health care and social services have resulted in a lower death rate.

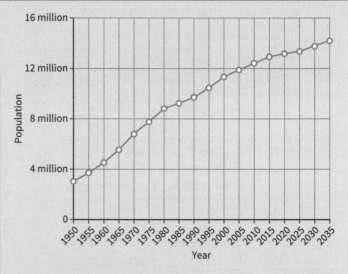

Figure 2 *The growth of Rio's population, 1950–2035 (projected)*

Internal migration

Most migrants move to Rio from other parts of Brazil, particularly from rural areas. This is the result of push and pull factors (see 13.2).

 Six Second Summary

- Rio de Janeiro is in the south-east of Brazil
- It is a major regional, national and international city
- It has grown because of internal and international migration, and natural increase

 Over to you

Draw a spider diagram with five 'legs' to show five reasons why Rio de Janeiro is an important city.

Student Book
See pages 168–9

You need to know:

- how urban growth has created social opportunities in Rio.

How has urban growth created social opportunities?

- High levels of investment in Rio have created features such as Rio's Olympics in 2016.
- Many of Rio's international migrants are skilled workers. They help to boost the diversity of the city.
- Money has been invested in health care and education.

	Rio	Brazil average
Life expectancy (years)	76.3	75.7
Infant mortality (per 1000)	6.2	12.4
Literacy rate (%)	99	93

Figure 1 *Social development indicators for Rio and Brazil*

Big Idea

Urban growth creates social opportunities. 'Social' refers to people's lives and well-being.

Access to services

Health

- Rio's residents enjoy free health care and better access to hospitals than in other parts of Brazil.
- Health cover has increased from 4 per cent to 70 per cent for people in some slum areas.
- 'Family health teams' have each provided health care for up to 3000 people.

Education

- Rio has over 1000 primary schools, 400 secondary schools and six universities.
- In the poorer favelas, NGOs such as 'Schools for Tomorrow' are working with communities to improve education provision.
- The government provides grants to help children remain in school.

Figure 2 *Family health clinic, Complexo do Alemão, Rio*

Access to resources

Water supply

- Rio has the largest water treatment works in the world.
- About 96 per cent of the city has safe piped water, though only 88 per cent of houses in favelas are connected.

Energy

- About 99 per cent of the city's residents have direct access to electricity.
- In the Santa Marta slum, a community energy programme has fitted over 150 solar panels to the roofs of many buildings which provide affordable, clean energy.

Six Second Summary

- Rio's urban growth creates social opportunities in access to health services, education, water supply and energy
- Social opportunities tend to be higher in Rio than in rural areas.

Over to you

Describe two opportunities for each of health services, education, water supply and energy in Rio.

CASE STUDY

Student Book
**See pages
170–1**

You need to know:

- how the industrial areas of Rio have become a stimulus for economic development.

Economic opportunities for growth

Rio's industrial growth has helped to stimulate economic development in the *formal economy*:

- Rio is Brazil's second most important industrial centre.
- With its growing population, there is a large labour supply.
- Existing industries stimulate the development of new industries (called the 'multiplier effect').
- A growing number of jobs are in the service sector and public services.
- The tourist and oil industries have helped to stimulate economic development.

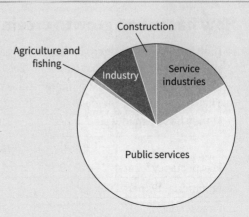

Figure 1 Types of employment in Rio

How have industrial areas stimulated economic development?

Rio has a diverse range of industries, including:

- a rapidly expanding service and quaternary sector.
- established traditional manufacturing industries such as printing, pharmaceuticals and food processing.

The industrial areas in Rio have stimulated economic development at a range of scales:

- The Brazilian and local governments have benefited from tax revenues and investment into the city.
- Local people have secure employment, increasing disposable incomes and better health care and education.
- Local communities, particularly the favelas, have benefited from investment and self-help projects, improving service provision.

These industrial areas benefit from Rio's port facilities (Figure **3**). Oil refining and shipbuilding employ many local people and encourage supply chain industries to set up.

Ternium steelworks, Sepetiba Bay

This giant steelworks is in Rio's West Zone. It has triggered significant multiplier effects, attracting construction and supply industries into the area and stimulating economic development.

Figure 2 Ternium steelworks, Sepetiba Bay, Rio

Figure 3 The port of Rio

Six Second Summary

- Rio's industrial areas have become a stimulus for economic development.
- Existing industries trigger a multiplier effect by attracting other industries.
- There are increased job opportunities for local people.

Over to you

Either: Draw your understanding of the economic opportunities in Rio. (No writing!)

Or: Create a mind-map of the economic opportunities in Rio.

CASE STUDY

You need to know:

- about the challenges associated with slums and squatter settlements in Rio.

The challenges of managing slums and squatter settlements

Rio has not been able to build enough housing for its rapidly growing population. The majority of the poorer population have to live in slums or squatter settlements.

Slums

Rio's slums are usually older, abandoned industrial or residential buildings. Often they:

- are dangerously overcrowded

- have inadequate services such as bathrooms and lighting
- are owned by landlords who charge high rents.

Squatter settlements

Squatter settlements are unplanned invasions of land by homeless people.

Favelas are the most common type of squatter settlement. They are self-built houses on public or private land. Over time, services such as water and electricity may be introduced.

The challenges of living in favelas

Construction
- Initially houses were poorly constructed. They are now mostly built from concrete and brick.
- Heavy rain can cause landslides on steep slopes.

Unemployment
- Unemployment rates are as high as 20%.
- Average incomes may be less than £75 a month.

Crime
- A high murder rate of 20 per 1000 people in many favelas.
- Drug gangs can dominate.

Services
In the non-improved favelas:
- 12% of homes have no running water
- 30% have no electricity
- 50% have no sewage connections.

Health
- Infant mortality rates are as high as 50 per 1000.
- Waste can build up in the street, increasing the danger of disease.

Figure 1 *A favela on a Rio hillside*

 Six Second Summary

- Many poorer people live in slums or squatter settlements.
- Slums are often overcrowded with inadequate services.
- Challenges in favelas include landslides, high unemployment and high infant mortality rates.

Over to you

Give the meaning of the term 'squatter settlement'.

List **seven** challenges that the people living in squatter settlements face.

Consider which **two** challenges would be most difficult to overcome and give one piece of evidence to support your ideas.

Student Book
See pages
174–5

CASE STUDY

You need to know:

- about providing clean water, sanitation systems and energy for Rio.

Water supply

Despite plentiful supply, around 12 per cent of Rio's population do not have access to clean running water.

- The city does not have a duty to supply water to households in favelas where there is no legal proof of ownership.
- Underground pipes are often accessed illegally.
- Poor maintenance and leakages result in water being cut off.

Sanitation systems

- The city's infrastructure (pipes and sewage treatment works) cannot cope with the volume of waste.
- About 35 per cent of Rio's sewage is transferred in open sewers and dumped into Guanabara Bay.
- About 150 metric tons of industrial wastewater, which may be toxic or contaminated with chemicals, flows into the bay.
- Many houses in favelas are not connected to the sewage system because of legal land ownership issues.

Energy

- About 99 per cent of all homes in Rio have access to electricity.
- In favelas, the illegal tapping of electricity supply is common. This can lead to fires, electrocution and blackouts.
- Demand for energy is rising rapidly, due to Rio's growing population and expanding industrial sector.

Big Idea

Urban growth has created challenges providing clean water, sanitation systems and energy.

Figure 1 *Makeshift water supplies in one of Rio's favelas*

Babilonia community scheme

In Babilonia favela, a non-governmental company, Revolusolar, has installed solar panels to provide energy to 35 families, two shops and one school (Figure **2**).

Figure 2 *Checking solar panels installed in Babilonia favela, Rio*

Six Second Summary

- Urban growth has created challenges with providing clean water, sanitation systems and energy.
- In favelas, land ownership issues mean many houses are not connected to services.
- Problems include water being cut off, sewage in the sea, and power cuts.

Over to you

Write down, with detail, one problem caused by **each** of these challenges:

- water supply
- sanitation systems
- energy.

You need to know:

- about the social challenges of providing access to health and education in Rio.

CASE STUDY

What are the challenges in health and education provision?

Rio has a youthful population. There are a large number of children, which puts pressure on the health and education systems.

Health

There is greater access to health care in Rio than in surrounding rural areas, but there are still only six hospitals and insufficient health clinics.

There are great social and economic inequalities across the city. Figure **1** compares Rio and two districts in the West Zone – Barra de Tijica is an affluent beach district and Cidade de Deus is a low-income area originally built to rehouse people from slum areas.

The challenges are particularly difficult in favelas:

- On average, favela residents live 13 years less than people in wealthier parts of Rio.
- There are just two health clinics for a favela population of about 100 000.
- Many people suffer from diseases because of poor sanitation and a lack of safe water.
- The Covid-19 pandemic had devastating impacts on people living in overcrowded favelas (Figure **2**).

District	Zone	Infant mortality (per 1000)	Pregnant females getting medical care	Average life expectancy
Cidade de Deus	West	21	60%	45
Barra da Tijuca	West	6	100%	80
Rio de Janeiro		19	74%	63

Figure 1 Health in two contrasting districts and Rio as a whole

Figure 2 Disinfecting the streets in a favela against Covid-19

Education

About 90 per cent of children aged 10 can read and write because there are more schools in Rio compared with rural areas. However, about 25 per cent of the poorest children do not attend school regularly.

Only about half of children in Rio continue with education beyond the age of 14. Reasons include:

- a shortage of local schools
- teenage pregnancy
- many children are expected to work.

Violence and drug-related crime in favelas may shut schools. Schools were closed during the Covid-19 pandemic but children lacked computers and internet access at home.

Six Second Summary

- Rio has greater access to services than rural areas.
- There are problems in accessing health care and education, especially in poorer areas.
- The Covid-19 pandemic impacted upon health and education, especially in favelas.

Over to you

From memory, time yourself talking for thirty seconds about the challenges of accessing health and education in Rio.

Student Book
**See pages
178–9**

You need to know:

- about the challenges of unemployment, crime and the environmental issues of waste disposal, pollution and traffic congestion in Rio.

CASE STUDY

Unemployment

- There are huge inequalities in unemployment rates in Rio (Figure **1**).
- Measuring unemployment accurately is impossible due to the large number of people employed in the *informal economy*.
- High rates of unemployment are due to:
  o economic recession in 2015
  o an economic crisis in 2018 when many people lost their jobs in public services
  o the 2016 Olympics created few long-term employment opportunities.

 **Big Idea**

The rapid growth of Rio's population has created unemployment, crime and environmental challenges. These three issues particularly affect low-income groups.

District	Zone	Unemployment rate
Barra da Tijuca (wealthy, middle-class)	West	2%
Complexo do Alemão (favelas)	North	Estimated 37%

Figure 1 *Unemployment rates in Rio*

Crime

- Robbery and violent crime occur regularly in Rio.
- Since 2017, the murder rate has increased by 20 per cent.
- Police regularly target drug gangs in the favelas.

Figure 2 *Traffic congestion in Rio*

Environmental challenges in Rio
Waste disposal

- Each year Rio produces 3.5 million tonnes of waste. Less than 2 per cent is recycled.
- In the favelas' narrow, steep streets, waste collection is difficult. Much of the waste enters rivers.

Water pollution

- Guanabara Bay is highly polluted, threatening wildlife, fishing and tourism.
- Many of the rivers flowing into the bay are heavily polluted with sewage and waste.
- Industrial waste, oil spills and other ship discharges contaminate the bay.

Traffic congestion and air pollution

- Rio is the most congested city in South America.
- Traffic delays cost businesses huge amounts of time and money.
- Air pollution is estimated to cause 5000 deaths per year.

Six Second Summary

- Unemployment rates in favelas can be very high.
- Robbery and violent crime occur regularly in Rio.
- Environmental challenges include waste disposal, water and air pollution, and traffic congestion.

Over to you

Describe **one** challenge in Rio for **each** of the following. Use no more than one sentence for each:

- unemployment
- crime
- waste disposal
- water pollution
- traffic congestion
- air pollution.

Student Book
See pages 180-1

CASE STUDY

You need to know:

- about improvements to slums and squatter settlements aimed at improving the quality of life for the urban poor in Rio.

The Favela Bairro Project

The Favela Bairro Project (1995–2009) was a US$1 billion 'slum-to-neighbourhood' project that aimed to integrate Rio's favelas into the fabric of the city.

Big Idea

This is an example of how urban planning is improving the quality of life for the urban poor. Quality of life describes the extent to which a person is comfortable, healthy and able to enjoy life.

Social
- Daycare and after-school care, enabling adults to seek secure employment.
- Improving adult literacy.
- Medical services for drug addiction, alcoholism and victims of domestic violence.

Economic
- Inhabitants can apply to own their properties legally.
- Access to credit to allow people to buy materials to improve their homes.

Aims of the Favela Bairro Project

Environmental
- Replacement of wooden buildings with brick, making them permanent and resistant to the weather.
- Removal of houses from dangerous steep slopes.
- Infrastructure improvements (water, sanitation and electricity).
- Improved access for waste collection and emergency services.

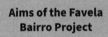

Figure 1 *Aims of the Favela Bairro Project*

How successful has the Favela Bairro Project been?

Successes	Issues
• By 2005 around 100 favelas were improved. • Residents were granted land ownership, roads paved and new childcare centres opened. • The quality of life, mobility and employment prospects of the inhabitants improved considerably. • Training was made available in hygiene, computing and community development.	• Basic literacy was not addressed. • Some of the new infrastructure improvements were costly and were not maintained. • Increased rents in some of the improved favelas. • New raised pavements have caused flooding of homes. • Deaths from vector-borne diseases (e.g. malaria) have not reduced.

Figure 2 *Successes and issues of the Favela Bairro Project*

Six Second Summary

- The Favela Bairro Project included social, economic and environmental aims.
- Successes included land ownership and improved employment prospects.
- Issues remain such as rents rising.

Over to you

List **three** aims, successes and issues of the Favela Bairro Project. Colour code each one to show whether it is social, economic or environmental.

You need to be able to:

- construct a line chart
- calculate percentage change
- extrapolate data
- interpret satellite images.

Student Book
See pages 182–3

SKILLS FOCUS

CASE STUDY

Using a line chart with a satellite image

Barra da Tijuca (Barra) is a coastal suburb in Rio's West Zone. It is one of the city's fastest growing neighbourhoods.

Figure **1** shows how the population of Rio has grown between 1950 and 2020. The two satellite images (Figures **2** and **3**) show the growth of Barra between 1984 and 2015.

Year	1950	1960	1970	1980
Population (millions)	3.0	4.5	6.8	8.8
Year	1990	2000	2010	2020
Population (millions)	9.7	11.3	12.4	13.5

Figure 1 *Population of Rio, 1950–2020*

Figure 2 *Satellite photo of Barra da Tijuca, 1984*

Figure 3 *Satellite photo of Barra da Tijuca, 2015*

Skills

1 Look at Figure **1**.
  a Between which two years did the population of Rio grow by:
    i 2 million
    ii the greatest percentage?
  b Is the rate of growth of Rio's population:
    i speeding up
    ii staying the same
    iii slowing down?

Give data to illustrate your answer.

2 Which of **a**) bar chart, **b**) pie chart or **c**) line graph, would be the **most suitable** graph to show the data in Figure **1**? Give a reason for your answer.

3 Look at the land use in Barra in 2015 (Figure **3**).
  a Name the features shown on this satellite photo in:
    i green
    ii dark blue
    iii beige/grey.
  b Assess the likely impact on the proportions of each of these features if Rio's population were to continue to increase.

Analysis

1 Look at Figure **1**.
  a Using the data, predict the changes in Rio's population between:
    i 2020 and 2030
    ii 2030 and 2040.
  b Explain how you could use a line graph to predict more accurately Rio's population by 2040.

2 Look at Figures **2** and **3**.
  a Explain the value of **i**) the forest, and **ii**) the coast, to the people living in this part of Rio.
  b Assess the threats of future urban sprawl to these areas of the city if rapid population growth continues.

Evaluation

How far do line graphs create better predictions of future populations than using tables of data?

Student Book
**See pages
184–5**

You need to know:

* about the distribution (how it is spread out) of population in the UK and the location of the major cities.

How is the UK population distributed?

* The UK's population is unevenly distributed.
* 84 per cent live in urban areas.
* One in seven of these urban dwellers live in London and the south-east of England.
* Many highland regions are very sparsely populated – upland areas are remote and can experience harsh weather conditions.

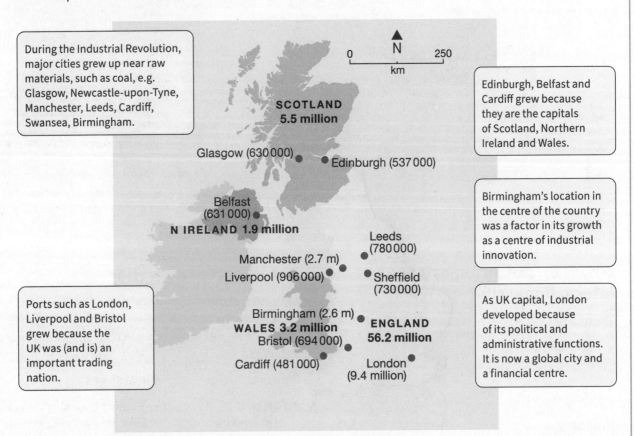

During the Industrial Revolution, major cities grew up near raw materials, such as coal, e.g. Glasgow, Newcastle-upon-Tyne, Manchester, Leeds, Cardiff, Swansea, Birmingham.

Edinburgh, Belfast and Cardiff grew because they are the capitals of Scotland, Northern Ireland and Wales.

Birmingham's location in the centre of the country was a factor in its growth as a centre of industrial innovation.

Ports such as London, Liverpool and Bristol grew because the UK was (and is) an important trading nation.

As UK capital, London developed because of its political and administrative functions. It is now a global city and a financial centre.

SCOTLAND
5.5 million
Glasgow (630 000)
Edinburgh (537 000)
Belfast (631 000)
N IRELAND 1.9 million
Leeds (780 000)
Manchester (2.7 m)
Liverpool (906 000)
Sheffield (730 000)
Birmingham (2.6 m)
WALES 3.2 million
ENGLAND 56.2 million
Bristol (694 000)
Cardiff (481 000)
London (9.4 million)

Figure 1 *The population of the UK and its major cities, 2021*

How might this distribution change?

* There has been a general drift towards London and south-east England.
* There is greater inward migration than outward migration. Net migration has declined every year from 2015 to 2021.
* In recent years, there has been a movement from urban to rural areas. Many older people choose to retire near the coast or in the country.

Six Second Summary

* The UK's population is unevenly distributed.
* 84 per cent live in urban areas.
* Cities grew near supplies of raw materials.
* There is now a general drift towards London and the south-east.

Over to you

On a blank map of the UK, mark the location of **nine** different cities. For at least **five** of those cities, write down why each one has grown.

Student Book
**See pages
186–7**

You need to know:

- where Bristol is located
- reasons why Bristol is important in both the UK and the wider world
- the impacts of national and international migration on a) the growth and b) the character of Bristol.

CASE STUDY

What makes Bristol a major UK city?

Bristol is the largest city in south-west England. It is important regionally and nationally.

 **Big Idea**

Bristol is a case study of a major city in the UK.

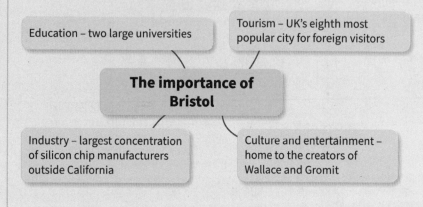

Education – two large universities

Tourism – UK's eighth most popular city for foreign visitors

The importance of Bristol

Industry – largest concentration of silicon chip manufacturers outside California

Culture and entertainment – home to the creators of Wallace and Gromit

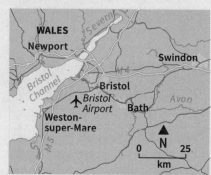

Figure 1 *Bristol is linked to Wales and London by the M4, and to the south-east and Midlands by the M5*

Why is Bristol an important international city?

Transport

- Good road and rail links
- Ferry services to Europe
- Two major docks
- Bristol airport links to Europe and the USA

Industry

- Global industries like aerospace and media
- Inward investment from abroad

Education

- Attracts international students

The impact of migration

Until 2015, about half of Bristol's population growth came from migration, including large numbers from EU countries. Migration has brought both opportunities and challenges.

Opportunities

- Part of a hard-working workforce.
- Enriching the city's cultural life.
- Mainly young migrants help to balance the ageing population.

Challenges

- Housing provision has not kept pace with population growth – so Bristol is very expensive for housing.
- Teaching children whose first language is not English.
- Integration into the wider community can be a challenge.

 Six Second Summary

- Bristol is important in the UK, e.g. education and tourism.
- Bristol is important in the wider world, e.g. industry and transport.
- Migration has brought both opportunities and challenges.

 Over to you

Under the headings **education**, **industry** and **culture**, explain:
- why Bristol is an important city
- the impact of migration on Bristol.

Student Book
See pages
188–9

You need to know:

- what urban changes are affecting Bristol
- how those urban changes have created cultural, recreation and entertainment opportunities.

CASE STUDY

Changes in Bristol

- Bristol's population is increasing
- Migration has created an ethnically diverse population.
- Improvements to transport links have increased Bristol's connectivity.
- Over 2 million people live within 50 km of the city

 **Big Idea**

Urban change in Bristol has created **social opportunities** associated with the city's cultural mix, recreation and entertainment.

Cultural mix

Bristol embraces the diverse backgrounds of its growing population.

Art

The city is well known for its street art. It is home to artists like Banksy.

Figure 1 *An example of Banksy artwork in a Bristol street*

Museums

Bristol has many museums including Aerospace Bristol and Brunel's ship *SS Great Britain*.

Food and music

The influx of migrants has led to diverse food outlets.

Bristol's youthful population contributes to a vibrant underground music scene.

Festivals

The city's culture is celebrated by festivals such as the Bristol International Balloon Fiesta and the Bristol Harbour Festival.

Recreational activities

Bristol provides a huge range of opportunities for outdoor recreation. Ashton Court and Clifton Downs are areas for walking, cycling and picnics.

Six Second Summary

- Bristol's cultural mix has created opportunities in art, museums, festivals, food and music.
- There are opportunities for outdoor recreation.
- Entertainment includes theatre, sport and shopping.

 Over to you

List **three** changes that have affected Bristol. Draw lines to link each one with a different social opportunity that has occurred.

Entertainment

The growth of Bristol has created demand for a wide variety of entertainment.

- Theatres include the Bristol Old Vic.
- Bristol has two professional football teams, a premiership rugby union team and is headquarters for Gloucestershire County Cricket.
- Shopping is a growing leisure activity. Shopping centres include Cribbs Causeway and Cabot Circus.

Figure 2 *The interior of Cabot Circus Shopping Centre*

You need to know:

- how urban changes in Bristol have created economic opportunities, such as employment.

CASE STUDY

How has urban change created employment opportunities in Bristol?

- Skilled entrepreneurs from UK and abroad have come to the city.
- There is a highly educated graduate labour force.
- Urban regeneration has made brownfield sites available for redevelopment.
- Bristol's Temple Quarter Enterprise Zone attracts government grants and tax relief.

How has employment in Bristol changed?

The closure of the city centre port meant its industry changed. Since then, major developments have been in tertiary (services) and quaternary (high-tech) sectors. This creates employment.

Why have high-tech industries developed in Bristol?

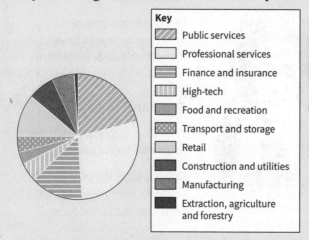

Key
- Public services
- Professional services
- Finance and insurance
- High-tech
- Food and recreation
- Transport and storage
- Retail
- Construction and utilities
- Manufacturing
- Extraction, agriculture and forestry

Figure 1 Bristol's employment structure

High-tech businesses have been attracted to Bristol because of:

- a government grant of £100 million to become a Super-Connected City with fast broadband download speeds
- advanced research in collaboration with local universities
- collaboration between high-tech companies and other sectors in research and development.

Brunel's Engine Shed

Brunel's Engine Shed is used for high-tech industries including micro-electronics, media and digital production companies.

Figure 2 The Aardman characters Wallace and Gromit

Aardman Animations

- Well-known for using stop-motion clay animation.
- More recently it has won Oscars for its computer-animated films.

Financial services industry

Bristol is now one of the main financial hubs outside London. This industry is supported by strong links with local universities.

 Six Second Summary

- Urban growth has brought skilled workers and urban regeneration.
- A growing number of people in Bristol are employed by high-tech companies.
- Employment is an economic opportunity created by the growth of high-tech industries.

 Over to you

Write your top **five** opportunities that urban change in Bristol has created. They can be social or economic.

Student Book
**See pages
192–3**

You need to know:

- how urban change in Bristol has created social, economic and environmental opportunities.

CASE STUDY

Bristol: Europe's Green Capital, 2015

The development of Bristol as a green city has led to further improvements in transport and urban greening.

Add a *WOW!* factor

Make sure you know which opportunities are economic, social and environmental. You may get asked a question which includes more than one category.

Bristol's Integrated Transport System

Bristol has developed an **integrated transport system (ITS)** to link its transport into a single network. It aims to reduce congestion from a growing population.

- The *Metrobus rapid transit system* aims to connect suburban housing areas with retail parks, motorway junctions, railway stations and universities.
- *Metrowest suburban rail scheme* links with areas surrounding the city.
- Bristol received £11.4 million from the government to construct cycle lanes and improve cycling facilities.

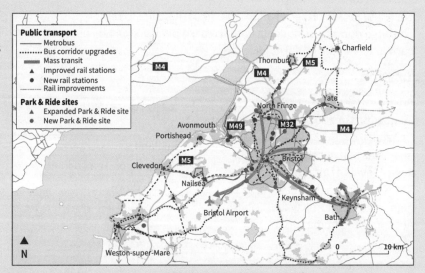

Figure 1 *Plans for developing Bristol's integrated transport system*

Urban greening

Urban greening can be defined as 'making urban spaces greener'.

- More than a third of Bristol is open space.
- Queen Square was once a dual carriageway, but is now an open space with cycle routes.
- The city council provides free vegetable plants for community groups in some of the more deprived parts of the city.
- In 2019, 'Replant Bristol' was launched, to plant 250 000 new trees by 2030.

Figure 2 *Bristol's Queen Square*

Six Second Summary

- Urban change has included population growth and the development of Bristol as a green city.
- Integrated transport systems provide social and economic opportunities.
- Urban greening is an environmental opportunity.

Over to you

Produce a Venn diagram of social, economic and environmental opportunities in Bristol. Explain why there may be cross-over between categories for some of the opportunities.

Student Book
See pages
194–5

CASE STUDY

You need to know:

- how urban change in Bristol has caused social and economic challenges.

What are the urban challenges resulting from urban change?

Urban deprivation in Bristol

Fifteen per cent of Bristol's residents live in some of the most deprived areas in England. Many of the council-run estates and high-rise flats are in urgent need of modernisation. These areas suffer relatively high levels of crime and unemployment.

Inequalities in housing

- In 2020, 13 000 families were on the council waiting list to be rehoused.
- There is also a shortage of affordable social housing to rent.
- The large number of students has increased pressure on housing, particularly in the rental market.

Figure 1 *Broadway in Filwood, one of Bristol's most deprived areas*

Education

- Bristol experiences significant inequalities in educational attainment.
- Generally, children living in areas of highest urban deprivation have the lowest levels of attainment.
- Rates of under-achievement can be high among children where English is not spoken at home.

Bristol Ward	Eight GCSE average attainment score (2019)
Redland	65.0
Westbury on Trym and Henleaze	63.5
Clifton Down	62.7
Avonmouth and Lawrence Weston	36.7
Filwood	34.0
Hartcliffe and Withywood	34.0

Figure 2 *Average GCSE attainment scores for selected wards in Bristol, 2019*

Health

The deprived wards of Hartcliffe and Withywood, Filwood (Figure **1**) and Lawrence Hill record lower than average levels of good health and life expectancy. The opposite is found in wealthier wards such as Clifton (Figure **3**) and Redland.

Employment

The employment rate for Bristol (77.6 per cent) is one of the highest in UK cities. However, there are high levels of unemployment in Lawrence Hill, Whitchurch Park and Filwood.

Figure 3 *Clifton – a wealthy area of Bristol*

 Six Second Summary

- Social and economic challenges include urban deprivation, inequalities in housing, education, health and employment.
- There are significant inequalities between deprived and wealthier areas in Bristol.

 Over to you

Write **three** questions about the material on this page so that you could test a friend. You have to know the answers too!

You need to be able to:

- interpret ground photos
- construct a pie chart
- construct a bar chart.

Student Book
See pages
196–7

What are the social inequalities between Stoke Bishop and Filwood?

Stoke Bishop and Filwood are two very different wards in Bristol. Stoke Bishop is an affluent suburb (Figure **1**), whereas Filwood is one of the most socially deprived areas in the city (Figure **2**). Figure **3** compares housing in Stoke Bishop and Filwood.

Figure 1 *The centre of Stoke Bishop*

Figure 2 *Empty shops in Filwood awaiting redevelopment*

Housing tenure and type	Filwood (%)	Stoke Bishop (%)
Owner occupied	46	75
Social rented	41	12
Private and other rented	13	13
TOTAL TENURE	*100*	*100*
Detached	4	28
Semi-detached	56	35
Terraced	30	8
Flats	10	29
TOTAL TYPES	*100*	*100*

Figure 3 *Housing tenure and type in Stoke Bishop and Filwood, 2011*

Skills

1 Use two pieces of evidence from Figure **2** to show that Filwood is a deprived area.

2 Study Figure **3** which compares data on housing tenure (whether people own or rent) and type.

  a Explain **how** you would construct two pie charts to compare data on housing Stoke Bishop and Filwood.

  b Draw a proportional bar chart to compare the data.

Analysis

1 Look at Figure **3** and your completed proportional bar chart from question **2b**.

  a Compare housing tenure between Stoke Bishop and Filwood.

  b Compare housing types between Stoke Bishop and Filwood.

  c Suggest reasons for differences in housing tenure. Use the word 'deprivation' in your answer.

Evaluation

1 Look at Figures **1** and **2**.

  a How might photos be misleading when describing **inequalities** in places?

  b Name two other forms of evidence that would help you to decide how the level of deprivation was greater in Filwood compared to Stoke Bishop.

2 'Data about housing can help to measure inequality in an area.' Do you agree with this statement? Explain your reasons.

You need to know:

- how urban change has created environmental challenges.

Student Book
See pages
198–9

CASE STUDY

Bristol's environmental challenges

Bristol's changing industries and growing population have created environmental challenges.

Dereliction

In the 1960s, the port moved from the city centre to Avonmouth on the Bristol Channel. Many inner-city warehouses, industrial buildings and workers' houses were abandoned.

Figure 1 Graffiti on an abandoned building in Stokes Croft

The inner city – Stokes Croft

- Squatters occupied empty houses.
- The area experienced riots and antisocial behaviour.
- Bristol City Council used lottery money to renovate buildings.
- The area has become an artistic hub.

Building on brownfield and greenfield land

	Brownfield sites	Greenfield sites
Advantages	It is land that has already been developed for building so doesn't use green land.	It has never been built on so requires less groundwork.
Disadvantages	Costly to clear waste, decontaminate the land and construct modern infrastructure.	Objections from local residents can delay the time taken to obtain planning permission by many years.
Example in Bristol	Finzels Reach is a former industrial area which now has office buildings, shops, restaurants and apartments.	The new town of Bradley Stoke, just to the north of Bristol.

Figure 3 Bradley Stoke greenfield housing development

Figure 2 Advantages and disadvantages of brownfield and greenfield sites

Waste disposal

Waste disposal is a major challenge in Bristol. Landfill sites are in short supply and incineration plants emit greenhouse gases.

Actions such as **waste recycling** and reducing packaging have reduced the amount of domestic waste by about 8 per cent per year.

 Six Second Summary

- Environmental challenges include dereliction, building on brownfield and greenfield sites, and waste disposal.
- Dereliction has been caused by de-industrialisation.
- There are advantages and disadvantages of brownfield and greenfield sites.

 Over to you

Decide whether it would be better to build on greenfield or brownfield sites. Explain your decision to a friend, making sure you include arguments about each type of site.

Student Book
See pages
200–1

You need to know:

- about the impact of urban sprawl and the growth of commuter settlements.

CASE STUDY

How has Bristol's urban change led to urban sprawl?

The physical outward growth of a city is called *urban sprawl*.

There are several reasons why urban change has caused urban sprawl in Bristol:

- A rapidly growing population.
- A shortage of affordable housing in the city centre.
- Competition for brownfield sites causing land prices to rise.

- Improvements in transport meaning people commute into the city centre.
- Many people wishing to live in semi-rural locations.

What is the impact of urban sprawl on the rural–urban fringe?

The building of large housing estates, motorways and services in the **rural–urban fringe** has been controversial. There are concerns about:

- loss of countryside
- impacts on wildlife and biodiversity
- increased levels of traffic congestion, noise and air pollution.

In 1966, the Bristol and Bath Green Belt was approved. Green belt land is protected from new building development by strict planning regulations.

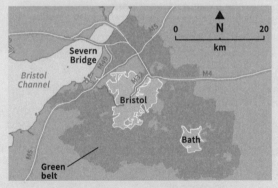

Figure 1 *The green belt around Bristol*

The green belt does not protect the entire rural–urban fringe. Developments on previously open countryside include:

- the M32, M4, M5 and M49 motorways
- the out-of-town retail park at Cribbs Causeway.

Growth of commuter settlements

Commuter settlements are places where a significant proportion of the residents commute to work elsewhere. Towns such as Clevedon in North Somerset and Wotton-under-Edge in Gloucestershire have expanded to become commuter settlements. People are also choosing to live in South Wales where property prices are lower.

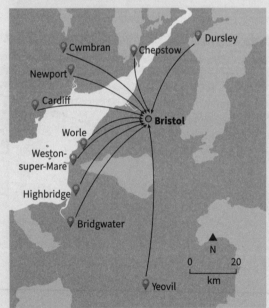

Figure 2 *Desire line map showing Bristol's top ten commuter towns (Comparemymove, 2019)*

✎ Over to you

List **three** developments that have taken place on the rural–urban fringe. For each one, link it to a possible impact on people or the environment.

⏱ Six Second Summary

- A growing population and competition for land have caused urban sprawl.
- A number of developments have been built on the rural–urban fringe.
- Commuter settlements have expanded.

Student Book
See pages
202–3

CASE STUDY

You need to know:

- why the Temple Quarter of Bristol was in need of regeneration.

What is urban regeneration?

Urban regeneration is an attempt to reverse the decline and decay of an urban area. It often involves the use of public (government) investment to improve the physical structure of an area. In Bristol, the Temple Quarter has been regenerated.

 Big Idea

The Temple Quarter is an example of an urban regeneration project.

Why did the Temple Quarter area need to be regenerated?

The Temple Quarter developed as an industrial area in the eighteenth century in the centre of Bristol, close to the Temple Meads railway station. To attract new employment, in 2012, much of this area became an Enterprise Zone (EZ), qualifying for government money to support a programme of regeneration.

Figure 1 *The smoky industrial landscape of central Bristol in 1936*

The main industries included rope factories and glassworks.

In the 20th century, terraced housing was demolished as part of slum clearance.

By the second half of the century, heavy industries were closing down.

City centre docks declined as new port facilities were built at Avonmouth and Portbury (where water was deeper and land cheaper).

Factories and railway sidings were abandoned. Many areas were contaminated with industrial pollution and waste.

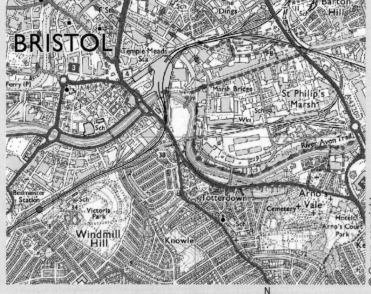
© Crown copyright

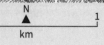

Figure 2 *Temple Meads Enterprise Zone (shown as a blue dotted line)*

 Six Second Summary

The Temple Quarter needed regeneration because:

- the heavy industries were closing down
- decline of the city centre docks
- many areas were contaminated.

Over to you

Explain on a spider diagram the reasons why Bristol's Temple Quarter needed regeneration.

Student Book
See pages
204–5

CASE STUDY

You need to know:

- about the main features of Bristol's Temple Quarter regeneration scheme.

What are the main features of the Temple Quarter regeneration scheme?

In 2012 much of the Temple Quarter area became an Enterprise Zone. This enabled businesses to benefit from tax relief, low rents and quicker and simpler planning procedures.

Figure 1 Regeneration projects in the Temple Quarter

Brunel's Engine Shed for high-tech and creative businesses (2013)

Temple Gate improvements completed (2019)

Glass Wharf office development (2015)

Paintworks workplaces and residential area (2015)

Brock's Bridge constructed – providing a link to Temple Island (2015)

Temple Meads station to receive a £10.2 million upgrade (due for completion in 2023).

University of Bristol Enterprise – car-free campus specialising in digital technologies and including a £43 million Quantum Technologies Information Centre – receives planning consent (2018)

The Temple Gate Scheme

The Temple Gate Scheme aims to revive the run-down area in front of Temple Meads railway station. The main features include:

- pedestrian and cycle routes
- better transport facilities and a new Metrobus stop
- creation of bus priority lanes to improve bus journey times and reliability.

How successful is the Temple Quarter regeneration?

So far, the Temple Quarter regeneration project has been considered a success:

- The transformation has created an attractive and accessible environment.
- More than 4000 jobs have been created.
- Almost 400 firms from the creative, digital and green industries have moved into the area.

Six Second Summary

The main features of the Temple Quarter regeneration project include:

- improved transport links
- encouraging business
- the creation of jobs.

Over to you

List **two** ways in which urban change in Bristol **has**, and **two** ways in which it **has not** created social and economic challenges.

Student Book
See pages
206–7

You need to know:

- about features of sustainable urban living.

What is urban sustainability?

Urban sustainability (**sustainable urban living**) involves creating an environment that meets the social, economic and environmental needs of existing residents without compromising the same for future generations.

Water conservation

A sustainable water supply conserves and recycles water. In cities, it could involve:

- water saving devices, including water meters
- collecting rainwater in tanks for watering the garden
- creating 'rain gardens' and green roofs.

Waste recycling

Recycling saves raw materials and reduces energy use. In 2020 the UK government set a legally binding target of recycling 65 per cent of waste by 2035, with no more than 10 per cent going to landfill sites.

Sustainable Drainage Systems (SuDS)

SuDS aim to reduce surface water flooding. This can be achieved by:

- using green roofs
- planting vegetation
- maintaining wetlands
- using permeable surfaces, such as pavements and driveways, to slow water transfer through the soil.

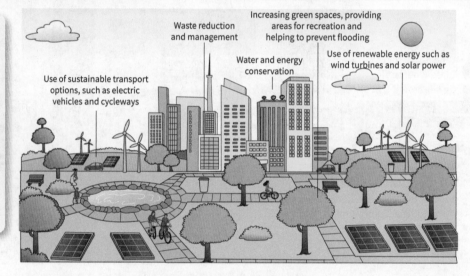

Figure 1 Urban sustainability

Energy conservation

Many cities are embracing energy conservation:

- Combined heat and power (CHP) technology captures heat produced when generating electricity.
- Energy efficiency of buildings can be increased by insulation and double glazing.
- Solar panels and wind turbines can be used to generate electricity.

Creating green space

The benefits of green spaces are that:

- they absorb carbon dioxide
- they provide areas of recreation
- they encourage wildlife habitats and biodiversity
- trees help to reduce the flood risk.

 Six Second Summary

Features of sustainable urban living include:

- water conservation
- energy conservation
- waste recycling
- creating green space.

 Over to you

Write out the four bullet points from the Six Second Summary as headings. Under each one write **three** sentences to explain how that feature can lead to sustainable urban living. Add pictures/sketches to help you to memorise them.

Student Book
See pages
208–9

You need to know:

- how urban transport strategies can reduce traffic congestion.

Impacts of traffic congestion

Examples of the impacts of traffic congestion may be:

- *Social* – people may become stressed
- *Economic* – delays take time and are expensive for businesses
- *Environmental* – reduces air quality.

Transport management strategies

Urban transport management strategies can be divided into 'carrot' (encouraging people) and 'stick' measures (preventing people).

'Carrot'	'Stick'
Encourage people to walk and cycle by widening pavements and creating more cycle ways.	Establish ultra-low emission zones (ULEZ) where highly polluting vehicles are banned or pay high charges.
Increase use of public transport, making it cheap, safe and pleasant to use.	Introduce a congestion charge to make it expensive for cars to enter.
Establish 'Park and Ride' schemes to keep cars out of city centres.	Restrict parking in city centres.

Figure 1 *'Carrot' and 'stick' transport management strategies*

Figure 2 *Congestion charging and ultra-low emission zone in London*

Singapore

- The public transport system is comfortable and efficient. By 2030 it is expected that 75 per cent of journeys will be made by public transport.
- Anybody wishing to buy a car has to purchase a Certificate of Entitlement costing nearly £40 000.
- An Electronic Road Pricing System (ERP) operates on expressways to regulate traffic flow. Pricing is determined by traffic conditions.

Beijing

Measures have been introduced to combat congestion in Beijing:

- Banning each car for one day a week, based on its registration plate.
- A rapid bus transit system and 30 new Metro lines.
- Bike parks at public transport hubs.
- These measures have resulted in a 20 per cent reduction in car use.

Figure 3 *Bike parking in Beijing*

 Six Second Summary

Sustainable traffic management strategies include:

- improving public transport
- restricting use of vehicles
- adding charges to make driving expensive.

 Over to you

List the bullet points from the Six Second Summary. Underneath each point, write two examples of that strategy.

Section B
The changing economic world

Your exam

Section B The changing economic world is part of Paper 2: Challenges in the human environment.

Paper 2 is a one-and-a-half hour written exam and makes up 35 per cent of your GCSE. The whole paper carries 88 marks (including 3 marks for SPaG) – questions on Section B will carry 30 marks.

You need to study all the topics in Section B – in your final exam you will have to answer questions on all of them.

Tick these boxes to build a record of your revision

Your revision checklist

Spec key idea	Theme	1	2	3
16 The development gap				
There are global variations in economic development and quality of life	16.1 Our unequal world			
	16.2 Measuring development			
	16.3 The Demographic Transition Model			
	16.4 Changing population structures			
	16.5 Causes of uneven development			
	16.6 Uneven development – wealth and health			
	16.7 Uneven development – international migration			
Various strategies exist for reducing the global development gap	16.8 Reducing the development gap			
	16.9 Reducing the gap – aid and intermediate technology			
	16.10 Reducing the gap – fair trade			
	16.11 Reducing the gap – debt relief and loans			
	16.12 Reducing the development gap – tourism			
Geographical skills	16.13 Skills Focus: Atlas maps and graphs			
17 Nigeria: a newly emerging economy				
Some LICs or NEEs are experiencing rapid economic development which leads to significant social, environmental and cultural change	17.1 Exploring Nigeria (1)			
	17.2 Exploring Nigeria (2)			
	17.3 Balancing a changing industrial structure			
	17.4 The impacts of transnational corporations			
	17.5 Nigeria in the wider world			
	17.6 The impacts of international aid			
	17.7 Managing environmental issues			
	17.8 Quality of life in Nigeria			
Geographical skills	17.9 Skills Focus: Graphs and statistical skills			
18 The changing UK economy				
Major changes in the economy of the UK have affected, and will continue to affect, employment patterns and regional growth	18.1 Changes in the UK economy			
	18.2 A post-industrial economy			
	18.3 UK science and business parks			
	18.4 Environmental impacts of industry			
	18.5 Changing rural landscapes in the UK			
	18.6 The UK's changing transport infrastructure (1)			
	18.7 The UK's changing transport infrastructure (2)			
	18.8 The north–south divide			
	18.9 The UK in the wider world (1)			
	18.10 The UK in the wider world (2)			
Geographical skills	18.11 Skills Focus: OS map skills and aerial photo interpretation			

Student Book
**See pages
210–11**

You need to know:

- there are global variations in economic development and quality of life.

What is development?

Development is the progress a country has made. As a country develops, it usually means that people's standard of living and quality of life will improve.

The **development gap** is the difference in standard of living between the world's richest and poorest countries.

Quality of life

Economic and social statistics give broad measures for countries rather than individuals. Quality of life also considers, for example, safety and security, freedom and the right to vote.

Measuring development

Gross National Income (GNI)

- **GNI** is an economic measure of development.
- It is the total value of goods and services produced by a country, plus money earned from, and paid to, other countries.
- It is expressed as per head (per capita) of the population.
- Some countries (NEEs) have begun to experience higher rates of economic development. For example, the BRICS (Brazil, Russia, India, China, South Africa) and MINT (Mexico, Indonesia, Nigeria, Turkey) countries.

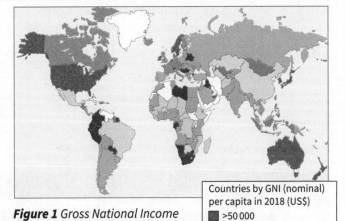

Figure 1 *Gross National Income per capita (US$), 2018*

Countries by GNI (nominal) per capita in 2018 (US$)

- ▮ >50 000
- ▮ 30 000–50 000
- ▮ 20 000–29 999
- ▯ 10 000–19 999
- ▮ 7 500–9 999
- ▮ 5 000–7 499
- ▮ 1 000–4 999
- ▯ <1 000
- ☐ Data unavailable

Human Development Index (HDI)

HDI is a social measure that is expressed in values 0–1, where 1 is the highest. It considers:

- **life expectancy** at birth
- number of years of education
- GNI per head.

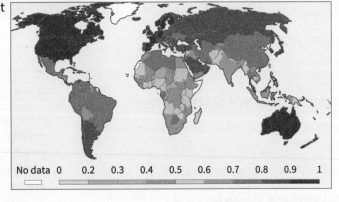

No data 0   0.2   0.3   0.4   0.5   0.6   0.7   0.8   0.9   1

Figure 2 *The Human Development Index, 2019*

Six Second Summary

- Development is a change that generally makes people's lives better.
- GNI per head is an economic measure of development.
- HDI is a social measure of development.

Over to you

- Write clear definitions of development, Gross National Income (GNI) and Human Development Index (HDI).
- Name the members of the a) BRICS b) MINT countries.
- Explain the difference between GNI and HDI.

Student Book
See pages
212–13

You need to know:

- how useful economic and social measures (or indicators) of development are
- examples of these measures
- some limitations of these measures.

How useful are measures of development?

Birth rate

As a country develops, women become more educated and want a career. They marry later and have fewer children.

Death rate

Developed countries tend to have older populations with a high **death rate**. Less developed countries may have very low death rates with proportionally more young people, having survived their early years.

Infant mortality

A useful measure of a country's health care system (as well as life expectancy and number of people per doctor).

Literacy rate

A high **literacy rate** means a good education system.

Access to safe water is an indication of modern infrastructure, e.g. water treatment plants.

	HICs	LICs
Birth rate	Low	High
Death rate	Depends on the ages of the population and health care availability	
Infant mortality rate	Low	High
Literacy rate	High	Low

Figure 1 *How measures of development vary with economic development*

Country	GNI per head (US$)	HDI	Birth rate (per 1000/yr)	Death rate (per 1000/yr)	Infant mortality (per 1000 live births/yr)	Literacy rate (%)
UK	42370	0.932	11.87	9.40	4.8	99
China	10410	0.761	11.62	7.44	7.7	97
Nigeria	**2030**	**0.539**	**34.59**	**12.40**	**94.3**	**62**
Bangladesh	1940	0.632	18.13	5.64	59.0	75
Zimbabwe	1390	0.571	33.57	10.20	32.3	89

Figure 2 *Measures of development for selected countries, 2020*

Limitations of economic and social measures

A single measure of development can give a false picture, as it gives the *average* for the whole country.

Other factors limit the usefulness of development measures:

- Data could be out of date, unreliable or hard to collect.
- Data may not take into account subsistence or informal economies.

Add a WOW! factor

Make sure you understand what each measure means and how it shows a country's level of development. You are not expected to memorise all the data but two or three examples could be useful. Trends in the data are more important.

 Six Second Summary

- Economic and social measures can show how developed a country is.
- There may be limitations to the usefulness of data if they are out of date or unreliable.

Over to you

Cover up everything on this page except for the table of data. Explain to somebody in your home what each measure shows about the level of development in those countries.

Student Book
See pages
214–15

You need to know:

- how levels of development can be linked to the Demographic Transition Model (DTM).

The Demographic Transition Model (DTM) shows changes over time in the population of a country.

The total population responds to variations in birth and death rates (natural change). It is also affected by migration. Migration is not shown on the DTM.

As a country becomes more developed, its population characteristics change.

Stage 1

- High birth rate
- High death rate
- Both fluctuate because of disease, famine and war
- Population fairly stable

Example: Traditional rainforest tribes with little contact with the outside world. There are now no Stage 1 countries in the world.

Stage 2

- Death rate decreases
- Birth rate remains high
- Population grows

Example: Afghanistan – many poor countries are in Stage 2.

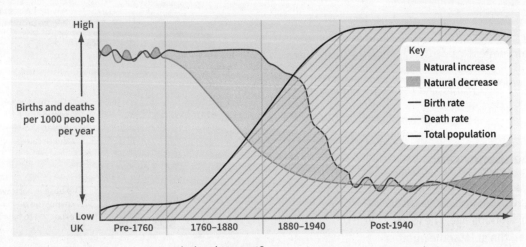

Figure 1 *What links the DTM with development?*

Stage 3

- Birth rate drops rapidly
- Death rate continues to decrease but more slowly
- Population still grows, but not quite as fast

Example: Nigeria – an NEE experiencing economic growth.

Stage 4

- Low birth rate
- Low death rate
- Birth rate can fluctuate depending on the economic situation

Example: USA – one of the most developed countries in the world, with good health care and women who pursue careers.

Stage 5

- Birth rate falls below death rate
- Death rate increases slightly because of ageing population
- Population decreases

Examples: Japan and Germany – well-developed countries with an ageing population.

Six Second Summary

- The DTM shows changes in birth rate, death rate and total population.
- As a country becomes more developed, these characteristics change.

Over to you

Draw the **five** stages of the DTM from memory and annotate it to show your understanding.

Student Book
**See pages
216–17**

You need to know:

- how the population structures of two contrasting countries are changing.

Population pyramids and the DTM

Countries at different stages of the DTM have population pyramids of different shapes.

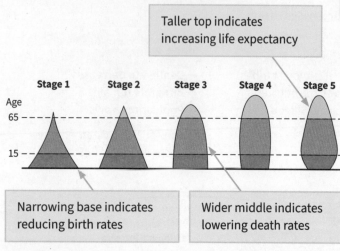

Taller top indicates increasing life expectancy

Narrowing base indicates reducing birth rates

Wider middle indicates lowering death rates

Figure 1 *Population pyramids for the stages of the DTM*

The dependency ratio

This is the proportion of people below (aged 0–14) and above (over 65) normal working age. The lower the number, the greater the number of people who work.

Six Second Summary

- Population pyramids show population structure by age and gender.
- Pyramids change with different stages of the DTM.

Over to you

Using your drawing of the DTM from 16.3, add diagrams of population pyramids appropriate for each stage.

Big Idea

Population structure considers how the number of men and women in different age groups is changing. It is studied using *population pyramids*.

Mexico's changing population structure (moving from stage 2 to 3)

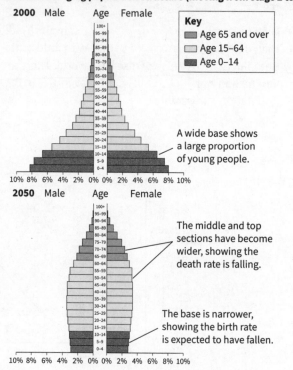

A wide base shows a large proportion of young people.

The middle and top sections have become wider, showing the death rate is falling.

The base is narrower, showing the birth rate is expected to have fallen.

Japan's changing population structure (moving from stage 4 to 5)

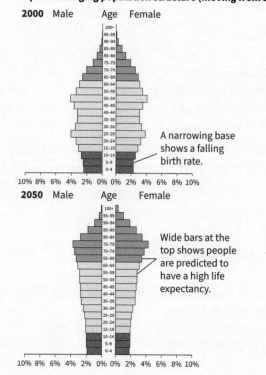

A narrowing base shows a falling birth rate.

Wide bars at the top shows people are predicted to have a high life expectancy.

Figure 1 *Mexico and Japan population pyramids 2000 and 2050*

Student Book
See pages 218–19

You need to know:

- the physical, economic and historical causes of uneven development.

Physical

- Landlocked countries are cut off from seaborne trade, which is important for economic growth.
- Climate-related diseases and pests affect the ability of the population to stay healthy enough to work.
- Extreme weather, such as tropical storms, droughts and floods, can slow development and it can be costly to repair damaged infrastructure.
- Lack of adequate supplies of clean water can affect farming and the health of workers (Figure **1**).

Figure 1 *Clean water is important for development*

Economic – trade

- Rich countries and large international companies often want to pay as little as possible for their raw materials – many of which come from LICs.
- Supply of raw materials often outstrips demand, which keeps prices low.
- Processing (which adds value) usually takes place in richer countries.
- The rich countries get richer and the development of poorer countries may be slowed.

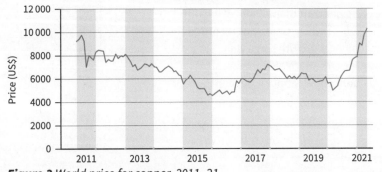

Figure 2 *World price for copper, 2011–21*

- LICs and NEEs have traditionally exported *primary products*; although in the last 20 years, many have developed manufacturing. Manufactured products now make up about 80 per cent of NEE exports.
- The price of raw materials fluctuates a lot (e.g. copper, see Figure **2**). In Zambia, copper accounts for over 60 per cent of the total value of exports.

Historical – colonialism

- Almost all the wealth produced during the colonial period (around 1650–1950) went to European powers.
- Since 1950 former European colonies have gained independence.
- Many former colonies did not have well-established political system, and rivalries between ethnic groups, corruption or financial mismanagement have affected development.

Six Second Summary

Causes of uneven development can be:

- physical (e.g. extreme weather or landlocked countries)
- economic (e.g. trade conditions)
- historical (e.g. colonialism).

Over to you

Talk for one minute about the causes of uneven development. Name and explain each cause, and give examples.

Student Book
**See pages
220–1**

You need to know:

- how uneven development leads to disparities of wealth and health.

Imbalances between rich and poor

Imbalances exist between countries. Some countries have lower levels of development and a poorer quality of life than others.

Imbalances also exist *within* countries. Areas of considerable poverty can be found in rich countries, and great wealth in areas of poor countries.

Figure 1 *A cartoon using exaggerated stereotypes to emphasise the inequalities that exist globally between HICs and LICs*

Disparities in wealth

- In 2020, the fastest growth of wealth was in North America, which now holds 34 per cent of total global wealth.
- Of the NEEs, China has recorded the highest growth since 2000.
- Africa's share of global wealth remains very small (about 1 per cent).

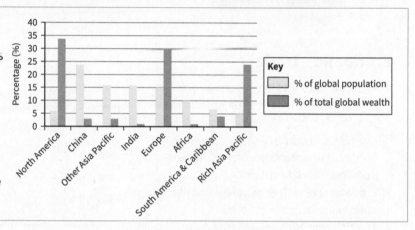

Key
- % of global population
- % of total global wealth

Figure 2 *Population and wealth by region, 2020*

Disparities in health

Levels of development are closely linked to health. In poor countries, health care is often patchy.

Children under 15 years account for 4 in every 10 deaths; the over 70s account for only 2 in 10 deaths.

Complications of childbirth are one of the main causes of death amongst under 5 year olds.

Low income countries

Infectious diseases are the main cause of death, e.g. lung infections, HIV/AIDS and malaria.

The over 70s account for 7 in every 10 deaths.

Main causes of death are chronic diseases, e.g. heart disease or cancer.

High income countries

Lung infections are the only main infectious cause of death.

Only 1 in every 100 deaths is among children under 15 years.

Six Second Summary

- Uneven development leads to disparities in wealth and health.
- Lower levels of development can affect the causes of death in different countries.

Over to you

- Create a mnemonic to help you learn the reasons for disparities in health.
- In two days' time, see how much you have remembered about this page before looking at it again.

Student Book
See pages
222–3

You need to know:

- how uneven development can lead to international migration.

What are the different types of migration?

Migration is the movement of people from place to place. It can be voluntary or forced. International migration is a consequence of uneven development, as people seek to improve their quality of life.

The following terms are important.

Immigrant – a person who moves into a country.

Emigrant – a person who moves out of a country.

Economic migrant – a person who moves voluntarily to seek a better life, such as a better-paid job.

Refugee – a person forced to move from their country of origin, often as a result of civil war or a natural disaster.

Displaced person – a person forced to move from their home but who stays in their country of origin.

Middle East refugee crisis, 2021

The Syrian civil war caused economic and social turmoil. Many Syrians were forced to flee to find employment and a better way of life.

By 2020, 6.6 million Syrians had fled the country. They mainly sought refuge in neighbouring countries such as Lebanon and Jordan. Thousands also settled in Europe.

Many people from Africa and the Middle East try to move in search of a better life.

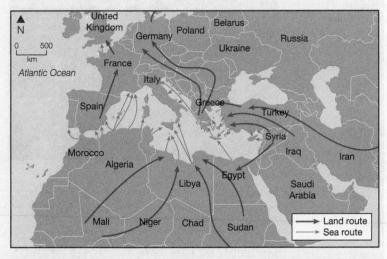

Figure 1 *Major migration routes to Western Europe from Africa and the Middle East*

Economic migration into the UK

- Until 2020 the majority of economic migrants to the UK came from the EU.
- When Britain left the EU in 2020, many migrants returned home.
- Many sectors of the UK economy have relied on economic migrants, who have also paid tax to the UK government.

Figure 2 *Migrant workers on a Lincolnshire farm*

Six Second Summary

- A consequence of uneven development is international migration.
- There are different types of migration.

Over to you

List as many causes and consequences of uneven development as you can.

Student Book
See pages
224–5

You need to know:

- how investment, industrial development and tourism can reduce the development gap.

What strategies can reduce the development gap?

Investment

Many countries and TNCs invest money and expertise in LICs (to increase their profits), which supports the LICs development by providing employment and income.

- An estimated 10 000 Chinese companies are now operating in Africa. Many are involved in massive infrastructure projects including railways and dam construction.
- There are many benefits, but some people think it is exploiting Africa's resources in order to benefit China's own economy.

Industrial development

Industrial development can bring employment, higher incomes and opportunities to invest in housing, education and *infrastructure* (e.g. transport networks, water and sewerage). The population then becomes better educated and healthier, which provides more opportunities to invest in industries and business. This circular process is called the *multiplier effect*.

Industrial development in Malaysia

- Malaysia has seen a dramatic growth in its wealth since the 1970s.
- It has made use of foreign investment to exploit its natural resources and develop a thriving manufacturing sector.
- Today, Malaysia has a highly-developed mixed economy.

Sector	Annual GDP growth rate 2019 (%)	% share of GDP in 2020
Services and others	6.1	58.9
Manufacturing	3.8	22.9
Construction	0.1	4.9
Agriculture	2.0	7.4
Mining	−2.0	6.8

Figure 1 *Malaysia's economic profile*

Tourism

- Many countries with tropical beaches, spectacular landscapes or abundant wildlife have become tourist destinations.
- This has led to investment and increased income from abroad, which can be used for improved education, infrastructure and housing.
- Tourism can generate a lot of income but is vulnerable in times of economic recession.

Figure 2 *A tourist village in the Seychelles*

Add a WOW! factor

Manipulate the data when describing a table of data (e.g. 'Services and others' had *more than twice* the percentage share of GDP in 2020 than manufacturing).

Six Second Summary

- Investment provides employment and income from abroad.
- Industrial development brings employment, higher incomes and opportunities to invest.
- Tourism has led to investment and increased income from abroad.

Over to you

Explain **three** ways in which investment can reduce the development gap.

Student Book
See pages
226–7

You need to know:

- how aid and intermediate technology can reduce the development gap.

What is aid?

International aid is when money, goods or services are given by governments or non-governmental organisations (NGOs) to help the quality of life and the economy of another country.

In 2020, the UK reduced its overseas aid budget to 0.5 per cent of its GDP. It is now 0.7 per cent below the target set by the United Nations.

In 2019, Pakistan received £305 million from the UK. It was spent mainly on education and to reduce hunger and poverty.

Aid can take the form of:

- money
- emergency supplies
- food or technology
- specialist skills (e.g. doctors or engineers).

Aid can reduce the development gap by:

- enabling countries to invest in development projects such as roads
- focusing on health care, education and services at a local scale.

Goat Aid from Oxfam

Goat Aid Oxfam was set up to help African families to buy a goat for meat and to produce milk (which can also be also used to make butter). This helps to generate food, fertiliser and income, and builds community spirit.

Intermediate technology

Intermediate technology is sustainable and appropriate to the needs, knowledge and wealth of local people. It takes the form of small-scale projects often associated with agriculture, water or health.

One such project is at Adis Nifas in Ethiopia where a small dam was built, creating a reservoir close to fields for irrigation.

There are benefits of this project:

- It used (and still uses) intermediate technology to build and run a small dam.
- It used local building materials.
- It provided local employment.
- It used local tools and knowledge.
- The irrigated land provides food for the villagers.

 Six Second Summary

- Aid can be invested in development projects or local-scale projects.
- Intermediate technology involves local people and is appropriate to their needs.

 Over to you

Record your understanding of aid and intermediate technology on a voice recorder so that you can listen to it again.

Student Book
See pages
228–9

You need to know:

- how fair trade can reduce the development gap.

Is trade fair?

Rich countries protect their **trade** using two main systems.

1 *Tariffs* are taxes paid on imports, making imported goods more expensive and locally produced goods more attractive.

2 *Quotas* are limits on the quantity of goods, usually primary products, that can be imported.

The trade in cocoa

The EU does not impose tariffs on imported cocoa beans. Tariffs are applied on processed goods, such as cocoa powder. This discourages processing industries in LICs.

Large producers of cocoa, such as Ghana, hope to reach trade agreements with the EU to reduce import tariffs on processed cocoa products.

Figure 1 Cocoa farmer in Ghana

What is free trade?

Free trade is when countries do not charge tariffs and have quotas. This has the potential to benefit the world's poorest countries.

Subsidies are a barrier to free trade. For example, rich countries can afford to pay subsidies to farmers, so their products are cheaper than those produced by poorer countries.

There are advantages of joining a *trading group* for poor countries:

- it encourages free trade between members
- members are able to get higher prices for their goods.

What is Fairtrade?

Fairtrade is an international movement that sets standards for trade and helps to ensure that producers in poor countries get a fair deal.

The farmer gets a fair price and all the money from the sale of the crop.

Farming is done in an environmentally friendly way.

COLOMBIA
FAIRTRADE
FLO-ID 19168

Part of the price is invested in local community development projects.

The product gains a stronger position in the global market.

Six Second Summary

- Free trade is when countries do not charge tariffs and quotas.
- Fairtrade is an international movement that helps producers in poor countries get a fair deal.

Over to you

Create a mind-map of **six** different methods that can be used to reduce the development gap.

Student Book
See pages
230–1

You need to know:

- how debt relief and microfinance loans can help reduce the development gap.

How have poor countries built up debt?

Many poor countries borrowed money to develop their economies. This led to a **debt crisis** because:

- low commodity prices reduced the value of their exports
- high oil prices increased the price of imports
- as a result of the above, interest rates rose.

These factors meant that their debt increased.

How can debt relief reduce the development gap?

- **Debt relief** has helped poor countries invest in development projects, such as infrastructure.
- Countries have used the money saved to provide services such as free education.

However, corrupt governments may keep the money for themselves. You can find out which of the world's governments are corrupt by searching for 'The world's most corrupt countries' in Google images.

What is microfinance?

- Microfinance is small-scale financial support.
- It is available from banks that are set up to help the poor.
- **Microfinance loans** enable individuals or families to start up small businesses.

The Grameen Bank in Bangladesh lends US$200 to village women to buy a mobile phone (Figure 1). Other villagers then pay the women to use the phones. However, when interest rates rise, it is more difficult to repay the loan.

Figure 1 *Using the village phone*

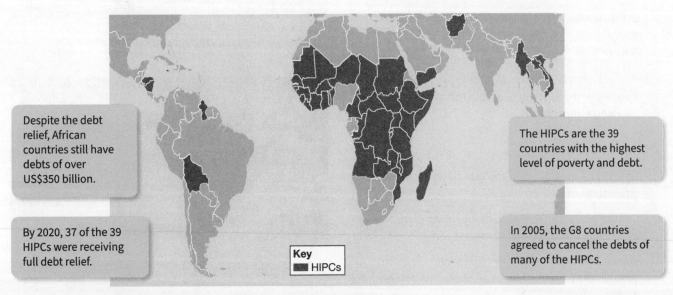

Despite the debt relief, African countries still have debts of over US$350 billion.

By 2020, 37 of the 39 HIPCs were receiving full debt relief.

The HIPCs are the 39 countries with the highest level of poverty and debt.

In 2005, the G8 countries agreed to cancel the debts of many of the HIPCs.

Key
■ HIPCs

Figure 2 *The highly indebted poor countries (HIPCs), 2020*

Six Second Summary

- Debt relief can help poor countries invest in development projects.
- Microfinance is small-scale financial support to help people start up small businesses.

Over to you

- Write a mini-test about ways of reducing the development gap.
- In a few days' time, see if you can answer the questions.

EXAMPLE

Student Book
See pages 232–3

You need to know:

- how tourism in Jamaica can help reduce the development gap
- that Jamaica is an example of the growth of tourism in an LIC or NEE.

How has tourism contributed to Jamaica's development

Over the last few decades, tourism has helped raise the level of development in Jamaica and reduce the development gap.

 **Big Idea**

Jamaica is an example of the growth of tourism in an LIC or NEE.

Economy

☺ In 2019, tourism contributed 35 per cent of Jamaica's GDP (Figure **1**).

☺ Income from tourism is US$2 billion each year and taxes contribute further to the development of the country.

Infrastructure

☺ Tourism has led to a high level of investment on the north coast.

☹ Improvements in roads and airports have been slower than other facilities.

☹ Some parts of the island remain isolated.

Quality of life

☺ In the northern tourist areas of Montego Bay and Ocho Rios, wealthy Jamaicans have a high standard of living (Figure **2**).

☹ However, large numbers of people live nearby in poor housing with inadequate access to fresh water, health care and education.

The environment

☺ Conservation and landscaping projects provide job opportunities.

☺ Community tourism and sustainable *ecotourism* is expanding in more isolated regions.

☹ Mass tourism can create environmental problems such as footpath erosion, excessive waste and harmful emissions.

Employment

☺ Tourism provides 200 000 jobs, either directly or indirectly.

☺ Employment in tourism provides income which helps to boost the local economy.

☺ Those in employment learn new skills.

Figure 1 *Tourism boosts the local economy*

Figure 2 *Turtle Beach, Ocho Rios, Jamaica*

 Six Second Summary

- Tourism creates employment and investment and can boost the economy.
- Tourism does not necessarily bring benefits for everyone.

Over to you

1 Revise the section headed 'Economy'.
2 Cover it and write down all you remember.
3 Check it against the book and note anything you have missed.
4 Repeat for the other headings.

Student Book
See pages 234–5

SKILLS FOCUS

You need to be able to:

- use an atlas map.
- construct a pie chart/proportional bar chart/pictogram.

Using an atlas map and a line graph

Malawi is a country in south-east Africa (Figure **1**). It is one of the world's least developed countries. In common with most LICs, Malawi's trade depends on the export of raw materials, particularly agricultural products which are processed and packaged in HICs (Figure **2**).

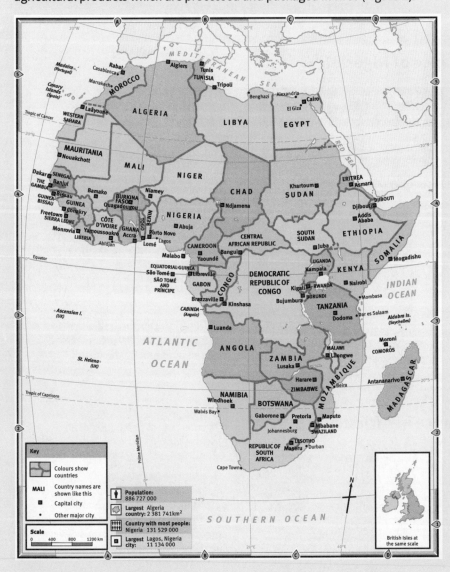

Figure 1 *Atlas map of Africa*

Export products	Percentage
Tobacco	
Sugar	9.4
Coffee and tea	9.2
Oil seeds	6.7
Vegetables	4.4
Fruit and nuts	3.5
Animal feed	2.9
Others	8.9
TOTAL	**100**

Figure 2 *Malawi's exports, 2019*

Skills

1 Locate Malawi on the atlas map (Figure **1**).
  a Describe Malawi's situation within Africa.
  b Name three countries that border Malawi.
  c What is special about Lilongwe as a city in Malawi?
2 Look at Figure **2**.
  a Calculate the percentage for tobacco.
  b Identify Malawi's three biggest exports, and calculate the combined percentage of these three exports.
  c Construct an appropriate graph to represent the data.

Analysis

1 Look at Figure **1**. Name three challenges that may face Malawi as a result of being land-locked.
2 Look at Figure **2** and your graph from question **2c**.
  a Assess the importance of tobacco in Malawi's exports.
  b Suggest two problems that could arise from such a reliance on farm products.

Evaluation

To what extent is a pie chart the most effective type of graph to use when representing the data in Figure **2**?

Student Book
**See pages
236–7**

CASE STUDY

You need to know:

- where Nigeria is located
- Nigeria's global and regional importance.

Where is Nigeria?

Nigeria is in West Africa, bordering four countries. It extends from the Gulf of Guinea in the south to the Sahel in the north (Figure **2**).

 Big Idea

Nigeria is a case study of a newly emerging economy (NEE) experiencing rapid economic development. Use this study wherever questions are asked about an NEE.

What is the global importance of Nigeria?

Year	Population	Annual change %	Fertility rate	Urban population %	Urban population	% of world pop
2020	206 139 589	2.58	5.42	51.96	107 112 526	2.64
1990	95 617 345	2.65	6.6	29.70	28 379 229	1.97

Figure 1 *How has Nigeria developed in 30 years?*

In 2020, Nigeria was the 27th largest economy in the world.

Nigeria supplies 2.2% of the world's oil. Much of the country's economic growth has been based on oil revenues.

It has developed a diverse economy, including financial services, telecommunications and media.

Nigeria has been a major contributor to UN peacekeeping missions around the world.

Nigeria's regional importance in Africa

Nigeria has one of the fastest-growing economies in Africa.

In 2020 it had Africa's highest GDP and the third largest manufacturing sector.

It has the largest population of any African country.

Nigeria has the highest farm output in Africa. In 2020, about 35% of the population were employed in agriculture; most are subsistence farmers.

Has huge potential despite problems with lack of infrastructure.

Figure 2 *The location of Nigeria*

 Six Second Summary

- Nigeria is in West Africa.
- Nigeria is an important oil producer and has experienced rapid economic development.
- Nigeria is important regionally in terms of its GDP, population and farm output.

Over to you

Annotate **six** features of Nigeria on a map to show its location and its importance globally and regionally. Stick it on your wall as a reminder.

Student Book
See pages
238–9

You need to know:

- the political, social, cultural and environmental contexts of Nigeria.

CASE STUDY

Political context

- During the colonial period, Europeans exploited Africa's resources and people. Nigeria was ruled by the UK as a colony. It became independent in 1960.
- Political instability after independence affected Nigeria's development and led to widespread corruption.
- Since 1999, it has had a stable government.
- Several countries are now starting to invest in Nigeria (e.g. China, USA).

Social context

- Nigeria is a multi-ethnic, multi-faith country – this is a strength, but has also been a source of conflict including a civil war between 1967 and 1970.
- Recently, economic inequality between the Islamic north and Christian south of Nigeria has created new religious and ethnic tensions. This has created an unstable situation with a negative impact on the economy.

Cultural context

- Nigerian music – e.g. the musician Fela Kuti.
- Nigerian cinema – 'Nollywood' – is the second largest film industry in the world, behind India.
- Well-known Nigerian writers include Wole Soyinka.
- The Nigerian football team has won the African Cup of Nations three times.

Environmental context

Nigeria's natural environments form a series of bands because of decreasing rainfall towards the north. Environmental challenges include deforestation, forest fires and oil spillages.

Figure 1 *Nigeria's natural environment*

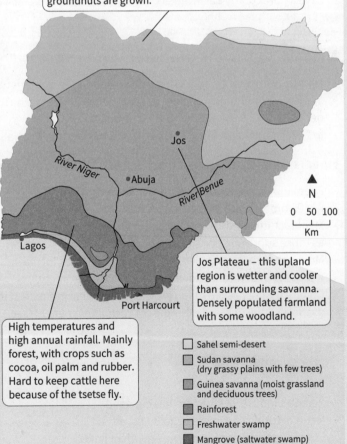

The far north east of the country is semi-desert. Further south, tropical grassland (savanna) dominates, mainly used for grazing cattle. Crops such as cotton, millet and groundnuts are grown.

Jos Plateau – this upland region is wetter and cooler than surrounding savanna. Densely populated farmland with some woodland.

High temperatures and high annual rainfall. Mainly forest, with crops such as cocoa, oil palm and rubber. Hard to keep cattle here because of the tsetse fly.

- Sahel semi-desert
- Sudan savanna (dry grassy plains with few trees)
- Guinea savanna (moist grassland and deciduous trees)
- Rainforest
- Freshwater swamp
- Mangrove (saltwater swamp)
- Montane (mountain slopes, with alpine vegetation)

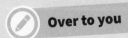

Six Second Summary

- There is considerable variety in Nigeria socially, culturally and environmentally.
- There have been political struggles but recently the government has been stable.

Over to you

Pick out **five** important pieces of information using sticky notes or by highlighting text on this page. Learn this information, and use the highlighting and sticky notes to jog your memory later.

You need to know:

- how Nigeria's economy is changing.

Student Book
See pages 240–1

CASE STUDY

Nigeria's sources of income

Traditionally, primary products such as cocoa and cotton were Nigeria's main source of income. Today, oil accounts for 90 per cent of Nigeria's export earnings.

 **Big Idea**

Nigeria's **industrial structure** (the proportion of the workforce employed in different sectors) is changing.

Does Nigeria have a balanced economy?

Industrial structure shows the contribution primary (agriculture), secondary (industry) and services sectors make to a country's GDP or employment.

Since 1991, there have been major changes in Nigeria's industrial structure. (Figure **1**).

With oil accounting for the majority of export revenues, Nigeria cannot be said to have a particularly balanced economy.

Rapid growth of communications, retail and finances has led to an expansion of the service sector.

The industrial sector accounts for about 27% of Nigeria's GDP. It has the fastest-growing industrial sector in Africa.

Employment in agriculture has fallen, due to increasing use of farm machinery and better pay and conditions elsewhere.

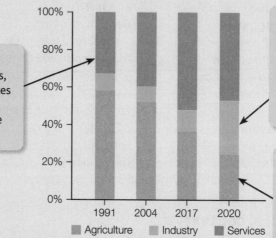

Figure 1 *Changes in Nigeria's employment structure, 1991–2020*

Nigeria's growing manufacturing sector

- Manufacturing involves making products from raw materials.
- In the past, manufacturing growth was hindered by Nigeria's dependence on the export of raw materials.
- In 2020, manufacturing accounted for 13 per cent of Nigeria's GDP.

How is manufacturing affecting economic development?

- Regular paid work gives people a more secure income. So there is a large home market for products manufactured in Nigeria, e.g. cars.
- Manufacturing industries stimulate growth for other companies, such as those supplying parts to make cars.
- More people are employed, so revenue from taxes increases.
- A thriving industrial sector attracts foreign investment.
- Oil processing has led to the growth of chemical industries, including soaps and plastics – an example of the *multiplier effect* (see 16.8).

Figure 2 *Peugeot factory, Kaduna, Nigeria*

 Six Second Summary

- Nigeria's industrial structure has changed.
- Manufacturing can increase incomes, attract investment and encourage the growth of linked industries – the multiplier effect.

 Over to you

- Add doodles to this page to help you remember the content – e.g. a tractor for primary sector.
- Draw a flow diagram to show Nigeria's economic multiplier effect.

Student Book
See pages
242–3

CASE STUDY

- the role of TNCs in Nigeria's industrial development.
- the advantages and disadvantages of TNCs to Nigeria (the host country).

What are the advantages and disadvantages of TNCs in Nigeria?

A **transnational corporation (TNC)** is a large company that operates in several countries.

A TNC usually has its headquarters in one country with production plants in several others.

Advantages

- 😊 Companies may provide employment and the development of new skills.
- 😊 Investment by companies in local infrastructure and education.
- 😊 Other local companies benefit from increased orders.
- 😊 Valuable export revenues are earned.

Disadvantages

- 😞 Local workers are sometimes poorly paid.
- 😞 Working conditions are sometimes very poor.
- 😞 Management jobs often go to foreign employees.
- 😞 Much of the profit goes abroad rather than being reinvested.

Shell Oil in the Niger Delta

Shell is one of the world's largest oil companies. It has extracted oil from the Niger Delta since 1958.

Advantages

- 😊 Shell provides direct employment for 2700 people and 9000 contractors, of whom 97 per cent are Nigerian.
- 😊 Over 90% of Shell contracts have been awarded to Nigerian companies.
- 😊 Around US$50 000 per year is spent on health care.
- 😊 Through its 'not-for-profit' enterprise, Shell finances renewable energy projects such as solar power.

Disadvantages

- 😞 Oil spills contaminate soils and cause water pollution, damaging agriculture and fishing.
- 😞 Most crude oil is exported to be refined in the USA and Europe, so most of the profits do not go to Nigeria.
- 😞 Oil theft and sabotage cost billions of dollars every year.
- 😞 Shell has reduced the tax paid in Nigeria by registering in countries such as Bermuda.

Figure 1 *An oil rig in the Niger Delta*

Figure 2 *Oil pollution at an illegal refinery, River State, Nigeria*

Six Second Summary

- Advantages of TNCs include employment and investment.
- Disadvantages include profit going abroad and environmental problems.

Over to you

Think of a favourite song and change the lyrics to remind you of the advantages and disadvantages of TNCs.

You need to know:

- about Nigeria's changing political and trading relationships with the wider world.

Student Book
**See pages
244–5**

CASE STUDY

How have Nigeria's political links changed?

- Until 1960, Nigeria was part of the British Empire.
- Since independence, Nigeria has become a member of the British **Commonwealth**.
- Nigeria is also a leading member of African political and economic groups, and international organisations.

OPEC (Organisation of Petroleum Exporting Countries): aims to stabilise the price of oil and to ensure a regular supply

ECOWAS (Economic Community of West African States): trading group

CEN-SAD (Community of Sahel-Saharan States): trading group and develops sporting links

Nigeria's political links

United Nations: Nigeria has a significant role in peacekeeping

African Union: economic planning and peacekeeping group

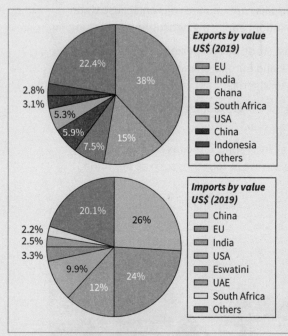

Exports by value US\$ (2019)
- EU
- India
- Ghana
- South Africa
- USA
- China
- Indonesia
- Others

38%, 22.4%, 2.8%, 3.1%, 5.3%, 5.9%, 7.5%, 15%

Imports by value US\$ (2019)
- China
- EU
- India
- USA
- Eswatini
- UAE
- South Africa
- Others

26%, 20.1%, 2.2%, 2.5%, 3.3%, 9.9%, 12%, 24%

Figure 1 *Nigeria's trading relationships*

Exports: crude and refined petroleum, natural gas, rubber, cocoa and cotton.

Imports: refined petroleum from the EU and the USA; cars from Brazil and the USA. Telephones from China is a fast-growing import.

What are Nigeria's global trading relationships?

Crude oil

- Crude oil dominates Nigeria's exports.
- Until recently, the greatest demand for Nigerian oil was from the USA.
- With the development of shale oil in the USA, demand for Nigerian oil has fallen.
- India is now Nigeria's biggest customer.

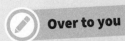

Six Second Summary

- Nigeria's political role used to be focused on the British Empire.
- It is now a member of African and international groups.
- Main trading partners include the EU and India.

Over to you

Write down **eight** pieces of information you've learnt from this page.

Agriculture

- The reliance on crude petroleum has reduced the importance of Nigeria's agricultural products.
- The top destinations for Nigeria's agricultural products are Vietnam, India, USA, Russia and the Netherlands.

Figure 2 *Crude palm kernel oil is a key agricultural export*

CASE STUDY

You need to know:

- the different types of aid
- the impact of international aid on Nigeria (the receiving country).

Student Book
See pages
246–7

Types of aid

Aid can be provided by individuals, charities, NGOs, governments and international organisations. There are two main types of aid:

- *Emergency aid* – following a natural disaster or conflict
- *Developmental aid* – long-term support aimed at improving quality of life

Why does Nigeria receive aid?

- Many people in Nigeria are poor and have limited access to services such as safe water, sanitation and a reliable electricity supply.
- Around 60 per cent of the population live on less that $1 (£0.63) per day.
- There are high birth rates and infant mortality with low life expectancy.
- Most aid is from UK and USA and also the World Bank.

What is the impact of aid in Nigeria?

The most successful aid projects are community-based, supported by small charities and NGOs. Aid has been used to benefit Nigeria in several ways.

In 2014, the World Bank approved a US$500 million loan to fund development projects and provide loans to businesses.

Aid from the USA helps to protect people against the spread of AIDS/HIV.

How does aid benefit Nigeria?

The Community Care in Nigeria project provides support for orphans.

Nets for Life (an NGO) provides education on malaria prevention and distributes anti-mosquito nets.

What prevents aid from being used effectively?

- Corruption has been a major factor in loss of aid.
- Donors may have political influence over what happens to aid.
- Money may be used to promote the commercial self-interest of the donor.

Improved health provision in SW Nigeria

One in eight Nigerian children die before the age of 5. A community development committee was set up by Christian Aid in 2017 in the state of Benue to target life-threatening diseases among very young children.

- One thousand local people were trained to provide treatment in people's homes.
- Between 2017 and 2019, 360 000 children under five years of age received life-saving treatment.
- Christian Aid has encouraged medical insurance schemes.

 Six Second Summary

- There are several different types of aid.
- Impacts of aid vary according to whether or not it is used effectively.

 Over to you

Try this 4-mark question.

Write down **two** reasons why aid may not always be effective. Explain your reasons fully.

Student Book
See pages
248–9

CASE STUDY

You need to know:

- the environmental impacts of economic development in Nigeria.

The effect of economic growth on the environment

Rapid economic growth, like in Nigeria, can bring many benefits. But it can also have a negative impact on the environment.

Industrial growth

- In Kano and Lagos, harmful pollutants go directly into water channels. They are harmful to people and ecosystems.
- Air pollution causes respiratory and heart problems. (Figure **1**).
- 96 per cent of Nigeria's forests have been destroyed through factors such as agriculture, urban expansion and industrial development.

Figure 1 *Air pollution in Lagos*

Commercial farming and deforestation

- In some places, there is water pollution due to chemicals, soil erosion and silting of river channels.
- Many species (e.g. cheetahs, giraffes) have disappeared in some areas because of deforestation.

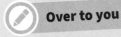
Six Second Summary

Environmental impacts of economic development include:

- air pollution
- damage to ecosystems
- oil spills.

Over to you

Design a poster which shows your understanding of **three** environmental impacts of economic development.

Urban growth

- Waste disposal is a major issue (Figure **2**).
- Traffic congestion leads to high levels of air pollution.
- The development of Abuja has resulted in areas of rich natural vegetation being replaced by concrete.

Figure 2 *Rubbish at the Olusosun dump in Lagos*

Mining and oil extraction

- Tin mining led to soil erosion. Local water supplies were polluted with toxic chemicals.
- Oil spills can cause fires, sending CO_2 and other harmful gases into the atmosphere, creating *acid rain*.

Ogale oil spills (2013–16)

Between 2013 and 2016 there were over 40 separate oil spills in Ogoniland in the Niger Delta. Ogale relies on the Ogale Stream for farming, drinking, washing and fishing. Oil contamination of the stream has had serious economic, social and environmental impacts on the community.

Figure 3 *A waterway in Ogale contaminated by oil*

Student Book
**See pages
250–1**

CASE STUDY

Quality of life

As a country's economy develops, the quality of life of ordinary people should improve.

Higher disposable income to spend (e.g. on schooling)

Improvements to infrastructure, such as roads

Better access to safe water and sanitation

Improved access to a better diet means higher productivity

Better-quality health care

Reliable electricity supplies

Reliable, better-paid jobs in manufacturing or services

Figure 1 The benefits of economic development

Have all Nigerians benefited from economic development?

Nigeria's HDI has been increasing steadily since 2005 and is expected to continue to rise (Figure 2). In 2019 it stood at 0.539. Most indicators suggest that economic development since 1990 has improved the quality of people's lives.

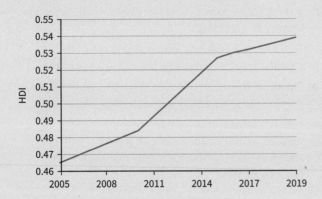

Figure 2 Changes in Nigeria's HDI, 2005–19 (1=most developed)

Has it all been good news?

- Many people in Nigeria are still poor.
- The gap between rich and poor has become wider.
- Corruption has been a major factor and the oil wealth was not used to diversify the economy as much as it should have been.
- Nigeria's over-dependence on oil could become a problem in the future.

Will quality of life continue to improve?

Sixty per cent of Nigerians live in poverty. To improve their quality of life, the following challenges must be met:

Political – there is a need for a continuing stable government to encourage inward investment.

Environmental – there are threats of desertification, pollution by oil spills and disease spread by the tsetse fly.

Social – historical distrust remains between tribal groups. Kidnappings by the militant group Boko Haram spread fear among Nigerians and potential investors.

Six Second Summary

- Quality of life has improved as a result of economic development.
- There are still challenges to overcome as a high proportion of the population still live in poverty.

Over to you

Meet with or message a friend and take it in turns to tell each other what you have learnt about Nigeria. Continue until you both run out of ideas.

Student Book
See pages
252–3

SKILLS FOCUS

You need to be able to:

- construct a scattergraph and draw a line of best fit
- construct a dispersion graph
- calculate central tendency (mean, median), range and inter-quartile range.

CASE STUDY

Constructing graphs of economic data

Figure **1** compares economic development in ten African countries, including Nigeria. Nigeria has a relatively high level of economic development with the highest GNI per capita (per person). Whilst the percentage of people employed in agriculture is high when compared with HICs, it is one of the lowest on the continent.

Country	GNI per capita (US$)	GDP annual growth (%)	Unemployment (%)	Employment in agriculture (%)
Nigeria	5710	2.2	7.9	37
Ghana	4650	6.5	4.5	41
Sierra Leone	1490	5.5	4.4	61
Cameroon	3700	3.7	3.4	62
Togo	1780	5.3	2.0	38
South Africa	3250	0.2	32.5	6
Kenya	3440	5.4	2.6	38
Uganda	1970	6.8	1.9	69
Niger	1300	5.9	0.5	75
Tanzania	3160	5.8	2.0	67

Figure 1 *Comparative economic development data for ten African countries, 2019*

Skills

1 a Using Figure **1**, sketch a scattergraph (see Student Book page 370) to show the relationship between GNI (*x*-axis) and employment in agriculture (*y*-axis).

b Sketch a best fit line (see Student Book page 370).

2 Use the data in Figure **1** to draw a dispersion graph (see Student Book page 375) to represent the data for GNI.

a The vertical line should extend from US$0 to US$6000.

b Plot each country's GNI as a cross on the vertical line. Write the name of the country alongside.

c Calculate the median, upper quartile and lower quartile.

d Indicate their positions on your graph.

Analysis

1 Look at Figure **1** and your completed scattergraph.

a Describe the relationship between GNI and employment in agriculture.

b Is this what you expect the relationship should be? Explain.

c Draw a circle around any anomalies (those points that are distant from the best-fit line).

d Suggest reasons why South Africa is an anomaly (also known as a residual).

2 Look at Figure **1** and your dispersion graph.

a Calculate the range (see Student Book page 375).

b Calculate the mean GNI. Compare this with the median value (see Student Book page 374).

c Which measure of central tendency, the mean or median, is more appropriate as a measure of a country's level of development? Explain possible reasons for this.

Evaluation

Look at Figure **1**. Explain two reasons why annual growth of GDP is not necessarily a good indicator of a country's economic development.

Student Book
See pages
254–5

You need to know:

- how the economy of the UK has changed
- the causes of economic change in the UK.

How has the economy of the UK changed?

Most people worked in farming or mining (*primary* sector).

During the Industrial Revolution, people made steel, ships or textiles (*secondary* or *manufacturing* sector).

A newly emerging *quaternary* sector has developed, with jobs in research and information technology.

A significant shift to the service (*tertiary*) sector.

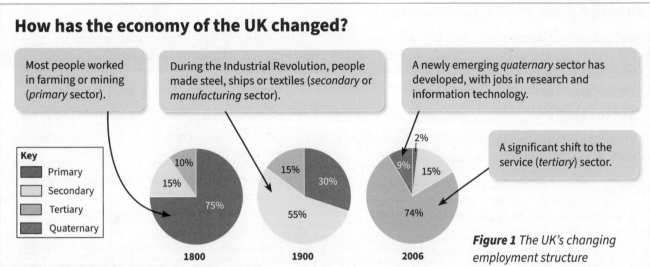

Key
- Primary
- Secondary
- Tertiary
- Quaternary

1800: 75%, 15%, 10%
1900: 30%, 55%, 15%
2006: 74%, 15%, 9%, 2%

Figure 1 The UK's changing employment structure

What are the causes of economic change in the UK?

De-industrialisation is the decline in traditional industries, such as manufacturing. This has happened because:

- machines and technology have replaced many people
- other countries (e.g. China) can produce cheaper goods because labour is less expensive.

Globalisation is the growth and spread of ideas around the world.

- Many people now work on global brands in the quaternary sector, e.g. in IT.
- Increased world trade and cheaper imported products have contributed to the decline in UK manufacturing.

Government policies

1945–79
- The government created state-run industries such as British Rail.
- Government money 'propped up' unprofitable industries.

1979–2010
- State-run industries sold to private shareholders. This is called *privatisation*.
- Many older industries closed down.
- New private companies brought innovation and change.

2010 onwards
'Rebalancing' the economy by stabilising the secondary sector and promoting opportunities in the less prosperous north of the UK. Policies have included:

- improvements to transport (e.g. HS2)
- more investment in manufacturing, such as high-tech engineering
- encouraging global firms to locate in UK.

Six Second Summary

- The UK economy has changed over time.
- De-industrialisation is the decline of manufacturing.
- Globalisation has increased the quaternary sector.
- Government policies have caused economic change.

Over to you

Make your own glossary of the key words (in bold and in italics) in this section.

Student Book
**See pages
256-7**

You need to know:

- what a post-industrial economy is
- how the development of information and technology, service industries, finance and research have moved the UK towards a post-industrial economy.

What is a post-industrial economy?

A **post-industrial economy** is where manufacturing industry declines and is replaced largely by the service sector and the development of a quaternary sector. This happened in the UK from the 1970s onwards.

Development of information technology

The use of **information technology (IT)** is a key factor in the UK's move to a post-industrial economy.

- Internet access enables people to communicate across the world and work from home.
- In 2019, 775 000 people were employed in IT-related industries.
- The UK is one of the world's leading digital economies.

Service industries and finance

The UK service sector has grown rapidly since the 1970s. In 2019, it contributed 81 per cent of UK economic output.

- Finance is an important part of the service sector.
- The UK is the world's leading centre for financial services.
- In 2019, the financial services sector accounted for almost 7 per cent of the UK's economic output.

Research

The UK research sector (part of the quaternary sector) employs over 250 000 (2018) highly qualified people and is estimated to contribute 1.7 per cent of the UK's GDP. This sector is likely to be one of the UK economy's main growth areas in the future.

Business and financial companies — NHS — Universities — Environment Agency — BBC — Charities — Engineering — Pharmaceutical

Figure 1 *Some UK research organisations*

British Antarctic Survey

The British Antarctic Survey (BAS) employs over 500 highly skilled people in Cambridge (UK), Antarctica and the Arctic. It is linked to the University of Cambridge and helps us understand the impact of humans on the Earth's natural systems.

Figure 2 *The BAS Halley VI Research Station in Antarctica*

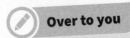 **Six Second Summary**

- Developments in IT have encouraged the growth of service and quaternary sectors.
- Finance is an important part of the service sector.
- Research employs highly qualified people.

Over to you

Explain **three** reasons why the UK is developing as a post-industrial economy.

Student Book
See pages 258–9

You need to know:

- what a science park is
- what a business park is
- how science and business parks are moving the UK towards a post-industrial economy.

What is a science park?

A **science park** is a group of scientific and technical knowledge-based businesses located on a single site. Most are associated with universities, enabling them to use research facilities and employ skilled graduates. Science parks may also include support services such as financial services and marketing.

University of Southampton Science Park

Southampton Science Park includes one hundred small science and innovation businesses including Jasper Therapeutics (a start-up pharmaceutical company) and Maverick Aviation Ltd (developing a wearable aerial mobility jet-pack).

Benefits

- Excellent transport links – close to M3, Southampton international airport and rail links
- Excellent links with the University
- Attractive location with green areas

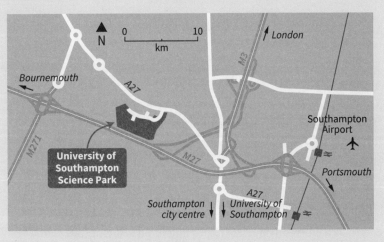

Figure 1 Southampton Science Park – transport links

What is a business park?

A **business park** is an area of land occupied by a cluster of businesses. Business parks are usually located on the edges of towns where:

- land tends to be cheaper and more available
- access is often better with less congestion
- businesses can benefit from working together.

Cobalt Business Park, Newcastle-upon-Tyne

Cobalt Park is the UK's largest business park, with support facilities including retail outlets and a fitness centre. The park is next to the A19, close to the A1 and 20 minutes from the international airport.

Businesses locating in Cobalt Park qualify for governmental assistance.

Companies in the park include Siemens, IBM and Santander.

Figure 2 Cobalt Business Park

Six Second Summary

- Science parks provide benefits such as links with universities and attractive locations.
- Business parks tend to be located on the edges of towns because land is cheaper, has better access and businesses can work together.

Over to you

Cover up everything apart from Figure 1. Use the map to explain the benefits of science parks.

Student Book
See pages
260–1

EXAMPLE

You need to know:

- what the impacts of industry are on the physical environment
- about an example of how modern industrial development can be made more environmentally sustainable – Torr Quarry in Somerset.

Impacts of industry on the physical environment

- Manufacturing plants can have a negative visual effect on the landscape.
- Industrial processes and waste products can cause air, water and soil pollution.
- The transport of raw materials and manufacturing products increases levels of air pollution.

How can industrial development be more sustainable?

- Natural ecosystems can be protected to encourage biodiversity.
- Technology can be used to reduce harmful emissions.
- Desulphurisation can remove harmful gases.
- Heavy fines can be imposed when pollution incidents occur.

Quarrying in the UK

Impacts of quarrying

- destroy natural habitats
- pollute water courses
- scar landscapes

Making quarrying more sustainable

- There are strict controls on blasting, removal of dust from roads and landscaping.
- Recycling is encouraged.
- Companies are expected to restore or improve a quarry after it has been used.

Torr Quarry, Somerset

Torr Quarry is a limestone quarry in the Mendip Hills. It employs over 100 people and contributes more than £15 million towards the local economy each year. Torr Quarry is an example of how modern industrial development can be more environmentally sustainable.

- The quarry is being restored to create wildlife lakes.
- The site is part of an initiative to create biodiversity-rich landscapes.
- Regular monitoring of noise, vibration, dust and **water quality**.
- Rail transport of quarried rock minimises the impact on local roads and villages.

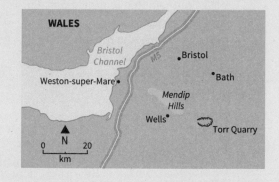

Figure 1 Location of Torr Quarry, Somerset

Figure 2 *Torr Quarry*

Figure 3 *Planned restoration of Torr Quarry*

 Six Second Summary

- Modern industry can cause pollution and destroy habitats.
- Torr Quarry aims to be environmentally sustainable by landscaping and monitoring.

 Over to you

Draw a field sketch of Figure **3** and annotate it to show how Torr Quarry is environmentally sustainable.

Student Book
See pages 262–3

You need to know:

- what social and economic changes are happening in the rural landscape in one area of population growth and also in one of population decline.

An area of population growth: South Cambridgeshire

What are the changes?

- The population of around 157 000 is increasing, due to migration into the area.
- Most migrants come from Cambridge and other parts of the UK; some have also arrived from Eastern Europe.
- The proportion of people aged 65 or over is growing.

Social effects

- Commuters use services at their place of work, having a negative effect on the local economy. Car ownership of 80 per cent leads to increased traffic on narrow roads.
- Housing developments on the edges of villages can lead to a reduction in community spirit.
- Young people cannot afford the high cost of houses and move away.

Economic effects

- A reduction in agricultural employment as farmers sell land for housing.
- Lack of affordable housing.
- High demand leads to high petrol prices.
- Increased population puts pressure on services.

Figure 1 *Location of South Cambridgeshire and the Outer Hebrides*

Figure 2 *The landscape of Cambridgeshire*

An area of population decline: the Outer Hebrides

What are the changes?

- The population has declined by more than 50 per cent since 1901.
- With limited employment, young people have moved away.

Social effects

- The expected fall in the number of children may result in school closures.
- An increasingly ageing population has fewer young people to support them (Figure **3**).

Economic effects

- Services are closing.
- Most small farms (crofts) can only provide work for two days a week.
- There has been an increase in tourism, but ...
- ... the current infrastructure cannot support the scale of tourism needed to provide an alternative source of income.

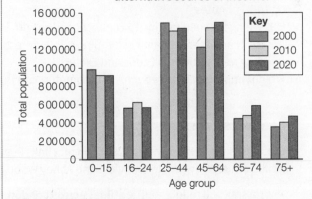

Figure 3 *Population structure of the Outer Hebrides, 2000, 2010 and 2020*

 Six Second Summary

- Social changes include increased traffic and fewer young people to support the elderly.
- Economic changes include lack of affordable housing and reduced employment.

Over to you

Draw a table comparing the social and economic changes happening in South Cambridgeshire and the Outer Hebrides.

You need to know:

- about improvements and new developments in road and rail infrastructure in the UK
- how those improvements will make a difference.

Student Book
See pages 264–5

Road improvements

New road schemes will create thousands of jobs and boost local and regional economies.

Future road schemes include:

- Improving connectivity (e.g. M42 improving links to Birmingham Airport).
- A better A14 link between the port of Felixstowe and the Midlands/North.
- Improving road design, e.g. the construction of additional lanes to reduce congestion.
- The A303 south-west 'super highway' (Figure **1**)

South-west 'super highway'

- A £2 billion road-widening project will take place on the A303.
- Converting the route to dual carriageway will create a 'super highway' to Exeter and beyond.

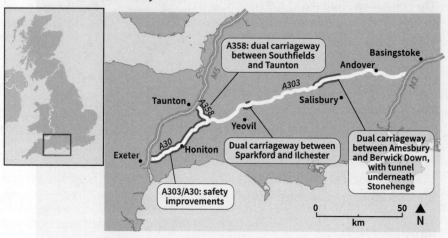

Figure 1 *Upgrading the A303*

Railway improvements

There are plans to stimulate economic growth in the north of the UK by improving rail links:

- Electrification of trans-Pennine rail links reducing journey times by up to 15 minutes.
- HS2 – a high-speed rail line to connect London with Birmingham (phase 1) and then to Manchester (phase 2) (Figure **2**).
- Building new stations in Leeds and Exeter.
- Freight improvements between Southampton and the Midlands.

London's Crossrail

Crossrail is a new railway across London that links Reading and Heathrow (to the west), to Shenfield and Abbey Wood (to the east).

- Crossrail will reduce journey times across London.
- It will bring an additional 1.5 million people within 45 minutes' commuting distance of London's key business districts.

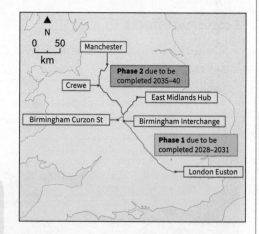

Figure 2 *Planned route for HS2*

Six Second Summary

- Improvements include building new rail lines and roads and adding lanes to motorways.
- These schemes can create jobs, reduce journey times and ease congestion.

Over to you

Create a Venn diagram to show the benefits of road and rail improvements.

Student Book
See pages 266-7

You need to know:

- how improvements and new developments will affect the UK's port and airport capacity
- how these can make a difference in the UK.

Developing the UK's ports

The UK ports industry is the largest in Europe. Most ports are run by private companies and handle a range of goods and services.

- Felixstowe – deals with 48 per cent of container trade. It has a new rail terminal and improvements to road connections are planned.
- Aberdeen – harbour improvements costing £350m to support the UK's offshore wind industry.

Liverpool2

In 2016 a new container terminal was opened at the Port of Liverpool, known as 'Liverpool2'.

The project more than doubled the port's capacity to over 1.5 million containers a year. The advantages of the terminal include:

- creating over 5000 jobs
- boosting the economy of the north-west
- reducing the amount of freight traffic on the roads.

Figure 1 *The container terminal at Liverpool2*

Airport developments

- Airports create vital global links
- They provide thousands of jobs
- They also boost economic growth both regionally and nationally.

Expanding London's airports

In 2015, a government report recommended a new third runway at Heathrow. The project is expected to cost £19 billion.

🙂 The Department of Transport expects the project to boost the regional economy by £61 billion and create up to 77 000 local jobs.

🙁 Hundreds of homes will have to be demolished to make way for the expansion. People living nearby are also concerned about increased noise levels.

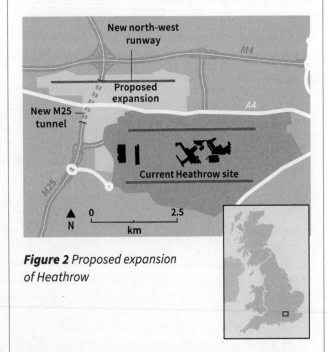

Figure 2 *Proposed expansion of Heathrow*

Six Second Summary

- Examples of improvements and new developments are Liverpool2 (a port) and a new runway at Heathrow (an airport).
- They are intended to create new jobs and boost the economy.

Over to you

Produce a **five**-sentence summary of what you have learnt from this page.

Student Book
See pages 268–9

You need to know:

- what is meant by the north–south divide
- why the north–south divide exists
- strategies used to try to resolve regional differences.

What is the north–south divide?

It refers to real or imagined cultural and economic differences between the south of England and the rest of the UK.

In general, the south enjoys higher incomes and longer life expectancy. But the south also has higher house prices and more traffic congestion.

Why is there a north–south divide in the UK?

- During the Industrial Revolution, the UK's growth was centred on coalfields, heavy industries and engineering in northern England, Wales and Scotland.

- Since the 1970s, many industries have declined, reducing prosperity in those areas.

- London and the South East developed rapidly due to a fast-growing service sector.

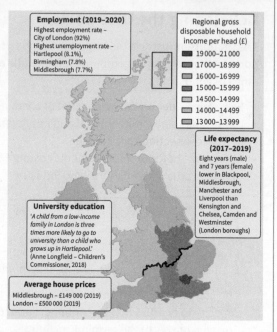

Employment (2019–2020)
Highest employment rate –
City of London (92%)
Highest unemployment rate –
Hartlepool (8.1%),
Birmingham (7.8%),
Middlesbrough (7.7%)

Regional gross disposable household income per head (£)
- 19 000–21 000
- 17 000–18 999
- 16 000–16 999
- 15 000–15 999
- 14 500–14 999
- 14 000–14 499
- 13 000–13 999

Life expectancy (2017–2019)
Eight years (male) and 7 years (female) lower in Blackpool, Middlesbrough, Manchester and Liverpool than Kensington and Chelsea, Camden and Westminster (London boroughs)

University education
'A child from a low-income family in London is three times more likely to go to university than a child who grows up in Hartlepool.'
(Anne Longfield – Children's Commissioner, 2018)

Average house prices
Middlesbrough – £149 000 (2019)
London – £500 000 (2019)

***Figure 1** North and south – some facts*

How can regional strategies address the issue?

Local enterprise partnerships (LEPs)

LEPs are voluntary partnerships between local authorities and businesses.

Their aim is to identify business needs and encourage companies to invest in order to boost the local economy and create jobs.

The Lancashire LEP is one example.

Lancashire LEP

The Lancashire LEP has secured a £1 billion growth plan.

- By 2021 around 11 000 new jobs were created.
- Construction of a major new road linking Preston and South Fylde to the M55 (£58m).
- Improvements to access and traffic flow in and around Blackburn (£12m).
- Improvements to the Blackpool Conference and Exhibition Centre (£15m).

Enterprise Zones

The aim of Enterprise Zones is to encourage new businesses and jobs. The government supports businesses in Enterprise Zones by:

- providing a business rate discount
- ensuring the provision of superfast broadband
- creating simpler planning regulations.

Six Second Summary

- The north–south divide refers to differences between the north and south of the UK.
- Local enterprise partnerships and Enterprise Zones are attempts to resolve regional differences.

Over to you

Write the words 'north-south divide' and, for each letter, write a word or phrase, relevant to this page's information, e.g. **N**orth–south divide, regi**O**nal strategies, Ente**R**prise Zones, and so on.

Student Book
**See pages
270–1**

You need to know:

- what links exist between the UK and the wider world, through trade, culture, transport and electronic communication.

What are the UK's links with the wider world?

In the past, the UK was one of the world's superpowers. Although its global position has declined, the UK is still an influential member of important international organisations such as the G7 and the UN Security Council.

Trade

- The UK's most important trading links are with the EU.
- The USA is an important historic trading partner.
- There has been a recent increase in trade with China.

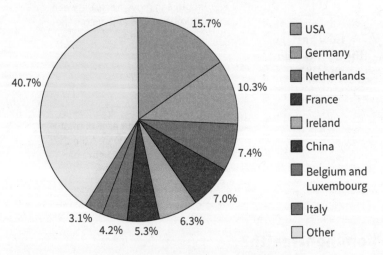

USA, Germany, Netherlands, France, Ireland, China, Belgium and Luxembourg, Italy, Other

15.7%, 10.3%, 7.4%, 7.0%, 6.3%, 5.3%, 4.2%, 3.1%, 40.7%

Figure 1 *The UK's major export destinations, 2018*

Transport

- London Heathrow is one of the busiest airports in the world.
- There are important transport links between the UK and mainland Europe via the Channel Tunnel and sea ferries.

Electronic communication

- 99 per cent of internet traffic passes along a network of submarine high-power cables.
- Connections are concentrated between the UK and USA.
- There is a further concentration in the Far East.
- A project known as Arctic Fibre plans to connect Asia, Canada and Europe.

Culture

- The global importance of the English language has given the UK strong cultural links with many parts of the world.
- Migrants have brought their own culture to the UK, such as food and festivals.

Television

Television is one of the UK's most successful media exports. In 2019–20, TV programmes and associated features accounted for £1.48 billion of the UK's export earnings. The USA, France and Australia are the largest markets. China is increasingly significant.

Figure 2 Dr Who – *a UK export success*

Six Second Summary

- The UK is connected to the wider world via trade, culture, transport and electronic communication.
- These links often generate more money for the UK.

Over to you

Talk for one minute about the links the UK has with the rest of the world.

Student Book
**See pages
272–3**

You need to know:

- about the UK's economic and political links with the European Union (EU) and the Commonwealth.

What are the UK's links with the European Union?

In 1973, the UK became a member of the European Union (EU). After a referendum, the UK formally left the EU in 2020. Whilst a free trade agreement has been reached with the EU, freedom of movement between countries no longer exists and the UK is no longer subject to EU rules and regulations.

In the past, membership of the EU has had many impacts on the UK.

Financial support for farmers and disadvantaged regions in the UK.

Goods, services, capital and labour can move freely between member states and encourage trade.

How has the EU affected the UK?

EU laws and controls on crime, pollution and consumers' rights.

In 2013, about 40% of total UK immigrants were from the EU. In 2019, this figure had fallen to 17%.

What are the UK's links with the Commonwealth?

The UK is a member of the Commonwealth, a voluntary association of 54 independent nations. The Commonwealth's roots go back to the British Empire, but today any country can join.

The Commonwealth Secretariat provides advice on a range of issues including human rights and social and economic development.

There are important trading and cultural links between the UK and the Commonwealth countries. There are also sporting connections, such as the Commonwealth Games.

Figure 1 *The Commonwealth Games in Australia, 2018*

 Six Second Summary

- The UK has both political and economic links with the EU and the Commonwealth.
- Economic links include trading links.
- Political links include laws or advice and support.

Over to you

- Highlight this page to show which links are economic and which are political.
- Create a Venn diagram to show these links.

Student Book
**See pages
274–5**

SKILLS FOCUS

You need to be able to:

- interpret an OS map (using grid references and symbols)
- draw a sketch map from an OS map (1:50 000)
- use a vertical aerial photo with an OS map (1:50 000).

Investigating Liverpool's docks

Liverpool is a coastal city located at the mouth of the River Mersey. It is naturally sheltered from the Irish Sea.

- Figure 1 is a 1:50 000 OS map extract dated 1997 showing the mouth of the River Mersey. You can see the docks lining the eastern bank of the river.
- To orientate yourself, locate the Royal Seaforth Dock on both Figure 1 and Figure 2.

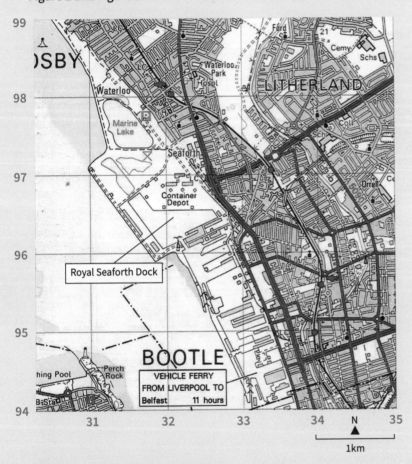

Figure 1 *OS map extract (1:50 000) of Liverpool docks, 1997*

Figure 2 *Vertical aerial photo of Royal Seaforth Dock, Liverpool*

Skills

1 Study Figures **1** and **2**. See page 208 for the key to map symbols.

 a What is the meaning of the symbol at 322961?

 b Give the six-figure grid reference for **each of** Royal Seaforth Dock, Gladstone Dock and Alexandra Dock in Figure **2**.

 c In which direction does the area of Litherland (grid square 3398) lie from **i)** the container depot (3296), and **ii)** the city centre (3395 and 3495).

2 Study Figure **1**.

 a Draw a sketch map showing the main docks in the area shown below.

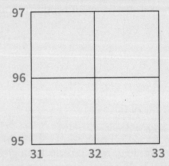

 b Use Figure **2** to help you locate, draw and label the new container terminal (Liverpool2) and the container cranes.

 c Label the docks that are named on Figure **2**.

 d Add a selection of buildings (mostly warehouses) shown on Figure **1**.

 e Complete your sketch map by writing a title, scale and north arrow. Label the gridlines.

Analysis

Using evidence from Figures **1** and **2**, suggest **three** reasons why Liverpool remains a good location for a major port (despite the fact that many other urban ports in the UK have closed).

Evaluation

1 Suggest how this OS map (Figure **1**) from 1997 is useful in understanding the changing port facilities at Liverpool.

2 Evaluate the advantages of using the vertical aerial photo (Figure **2**) alongside Figure **1** when interpreting the changing dockside of Liverpool.

Section C
The challenge of resource management

Your exam

Section C The challenge of resource management is part of Paper 2: Challenges in the human environment.

Paper 2 is a one-and-a-half hour written exam and makes up 35 per cent of your GCSE. The whole paper carries 88 marks (including 3 marks for SPaG) – questions on Section C will carry 25 marks.

You need to study resource management and one topic from food, water or energy in Section C – in your final exam you will have to answer Question 3 and one other question.

Tick these boxes to build a record of your revision

Your revision checklist

Spec key idea	Theme	1	2	3
19 Resource management				
Food, water and energy are fundamental to human development	19.1 The global distribution of resources			
The changing demand and provision of resources in the UK create opportunities and challenges	19.2 Provision of food in the UK (1)			
	19.3 Provision of food in the UK (2)			
	19.4 Provision of water in the UK (1)			
	19.5 Provision of water in the UK (2)			
	19.6 Provision of energy in the UK (1)			
	19.7 Provision of energy in the UK (2)			
Geographical skills	19.8 Skills Focus: OS map and decision-making exercise			
20 Food management				
Demand for food resources is rising globally but supply can be insecure, which may lead to conflict	20.1 Global food supply			
	20.2 Factors affecting food supply/Skills Focus			
	20.3 Impacts of food insecurity			
Different strategies can be used to increase food supply	20.4 Increasing food supply			
	20.5 The Indus Basin Irrigation System			
	20.6 Sustainable food production (1)			
	20.7 Sustainable food production (2)			
21 Water management				
Demand for water resources is rising globally but supply can be insecure, which may lead to conflict	21.1 Global water supply			
	21.2 Factors affecting water availability/Skills Focus			
	21.3 Impacts of water insecurity			
Different strategies can be used to increase water supply	21.4 How can water supply be increased?			
	21.5 The Lesotho Highland Water Project			
	21.6 Sustainable water supplies			
	21.7 Wakal River Basin Project			
22 Energy management				
Demand for energy resources is rising globally but supply can be insecure, which may lead to conflict	22.1 Global energy supply and demand			
	22.2 Factors affecting energy supply/Skills Focus			
	22.3 Impacts of energy insecurity			
Different strategies can be used to increase energy supply	22.4 How can energy supply be increased?			
	22.5 Gas – a non-renewable resource			
	22.6 Sustainable energy use			
	22.7 The Chambamontera micro-hydro scheme			

Student Book
See pages
276-7

- why food, water and energy are significant for economic and social well-being
- that resources are distributed unevenly around the world.

What is a resource?

- A resource is a stock or supply of something that has value or purpose.
- Food, water and energy are the most important resources for human development.
- Most HICs have plentiful resources, many of them imported.
- Many poorer countries lack resources and struggle to improve quality of life.

Big Idea

Population growth presents many challenges for **resource management**.

	Why are resources significant?	What are the global inequalities?
Food 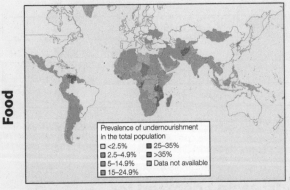 **Figure 1** *Areas where hunger was a problem in 2020*	• A poorly balanced diet can cause illness. • People need to be well fed to be productive. • Obesity is an increasing problem, especially in HICs.	• Over one billion people do not get enough calories. • **Undernutrition** (malnutrition) affects a further two billion. • There can still be hunger, even in countries that produce a lot of food.
Water 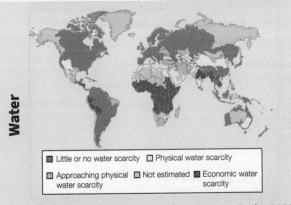 **Figure 2** *Projected areas of water scarcity by 2025*	• Essential for drinking. • Vital for crops. • Used to produce energy.	• Variations in climate and rainfall affect supply. • Capture, storage and extraction are expensive. • Many poor countries have water shortage. • LICs/NEEs use most water for agriculture • HICs use most water in industry.
Energy 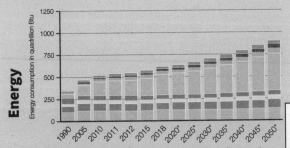 **Figure 3** *Global energy consumption by region 1990–2050 (quadrillion British thermal units)*	• Needed for light, heat and power. • Powers factories. • Provides fuel for transport.	• Richer countries consume more energy than poorer countries. • The Middle East is a major oil supplier; its own consumption is low. As NEEs become more industrialised, the demand for energy will increase.

Six Second Summary

- Richer countries use more resources than poorer countries.
- Many of the world's poorer countries lack resources and struggle to improve quality of life for their people.

Over to you

Annotate a blank world map to show the global inequalities in resource supply and consumption.

Student Book
**See pages
278–9**

You need to know:

- the growing demand for high-value food exports from LICs
- the all-year demand for seasonal food
- the increasing demand for organic produce.

Growing demand for high-value food from LICs

- In 2019, 12 per cent of the food eaten in the UK came from LICs.
- A growing proportion of imported food consists of high-value products, e.g. vanilla and saffron.
- The food might be produced cheaply in LICs but high storage and transport costs result in high prices in UK shops.
- Many farmers in LICs and NEEs earn little from growing these products.

Stage	Price per tonne (£)	% of final price
Producer	630	12
Exporter	290	6
Packaging	280	5
Air freight/handling	1040	20
Importer	620	12
Supermarket	2500	45
Total price	**5360**	**100**

Figure 1 *Price breakdown of one tonne of Kenyan mangetout*

All-year demand for seasonal food

Today there is a growing demand for seasonal foods (e.g. strawberries) to be available throughout the year.

Foods that are out of season have to be imported, and are more expensive. They are usually transported by air, which creates a considerable carbon footprint.

Increasing demand for organic produce

Organic produce is grown without the use of artificial chemicals.

Organic food has become increasingly popular in the UK. Higher labour costs often make it more expensive. Organic food can often be local and seasonal.

Riverford Organic Farms

- Began as an organic farm in Devon.
- Now delivers organic vegetables from farms in Devon, Yorkshire, Peterborough and Hampshire.
- This reduces food miles and provides local employment.

Six Second Summary

There is a growing demand for:

- high-value foods from LICs
- seasonal food throughout the year
- organic produce.

Over to you

List the opportunities and challenges created by the changing demand for food in the UK.

Figure 2 *A Riverford organic vegetable box*

Student Book
See pages 280–1

You need to know:

- how and why increasing 'food miles' leads to larger carbon footprints
- about moves towards local sourcing of food
- the trend towards agribusiness.

How does food demand affect the UK's carbon footprint?

Figure **1** shows the distances travelled by selected foods imported to the UK. This is known as **food miles**. Air transport is expensive and adds to the country's **carbon footprint**.

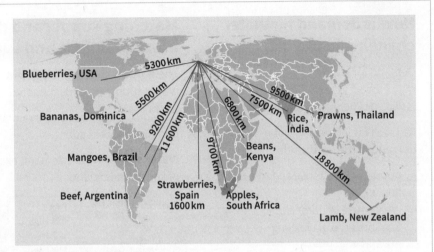

Figure 1 Distances travelled by food imported to the UK

Local sourcing of food

There has been a move towards local sourcing of food in the UK. This can significantly reduce food miles and greenhouse gas emissions.

Farm shops and farmers' markets sell directly from the farm to the public. They help to support the local economy. The carbon footprint is reduced by cutting down food miles, with less processing and packaging needed.

Agribusiness

- **Agribusinesses** are large commercial farms with high levels of investment.
- They are often part of a larger national or international business.
- They use modern technology, scientific research and chemicals to maximise production.
- They benefit from being large – they are able to buy seeds and chemicals in bulk, and use large and efficient machines.

Figure 2 Using modern technologies to maximise production at an agribusiness

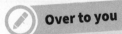 **Six Second Summary**

- If large numbers of 'food miles' are travelled, it increases the UK's carbon footprint.
- There has been a move towards local sourcing of food in the UK.
- Agribusinesses are large commercial farms with high levels of investment.

Over to you

In no more than **five** sentences, summarise how:

- food miles contribute to the UK's carbon footprint
- local sourcing of food can help reduce the carbon footprint.

Student Book
See pages
282–3

You need to know:

- how and why demand for water in the UK is changing
- how supply and demand are matched
- how water transfer schemes help to maintain supplies.

How is demand for water changing in the UK?

Demand for water is high. By 2034 it may exceed supply. Climate change is likely to increase the problem.

Reasons for increasing water demand in the UK include:

- population increase and more houses
- greater use of domestic appliances, e.g. washing machines
- increased demand for irrigation.

Water transfer schemes

Water transfer schemes move water from areas with a water surplus to areas with a water deficit. There is opposition because of:

- high costs
- potential damage to ecosystems
- greenhouse gases produced to generate electricity to pump water.

Matching supply and demand – areas of deficit and supply

The north and west (where rainfall is higher) has a **water surplus** where supply exceeds demand.

The south and east (where rainfall is lower) has a **water deficit** where demand exceeds supply.

Water stress (where demand exceeds supply) is experienced in much of southern England.

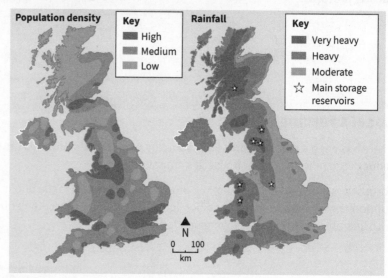

Figure 1 *UK population density and water supply*

The Thirlmere water transfer scheme

Recently, West Cumbria has experienced problems with the quantity and quality of its water supplies. The Thirlmere scheme (2017–22) will transfer water from Thirlmere to West Cumbria. Water will be transferred using gravity flow rather than pumps, to reduce the environmental impact.

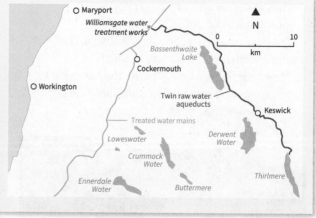

Figure 2 *The Thirlmere water transfer scheme*

Six Second Summary

- Demand for water is increasing.
- The UK has areas of water surplus and water deficit.
- Water transfer schemes move water from areas of surplus to areas of deficit.

Over to you

Cover everything apart from the maps on this page. Use them to suggest how far the UK's water supply meets demand.

Student Book
See pages
284–5

You need to know:

- about the quality of water in the UK
- the causes of water pollution
- how water pollution is managed.

Water quality

The UK has high quality, safe tap water. Yet despite effective water treatment, a report in 2020 stated that no rivers in the UK were pollution-free. Figure **1** shows the main causes of water pollution. There are three main types.

1 Agricultural pollution

Organic matter such as animal slurry is highly polluting to watercourses. The bacteria in water use its organic matter to multiply, and at the same time remove oxygen from the water. Without oxygen, fish and other freshwater species cannot survive.

2 Urban water pollution

Detergents from washing machines, minute plastics, and runoff from houses and streets are the main sources of water pollution in urban areas.

3 Industrial pollution

An example is when highly toxic mine water contaminated local water supplies in South Wales.

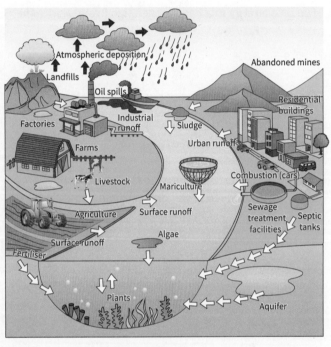

Figure 1 *Sources of water pollution*

Managing water pollution

The Environment Agency manages water quality in the UK.

1 Agricultural pollution

Since 2018, the law requires farmers to:

- restrict the amount of chemicals they use
- keep animals at least 50 m away from sources of water
- control the use of manure.

2 Urban water pollution

Sustainable Drainage Systems (SuDS) (see 15.1) reduce urban water pollution. The Belfast Sewers Project has upgraded Belfast's sewer networks, which has reduced the pollution in the River Lagan.

3 Industrial pollution

The Coal Authority built a treatment system to prevent iron from entering the river. In addition, strict government legislation aims to control water pollution from manufacturing and chemical industries.

 Six Second Summary

- Water quality is high in the UK but there is still pollution.
- Causes of pollution include organic matter, runoff and mine water.
- Pollution management strategies include government rules and improved sewer networks.

Over to you

Create two mind-maps: one to show the causes of water pollution and one to show how water pollution can be managed.

You need to know:

- about the changing energy mix in the UK
- about the reliance on fossil fuels and the growing significance of renewables
- why there are reduced domestic supplies of coal, gas and oil.

Student Book
See pages 286–7

The UK's changing energy mix

Energy consumption in the UK has declined, mainly because of increased efficiency in transport, homes and workplaces.

The UK's **energy mix** has changed significantly since the 1990s (see Figure **1**).

Recent developments in the UK's energy sector

The UK's renewable energy sector is dominated by wind. In 2018, construction started on Hornsea One, the world's largest offshore wind farm. It will produce enough electricity to power one million homes.

Biomass is an important source of energy for electricity generation.

By 2030 most of the UK's nuclear reactors will have closed. However, nuclear power will remain a part of the UK's energy mix.

Reduced domestic sources of energy

The UK is no longer self-sufficient in energy.

- About 75 per cent of the UK's known oil and natural gas reserves have been exhausted.
- In 2019, the UK imported 35 per cent of its energy.
- The UK's **energy security** is affected as it becomes increasingly dependent on imported energy.

Big Idea

Energy mix means the types and proportions of different energy sources that are used.

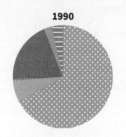
1990

In 1990 almost three-quarters of UK energy came from coal and oil – 'fossil' or **non-renewable fuels**.

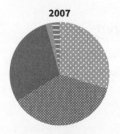
2007

By 2007 there was an equal mix of coal, gas and nuclear – all non-renewabel sources

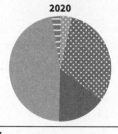
2020

By 2020 renewable sources, such as wind and solar energy, had become more important (graph **B**).

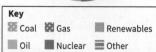
Key
Coal | Gas | Renewables
Oil | Nuclear | Other

Figure 1 *The UK's sources of energy, 1990–2020*

Six Second Summary

- There is less dependence on fossil fuels.
- Renewable sources, especially wind, have become more important.
- Domestic supplies of fossil fuels have reduced so the UK relies on imported energy.

Over to you

Use the pie charts on this page to **describe** how the UK's energy mix has changed. Then **explain** to a friend some reasons why this has happened.

Student Book
See pages
288–9

You need to know:

- the economic and environmental issues that are associated with exploiting energy sources.

Exploiting new energy sources

Source of energy	Economic impacts	Environmental impacts
Fossil fuels	• Finite • Creates employment	• Greenhouse gas emissions • Danger of oil spillages
Nuclear	• Costly to build, and manage waste • Fuel non-renewable but is recyclable	• No greenhouse gases • Warm cooling water affects ecosystems
Renewable	• Electricity produced can be variable • Cost of installation is falling significantly	• Negative visual impact on landscape • Noise pollution with wind turbines

Economic and environmental issues with fossil fuels

Fracking

The UK has natural gas trapped deep underground. To extract it, high pressure liquids are injected into the rock, a process called *fracking*.

In 2011, test drilling in Lancashire triggered a small earthquake, leading to protests. There were also concerns about greenhouse gas emissions and noise. The UK government banned fracking in 2019.

A new coal mine for Cumbria?

In 2017, planning permission was granted for a new deep coal mine in Cumbria. Despite economic benefits, there were large-scale protests. In May 2021, Cumbria County Council withdrew planning permission, arguing that it would break greenhouse gas emission reduction targets.

Economic and environmental issues with carbon-neutral energy sources

	Economic	Environmental
Nuclear	• Nuclear power plants are expensive to build. • Decommissioning old plants is expensive. • New plants provide job opportunities.	• Safe processing and storage of radioactive waste is a big problem. • Warm waste water can harm local ecosystems.
Wind farms	• High construction costs. • May reduce tourist visitor numbers. • Local homeowners can have lower energy bills.	• Visual impact on the landscape. • Help reduce the carbon footprint. • Noise from wind turbines.

 Six Second Summary

- There are positive and negative economic and environmental impacts of energy source exploitation.

 Over to you

Highlight the impacts of energy source exploitation to show whether they are **positive** or **negative**.

SKILLS FOCUS

You need to be able to:

- use a 1:50 000 Ordnance Survey map (use of symbols, grid references, height and calculating area)
- interpret a rainfall graph
- evaluate evidence to reach and justify a conclusion.

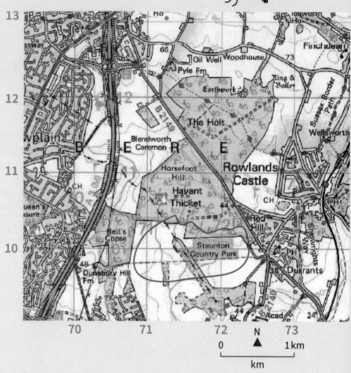

Student Book
See pages
290–1

Should a new reservoir be constructed in Havant Thicket, Hampshire?

Portsmouth Water is responsible for supplying water to parts of Southern England, a region suffering from water stress. By 2045, the population in this area is expected to increase by 15 per cent.

To meet demand, Portsmouth Water aims to construct a new reservoir at Havant Thicket, an area of ancient woodland (Figure **1**).

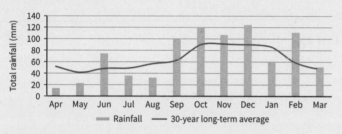

Figure 2 *Total monthly rainfall for Havant, Hampshire, 2019/20*

Figure 1 *The location of Havant Thicket Reservoir (outlined in red)*

Arguments for and against the new reservoir include:

For	Against
Increases water storage to meet future demand and avoid water stress as rainfall becomes more unreliable (Figure **2**).	The site is home to the Forest of Bere: a unique ecosystem supporting thousands of species of plants and animals.
The reservoir will be fed by local springs which normally run out to the sea.	Car park charges must be moderate or visitors will park on nearby residential roads.
Bills will not increase for Portsmouth Water's customers.	Boating should be restricted to canoeing and kayaking, with noisy motor boats banned.
Opportunities for recreation will be increased.	The B2149 is already busy, as a quick route from the coast to the A3(M).

Skills

1 Look at the OS map, Figure **1**.
   a Give the four-figure grid reference of Red Hill.
   b Name the footpath that runs to the east of Red Hill.
   c Describe the location of The Holt.
   d What does the symbol at 712106 mean? Name the areas that this symbol relates to.
   e Several streams start in Havant Thicket. Why might this be advantageous to the new reservoir?
   f Calculate the shortest distance of the A3(M) from the station at Rowlands Castle.

Analysis

1 Using evidence from Figure **1**, suggest why some people might object to the proposal.
2 Figure **2** presents recent rainfall data for Havant.
   a Describe the pattern of rainfall for 2019–20.
   b How does this compare with the 30-year long-term average?
   c Suggest why variable monthly rainfall creates problems for water supply.
   d How will a new reservoir increase resilience as climate change leads to changing patterns of rainfall?

Evaluation

Comment on the validity of Figure **2** in its representation of rainfall variability.

Student Book
See pages
292–3

You need to know:

- how calorie intake and food supply vary around the world
- why there is increasing food consumption
- what is meant by food security.

Global patterns of food consumption

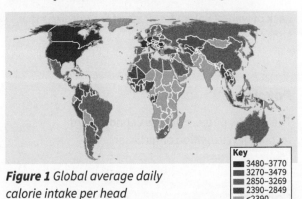

Key
- 3480–3770
- 3270–3479
- 2850–3269
- 2390–2849
- <2390

Figure 1 *Global average daily calorie intake per head*

Figure **1** shows global food consumption.

- Canada, USA and Europe consume the most calories.
- In parts of sub-Saharan Africa, daily calorie intake per head is below the recommended daily intake of 2000–2400 calories.

Global food consumption is increasing because of:

- *Economic development* – higher standards of living mean that demand for food has increased.
- *Population growth* – with more people to feed, demand for food increases.
- *Greater availability of food* – improvements in transport and storage have increased the availability of food.
- *Dietary changes* – rising incomes tend to increase demand for meat and proteins.

Global patterns of food supply

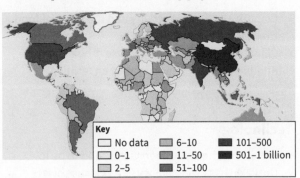

Key
- No data
- 0–1
- 2–5
- 6–10
- 11–50
- 51–100
- 101–500
- 501–1 billion

Figure 2 *Global cereal production in million tonnes, 2018*

Figure **2** shows cereal production across the world.

- Countries such as China, the USA, Brazil, Russia and much of Europe have sufficient rain and sunshine for growing cereals.
- They use intensive farming methods and have high capital investment, which encourage high yields.

Many countries in Africa and the Middle East have lower crop yields because:

- rainfall is often less reliable
- farming has low investment (caused by low incomes)
- a general lack of training in farming methods.
- climate change is increasingly impacting food production as droughts and floods become more frequent.

What is meant by food security?

Food security – having access to enough affordable, nutritious food to maintain a healthy life.

Countries which produce more food than is needed by their population have a *food surplus*.

Countries that do not produce enough food to feed their population and have to rely on imported food have a *food deficit*. Many of these countries also experience **food insecurity**.

Six Second Summary

- Food consumption and supply vary around the world.
- Reasons for increasing food consumption include economic development and rising populations.

Over to you

- Describe **four** points about global patterns of a) food consumption, b) food supply.
- Create a mind-map of the reasons why food consumption is increasing.

You need to know:

- factors that affect food supply
- how those factors affect food supply.

Student Book
**See pages
294–5**

Climate

- Climate affects productivity and the types of food that can be grown.
- Climate change is causing worse droughts and flooding, which have an impact on farming.

Technology

- Without technology, food yields tend to be low.
- Unskilled use of technology (e.g. poor use of irrigation) can lead to waterlogging and salinisation.

Pests and diseases

In some warm climates:

- pests such as locusts can devastate food crops
- the tsetse fly causes widespread death in cattle.

Rising global temperatures are causing pests and diseases to spread from the Tropics.

Water stress

Lack of water (water stress) affects many areas that suffer food scarcity.

Poverty

The world's poorest people cannot afford technology, irrigation or fertilisers

Conflict

Political conflicts can result in the destruction of crops/livestock and disrupt transport networks.

 Six Second Summary

Factors that affect food supply include climate, technology, pests and diseases, water stress, conflict and poverty.

Bar graphs

You need to be able to:

- construct a bar graph showing positive and negative trends
- calculate range.

The Food Security Index (FSI)

The FSI assesses a country's level of food security. It is calculated using indicators including food affordability and quality (Figure **1**).

Skills

1 Use the data in Figure **1** to sketch out a bar graph showing positive and negative trends in FSI score. See page 295 of the Student Book for guidance.

Analysis

1 Suggest **one** reason why a country's food security may
   a) improve b) worsen.

2 Explain **two** reasons why the majority of countries experiencing positive changes in FSI were NEEs.

3 Explain **two** reasons why the majority of countries experiencing negative changes in FSI were LICs.

Country	Change 2019–20 (%)
Haiti	+4.7
Kazakhstan	+2.7
Pakistan	+2.6
Romania	+2.6
Paraguay	+2.3
Chile	−2.8
Guinea	−3.1
Colombia	−4.1
Egypt	−4.3
Norway	−4.4

Figure 1 *Changes in food security index (FSI) 2019–20 for selected countries*

Evaluation

1 Discuss the effectiveness of bar graphs (as in Skills question 1) in comparing percentage change in data.

2 Explain **two** benefits of using a simple FSI figure to show food security for every country.

Student Book
**See pages
296–7**

You need to know:

- what the impacts of food insecurity are.

What are the impacts of food insecurity?

Food insecurity occurs when a country can't supply enough food (home grown and imported) at an appropriate price to feed its population.

Famine

Famine is a widespread lack of access to food often causing malnutrition, starvation and death.

Famine in Somalia (2010–12)

The UN estimates that 258 000 people died in Somalia as a result of food insecurity during the famine of 2010–12.

The famine had two main causes:

- Two successive seasons of low rainfall, poor harvests and the death of livestock.
- In southern and central Somalia, the al-Shahab militant group blocked aid, making the crisis worse.

Rising prices

Food prices are rising, mainly due to higher prices for fertilisers, food storage and transportation.

LICs and the poorest people in NEEs are hardest hit by higher food costs.

Many countries that experience food insecurity are dependent on foreign food imports. The Covid-19 pandemic impacted food supply chains, causing a significant increase in the cost of food.

Soil erosion

Soil erosion involves the removal of fertile topsoil by wind and water. Food insecurity can contribute to soil erosion (Figure **1**).

Overgrazing by animals reduces the amount of vegetation, leaving soil exposed.

Cultivation of marginal land to increase food production can reduce soil fertility and destroy vegetation.

Over-cultivation can exhaust soils, making them infertile.

Deforestation for farming (as in the photo) removes the protective covering of the trees and increases surface run off.

Figure 1 What causes soil erosion?

Undernutrition

Undernutrition is the lack of a balanced diet, and deficiency in minerals and vitamins.

It causes around 300 000 deaths per year and contributes to half of all child deaths, particularly in southern Asia and sub-Saharan Africa.

Social unrest

Incidents of social unrest ('food riots') are often linked to large increases in the price of food.

In 2011, the price of cooking oil and flour doubled. In Algeria, this led to five days of rioting, with four people killed.

 Six Second Summary

- Impacts of food security include: famine, undernutrition, soil erosion, rising prices and social unrest.

Over to you

Create a mnemonic for the impacts of food insecurity. Add an example for each impact.

Student Book
See pages
298–9

You need to know:

- what strategies are used to increase food supply
- how each strategy works to increase food supply.

How can food supply be increased?

Irrigation

Irrigation is the artificial watering of land. Irrigation projects can involve the construction of expensive dams and reservoirs, such as in the Indus Valley in Pakistan (see 20.5). They often benefit larger commercial farming.

There are smaller schemes such as in Makueni County in eastern Kenya. Pipelines and storage tanks enable drip irrigation to support domestic food cultivation.

The 'new' green revolution

The 'new' **green revolution** focuses on sustainability and community. It uses techniques such as:

- water harvesting and irrigation
- soil conservation
- improving seed and livestock quality using science and technology.

Along with improved rural transport and affordable credit, these innovations have enabled the Indian state of Bahir to double its rice output.

Aeroponics and hydroponics

Aeroponics – plants are sprayed with a fine mist containing nutrients, which enables small-scale farmers to increase yields and lower production costs.

Hydroponics – plants are grown in gravel or mineral-rich water (Figure **1**).

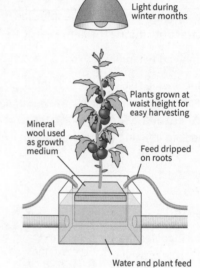

Light during winter months

Plants grown at waist height for easy harvesting

Mineral wool used as growth medium

Feed dripped on roots

Water and plant feed

Figure 1 How hydroponics works

Appropriate technology

- **Appropriate technology** means using skills or materials that are cheap and easily available to increase output without putting people out of work.
- Particularly useful for people living in poorer countries.

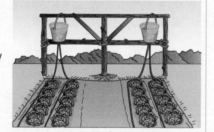

Figure 2 Bucket kit irrigation delivers water directly to plants

Biotechnology

- Uses living organisms to make or modify products or processes.
- Includes the development of genetically modified (GM) crops, which produce higher yields and use fewer chemicals.
- In the UK, there is opposition to GM crops. They are widely grown in other countries.
- Biotech crops have increased productivity by over 800 million tons.

Six Second Summary

- Strategies used to increase food supply include: irrigation, aeroponics and hydroponics, the new green revolution, biotechnology and appropriate technology.

Over to you

- Make clear definitions of all the terms listed in the Six Second Summary.
- Learn these over five minutes, then write them out from memory.

Student Book
**See pages
300–1**

You need to know:

- about the Indus Basin Irrigation System, a large-scale agricultural development
- that the aim of this development is to increase food supply
- the advantages and disadvantages of this development.

The Indus River runs from the Tibetan Plateau, through Pakistan to the Arabian Sea.
With its tributaries, it supplies water to irrigate the drier agricultural land further south.

What is the Indus Basin Irrigation System (IBIS)?

- The IBIS is the largest continuous irrigation scheme in the world.
- Three large dams and over a hundred smaller dams regulate water flow.
- Link canals enable water to be transferred between rivers.
- Smaller canals distribute the water across the countryside.
- Over 1.6 million km of ditches and streams provide irrigation for Pakistan's agricultural land.

Big Idea

The Indus Basin Irrigation System is an example of a large-scale agricultural development.

EXAMPLE

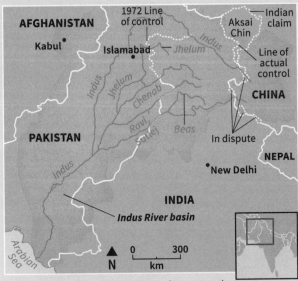

Figure 1 The Indus River basin (in orange)

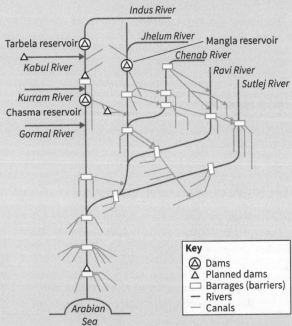

Figure 2 Topological map of the IBIS

What are the advantages and disadvantages of the IBIS?

Advantages

- Improves food security for Pakistan, making 40 per cent more land available for cultivation.
- Irrigation has increased crop yields.
- Many people's diets have improved as a greater range of food products is available.
- HEP is generated by the large dams.

Disadvantages

- Some farmers take an unfair share of water.
- Poor irrigation techniques mean water is wasted. *Salinisation* (increased saltiness) can damage the soil.
- Population growth will increase the demand for water.
- High costs to maintain reservoir capacity.

Six Second Summary

- The Indus Basin Irrigation System (IBIS) is an example of a large scale agricultural development to increase food supply.
- It has improved food security, but some farmers take an unfair share of the water.

Over to you

- Write down **two** advantages and **two** disadvantages of the IBIS.
- For each statement, explain why it benefits/does not benefit people in Pakistan.
- State which was the most significant advantage and disadvantage, and explain why.

Student Book
See pages 302–3

You need to know:

- what a sustainable food supply is
- how different strategies can create the potential for sustainable food supplies.

What is sustainable food supply?

A **sustainable food supply** ensures that fertile soil, water and environmental resources are available for future generations.

Organic farming

Organic farming is growing crops or rearing livestock without the use of artificial chemicals. Many people choose to pay higher prices for *organic produce.*

Permaculture

Permaculture is a system of food production which follows the patterns and features of natural ecosystems.

Permaculture practices include:

- harvesting rainwater
- crop rotation
- managing woodland.

Urban farming

Urban farming is the cultivation, processing and distribution of food in and around settlements.

The Michigan Urban Farming Initiative

- The Michigan Urban Farming Initiative in the USA aims to address problems of urban decay, poor diet and food insecurity in Detroit.
- Urban communities are encouraged to work together to turn wasteland into productive farmland, providing jobs and easier access to healthy food.

Figure 1 Urban farming in Paris, France

Fish from sustainable sources

Increasing demand for food and technological improvements have resulted in greater catches of fish.

Sustainable fishing involves setting catch limits (quotas) and monitoring fish breeding and fishing practices.

In Norway, salmon farms are spread out to reduce the possible spread of disease.

Meat from sustainable sources

Sustainable meat production involves small-scale livestock farms, using free-range or organic methods.

Prices may be higher in the shops but quality and animal welfare standards are higher.

Six Second Summary

- Organic farming, permaculture, urban farming and consuming fish and meat from sustainable sources can all create potential for sustainable food supplies.

Over to you

- Make a list of the different strategies to create sustainable food supplies.
- Add **two** sentences to each strategy to explain how it creates the potential for sustainable food supplies.

Student Book
See pages 304–5

EXAMPLE

You need to know:

- how seasonal food consumption and reducing food waste and losses can create sustainable food supplies
- about a local scheme to increase sustainable supplies of food in an LIC or NEE.

Seasonal food consumption

In the past, food was bought from local sources when 'in season'. It is now possible to eat every type of food throughout the year.

Local food sourcing is more sustainable. It reduces both 'food miles' and our carbon footprint.

 **Big Idea**

Food miles describe the distance covered supplying food to customers.

Carbon footprint is the measurement of the greenhouse gases that each individual produces, through the direct or indirect burning of fossil fuels.

Reducing food loss and waste

Each year about a third of all food produced globally is lost or wasted.

By halving the amount of food waste, the gap between food supply and demand could be reduced by 22 per cent by 2050.

Improved food storage and distribution using refrigerated containers

Clearer food labelling, such as 'Best before' or 'Use by'

Processing surplus food to increase shelf life

Reducing food waste

The use of cooling systems where there is no refrigeration

Using sealed plastic bags to make fresh food last longer

More sensible approach to using food that is past its 'Sell by' date

The Makueni Food and Water Security Programme

The programme provided direct help to two small villages and Kanyenoni Primary School in Makueni County, Kenya.

The programme included:

- improving water supply by building sand dams for each village
- providing a reliable source of water for crops and livestock
- a training programme to support local farmers
- growing trees to reduce soil erosion.

Sand dams store water in the ground, filtering and cleaning the rainwater as it soaks into the soil. They are cost-effective and sustainable.

The project has been very successful.

- Crop yields and food security have increased.
- Waterborne diseases have been reduced.
- Less time is wasted fetching water.

 Six Second Summary

- Seasonal food consumption and reducing food waste can make food supplies more sustainable.
- Sand dams have helped to improve food security in Makueni County, Kenya.

 Over to you

Create a mind-map to show how the Makueni Food and Water Security Programme has increased sustainable supplies of food in that area.

Student Book
**See pages
306–7**

You need to know:

• what is meant by 'water security' and 'water insecurity'
• how water surpluses and deficits vary around the world
• why there is increasing water consumption.

Water security/insecurity

Water security means having access to enough clean water to sustain good health and economic development.

Water insecurity (water scarcity) is where regions do not have access to sufficient water supplies. This may be caused by physical and human factors. Figure **1** shows areas of:

• physical scarcity (where there is low rainfall)
• economic scarcity (where economic factors such as lack of infrastructure prevent exploitation of water supplies.

Countries begin to experience **water stress** when less than 1700 m³ is available per person per year. Regions with high water stress include several Caribbean islands and the Middle East.

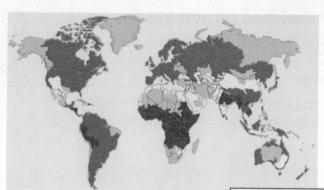

Figure 1 *Global physical and economic water scarcity (insecurity)*

Key
■ Little or no water scarcity
□ Physical water scarcity
▨ Approaching physical water scarcity
■ Economic water scarcity
▨ Not estimated

Global patterns of water surplus and deficit

Regions with a **water surplus** have a supply of water which exceeds demand.

Other regions have a **water deficit**, where demand exceeds supply. Areas of water deficit may have:

• low rainfall
• high densities of population and/or industry, increasing demand.

Key

Water deficit

Water surplus

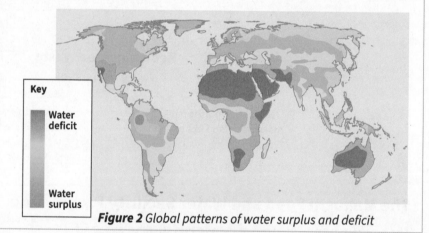

Figure 2 *Global patterns of water surplus and deficit*

Why is water consumption increasing?

Global water demand is expected to increase by 20–30 per cent by 2050. Water consumption is increasing because of:

• *Economic development* – increasing levels of development mean that demand for water has increased.
• *Population growth* – more people will increase the demand for water.
• *Increased demand for food* – demand for irrigation and food processing is likely to increase.
• *Increased urbanisation* – more people in urban areas increases pressure on water supplies.

Six Second Summary

• Areas of water surplus often experience water security. Areas with a water deficit often experience water insecurity.
• Water surplus and deficit patterns vary around the world.
• Reasons for increasing water consumption include economic development and rising populations.

Over to you

Make a list of: **one** place with water insecurity, **two** places with water surplus and **three** reasons why water consumption is increasing. Add a sentence to explain each one.

Student Book
**See pages
308–9**

You need to know:

- factors that affect water availability
- how those factors affect water availability.

Over-abstraction

Over-abstraction occurs when water is used faster than it is replaced by rainfall. It is often the result of irrigation and industrial processing.

Geology

Percolation of water through permeable rocks forms huge underground reservoirs called aquifers. Some aquifers are under threat from unsustainable demand, particularly from agriculture.

Pollution of supply

Increasing amounts of waste and chemicals in farming have led to more pollution in rivers and aquifers.

In some LICs and NEEs water sources can be used as sewers leading to the spread of **waterborne diseases**.

Climate

Regions with high and reliable patterns of rainfall rarely experience physical water scarcity.

Limited infrastructure

Limited infrastructure (e.g. pumping stations, pipes) may result in economic scarcity, particularly in LICs and NEEs.

Poverty

Many poorer communities in LICs and NEEs do not have access to safe water.

Six Second Summary

Factors that affect water availability include climate, geology, pollution of supply, over-abstraction, limited infrastructure and poverty.

Bar graphs

You need to be able to:

- construct a bar graph showing positive and negative trends
- calculate range.

What is the projected global use of water?

Over the next 30 years global demand for water is expected to increase. Agriculture will remain the largest user, but reduce slightly as water is used more efficiently. Industrial and domestic demand is expected to rise at a much faster rate (Figure **1**).

Water use	2030 (% change)	2050 (% change)
Domestic	+36.5	+65.1
Industry	+53.3	+119.8
Agriculture	−3.6	−6.9

Figure 1 *Predicted trends in water use to 2030 and 2050*

SKILLS FOCUS

Skills

1 Using Figure **1**, calculate the range in percentage change in global water use in 2050.
2 Use the data in Figure **1** to sketch a bar graph showing positive and negative trends in water use. See page 309 of the Student Book for guidance.

Analysis

Suggest **two** reasons why domestic and industrial water use is expected to increase at a high rate. Give examples.

Evaluation

1 Discuss the effectiveness of bar graphs (as in Skills question **2**) in comparing percentage change in data.
2 Explain **two** benefits of using a graph to show positive/negative change in water use, like the one you have drawn.

Student Book
See pages
310–11

You need to know:

- the impacts of water insecurity on waterborne disease, pollution levels, food production, industry and conflict.

Waterborne disease and water pollution

Contaminated drinking water can cause diseases such as cholera.

Queuing to get clean water wastes time and reduces levels of productivity.

Water pollution: the River Ganges, India

- Over one billion litres of raw sewage enter the River Ganges each day.
- Factories discharge 260 million litres of untreated wastewater into the river daily.
- Toxic chemicals, pesticides and fertilisers leak into the river.

Bathing in and drinking the river's water have become very dangerous.

Food production

Agriculture uses about 70 per cent of global water supply and suffers the most from water insecurity.

The River Nile is Egypt's main source of water. Climate change and the demands of countries upstream are expected to reduce its flow by 10–90 per cent by 2095. Egypt currently has to import about 40 per cent of its food and agricultural products.

Industrial output

Industry is the second largest consumer of water. It is predicted to increase in demand by nearly 120 per cent by 2050.

Growth in manufacturing and processing, particularly in NEEs, will account for much of this predicted demand.

Water conflict

Water sources, such as rivers and groundwater aquifers, cross national and political borders. Issues such as reservoir construction and pollution can impact on more than one country and create conflict.

Turkey built a large number of dams on the Tigris and Euphrates Rivers, causing anger in Iraq and Syria.

Israel draws water from the Sea of Galilee. Groundwater is polluted and in short supply. Israel buys water from Turkey.

Lake Chad has shrunk to 5% of its former size, due to climate change and over-abstraction.

The Nile flows through eight countries. Egypt will not allow the other seven countries to affect the Nile's flow (e.g. build dams). This causes tension as countries argue over water rights.

India has built barriers to control the flow of water in the River Ganges, affecting water supply to Bangladesh.

Figure 1 *Some of the world's potential water conflict zones*

Six Second Summary

Impacts on water insecurity include: waterborne disease, water pollution, food production, industrial output and conflict.

Over to you

Create a Venn diagram of social, economic and environmental problems caused by water insecurity.

Student Book
See pages
312–13

You need to know:

- what strategies are used to increase water supply
- how each strategy works to increase water supply.

Diverting water and increasing storage

Water supplies can be artificially diverted and stored for use over longer periods. In Oklahoma, USA, rainfall is infrequent but heavy. Surface water quickly evaporates. So it is collected and diverted, and stored in underlying alluvial soils.

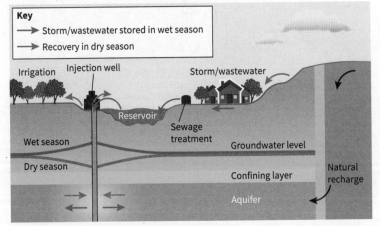

Figure 1 *Aquifer storage and recovery*

Water transfer

Schemes move water from areas of surplus to areas of deficit.

China has built two canal systems to transfer water from the Yangtze River in the south to the Yellow River Basin in the arid north. A third controversial system, the western route, is still at the planning stage. It involves building dams and tunnels through the Bayankala Mountains.

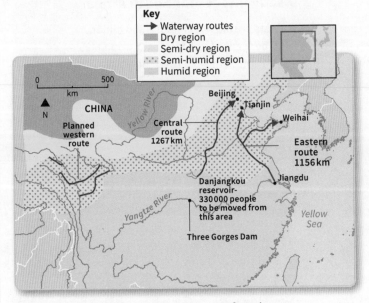

Figure 2 *China's south–north water transfer scheme*

Dams and reservoirs

Dams bring advantages:

- They control river flow by storing water in reservoirs.
- The control of water flow enables it to be transported and used for irrigation.
- They help to prevent flooding.

However, large dams:

- are expensive
- can lead to the displacement of large numbers of people
- may reduce the flow of water downstream.

In hot and arid regions, reservoirs can lose a lot of water through evaporation.

Desalination

- Desalination means removing salt from seawater to produce fresh water.
- This is a very expensive process.
- It is used only when there is a serious shortage of water with few alternatives to increase water supply.
- Both Saudi Arabia and UAE have developed desalination plants.

Six Second Summary

- Strategies used to increase water supply include: diverting supplies and increasing storage, dams and reservoirs, water transfers and desalination.

Over to you

Design a poster to show how water supply can be increased.

You need to know:

- about the Lesotho Highland Water Project, a large-scale water transfer scheme
- the advantages and disadvantages of this development.

EXAMPLE

Lesotho is a highland country, surrounded by South Africa. It is heavily dependent economically on South Africa.

Despite food insecurity, Lesotho has a water surplus due to high rainfall in the mountains, and low demand for water.

What is the Lesotho Highland Water Project?

- It is a huge water transfer scheme aimed to help solve the water shortage in South Africa.
- 40 per cent of the water from the Segu (Orange) River in Lesotho will eventually be transferred to the River Vaal in South Africa.
- It involves the construction of dams, reservoirs and pipelines as well as roads, bridges and other infrastructure.

Student Book
See pages 314–15

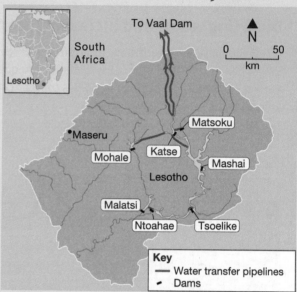

Figure 1 *Map of the Lesotho Highland Water Project*

What are the advantages and disadvantages of the scheme?

Advantages for Lesotho

- Provides 75 per cent of Lesotho's GDP.
- Supplies all Lesotho's hydro-electric (HEP) requirements.
- Sanitation coverage will increase from 15 to 20 per cent.

Disadvantages for Lesotho

- Building the first two dams displaced 30 000 people.
- Destruction of a unique wetland ecosystem.
- Corruption has prevented money reaching those affected by the construction.

Advantages for South Africa

- Provides water to an area with regular droughts.
- Fresh water reduces the acidity of the Vaal River Reservoir.
- Provides safe water for the 10 per cent of the population that does not have access to safe water.

Disadvantages for South Africa

- Costs are likely to reach US$4 billion.
- 40 per cent of water is lost through leakages.
- Corruption has plagued the whole project.

  Six Second Summary

- The Lesotho Highland Water Project is an example of a large-scale water transfer scheme.
- It generates energy and water supplies but people have been displaced and the project has suffered from corruption.

Over to you

List your top **eight** facts to remember about this project.

Student Book
See pages
316–17

You need to know:

- how different strategies can help to create sustainable water supplies and move towards a sustainable resource future.

What is sustainable water supply?

Sustainable approaches to water supply focus on:

- management of water resources
- reducing waste and excessive demand.

Groundwater management

Groundwater is stored in underground aquifers.

To ensure sustainability, water abstraction (loss) must be balanced by recharge (gain).

If groundwater levels fall, water can become contaminated, making expensive water treatment necessary.

Participatory Groundwater Management (PGM), India

The PGM scheme involves:

- training local people to monitor rainfall and groundwater levels
- helping farmers to plan how much water to use for irrigation
- encouraging farmers to plant crops to fit in with periods when water is available.

Through PGM, rural communities have balanced water supply and demand using sustainable practices.

Recycling

Water recycling involves re-using treated wastewater for purposes like irrigation and industry.

- In Kolkata in India, sewage water is re-used for fish farming and agriculture.
- Some nuclear power plants – such as in Arizona, USA – use recycled water for cooling.

Ways to conserve water

- Reduce leakages
- Improve public awareness of the importance of saving water
- Water meters
- Prevent pollution
- Turn off tap when brushing teeth

Using grey water

- **Grey water** is taken from bathrooms and washing machines.
- If used within 24 hours it contains fertiliser for plants.
- Water from toilets cannot be used in this way.
- In Jordan, 70 per cent of the water used for irrigation and gardens is grey water.

Figure 1 *Re-using grey water*

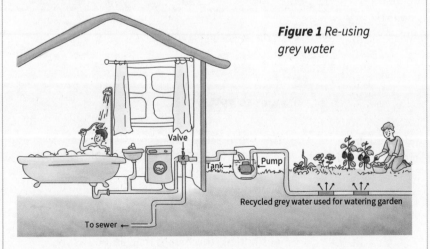

Six Second Summary

Water conservation, groundwater management, recycling and using grey water can all help to create sustainable water supplies

Over to you

Write the water supply strategies on brightly coloured pieces of card or on sticky notes. Place them around your home to help remind you of these strategies.

Student Book
See pages
318–19

EXAMPLE

You need to know:

- about the Wakal River Basin Project, an example of a local scheme in an LIC or NEE
- how the Wakal River Basin project increases sustainable supplies of water.

The Wakal River Basin is in north-west India in the south of Rajasthan – the driest and poorest part of India. The rainfall of less than 250 mm per year quickly soaks away or evaporates.

What are the issues with water supply?

- Water management in the region has generally been poor.
- Over-use of water for irrigation has led to waterlogging and salinisation.
- Over-abstraction from unregulated pumps has resulted in falling water tables in aquifers.
- Some wells have dried up.

Figure 1 Location of Rajasthan

Increasing water supply in the Wakal River Basin

The United States Agency for International Development has been working with local people in the Wakal River Basin. The project aims to improve water security and overcome the problems of water shortages by encouraging greater use of rainwater harvesting techniques.

- *Taankas* – underground storage systems which collect surface water from roofs.
- *Johad* – small earth dams that capture rainwater.
- *Pats* – irrigation channels that transfer water to the fields (Figure **2**).

How does the *pat* system work?

A small stone dam lined with leaves, called a bund, diverts water from the stream towards the fields. Villagers take turns to irrigate their fields in this way. Maintenance, making sure the bund does not break up or the channels become clogged with silt, is done by the villager whose turn it is to receive the water.

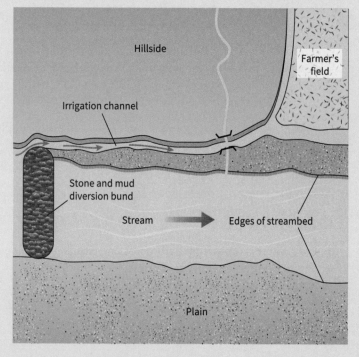

Figure 2 The pat irrigation system

Six Second Summary

- Earth dams, irrigation channels and underground storage systems have helped water security to increase in the Wakal River Basin.

Over to you

- Write down **three** ways in which the Wakal River Basin Project is increasing sustainable supplies of water.
- For each way, add the words 'this means that …' and finish the sentence to explain why it is increasing sustainable supplies of water.
- Keep adding 'this means that' as long as you can to add depth to your answer.

Student Book
See pages
320–1

You need to know:

- how energy supply and consumption can create areas of surplus (security) and deficit (insecurity)
- how energy consumption and supply vary around the world
- why there is increasing energy consumption

Global energy consumption and supply

A country's **energy security** depends on its supply and consumption. If supply exceeds demand, it has an *energy surplus*. If demand exceeds production, it has an *energy deficit* and the country is *energy insecure*.

- Consumption is highest in North America and parts of the Middle East.
- Consumption is lowest across most of Africa and parts of south-east Asia.
- North America has large coal reserves.
- Russia has large reserves of natural gas and oil.
- Sub-Saharan Africa depends on overseas TNCs to exploit reserves.

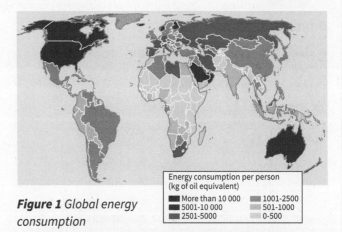

Figure 1 *Global energy consumption*

Energy consumption per person (kg of oil equivalent)
More than 10 000 | 1001–2500
5001–10 000 | 501–1000
2501–5000 | 0–500

Why is energy consumption increasing?

Global energy consumption has increased significantly in recent years. This trend is expected to increase to 2050 (Figure **3**). The contribution from renewables is expected to grow.

Global energy consumption is increasing because of:

- *Economic development* – as countries develop, their demand for energy supplies rises. NEEs will account for more than 90 per cent of the growth in demand for energy to 2035.
- *Population growth* – the growing number of people will increase the demand for energy.
- *Technology* – the increasing use of technology means a greater demand for electricity. Also, with improved quality of life, the demand for lighting, heating and air-conditioning also increases.

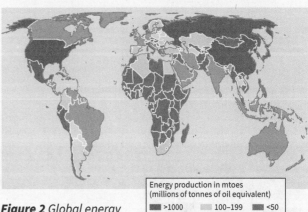

Figure 2 *Global energy supply (production)*

Energy production in mtoes (millions of tonnes of oil equivalent)
>1000 | 100–199 | <50
200–999 | 50–99

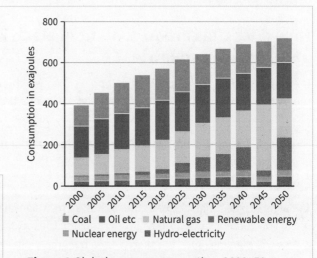

Figure 3 *Global energy consumption, 2000–50*

Six Second Summary

- Energy consumption and supply vary globally.
- Physical and political factors affect energy supply.
- Increasing energy consumption results from development and rising populations.

Over to you

Use the maps to describe the global distribution of energy consumption and supply.

Student Book
**See pages
322–3**

You need to know:

- factors that affect energy supply
- how those factors affect energy supply.

Physical factors

- Geology determines the location of fossil fuels.
- Geothermal energy is produced in areas of tectonic activity like Iceland.

Technology

- Technological advances have allowed exploitation of energy sources in remote environments.
- Technology has enabled the process of fracking, and the development of renewable energy.

Six Second Summary

Factors that affect water availability include physical factors, cost of exploitation and production, technology, and political factors.

Costs

Most energy sources are very expensive to develop. An oil rig at sea averages about US$650 million. The new Hinkley Point C nuclear power station in Somerset is expected to cost up to £23 billion!

Political factors

Political factors affect decisions about which energy sources to exploit.

- Political instability in the Middle East has meant that many oil-consuming countries are looking for alternative sources of energy.
- Some countries currently want to stop Iran developing nuclear power. They fear it will be used for non-peaceful purposes.

Bar graphs

You need to be able to:

- construct a bar graph showing positive and negative trends
- calculate range.

SKILLS FOCUS

How does the carbon content of electricity vary between countries?

Burning fossil fuels produces high carbon emissions, whereas renewable and nuclear energy sources produce low carbon emissions.

Figure **1** lists the changes in the carbon content of electricity, which is reducing for most countries as they increasingly adopt renewable energy sources.

Skills

1 Calculate the range between the highest percentage change in carbon content of electricity (Indonesia) and the lowest (UK).
2 Use the data in Figure **1** to sketch out a bar graph showing positive and negative changes in carbon content of electricity. See page 323 of the Student Book for guidance.

Analysis

1 Suggest one reason why a country may **a)** increase, or **b)** decrease the carbon content it uses in producing electricity.
2 Most countries recorded a decrease in the carbon content of electricity. Suggest **two** reasons for this trend.

Country	Change in carbon content of electricity 2008–17 (g/kWh)
Indonesia	+60
Japan	+55
India	+53
Norway	+3
Mexico	−30
Canada	−50
Germany	−80
China	−125
USA	−140
UK	−260

Figure 1 *Change in carbon content of electricity for selected countries, 2008–17*

Evaluation

1 Discuss the effectiveness of bar graphs (as in Skills question **2**) in comparing percentage change in data.
2 Explain **two** benefits of using a table like Figure **1**, to show changes in carbon content usage for every country.

Student Book
See pages 324–5

You need to know:

- the impacts of energy insecurity.

Exploration of difficult and environmentally sensitive areas

Energy resources have been extracted from increasingly challenging environments, such as beneath the North Sea. Future exploration in these areas will depend on:

- developing technologies that make exploitation cost-effective
- environmental implications of **energy exploitation** in easliy damaged areas.

Economic and environmental costs

Imports of oil and gas can be very expensive – a major cost of energy insecurity. A country may also look to exploit resources in environmentally sensitive areas.

The Arctic has potential to supply energy in the future, but there are costs:

Economic costs

Exploitation is difficult and expensive.

People demand higher wages to work there.

Long distances and limited transportation increase transport costs.

Environmental costs

The environmental consequences of an oil spill would be catastrophic for the fragile Arctic ecosystem.

Strict environmental controls are needed.

Drilling equipment may sink during the summer thaw.

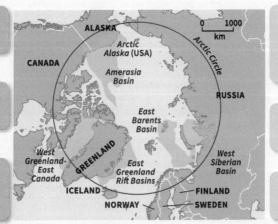

Figure 1 *Oil and natural gas resources in the Arctic (yellow shading)*

Impacts on food production

- Using biofuels like maize and sugar cane for energy have led to increased food prices.
- Biofuels are often grown on land previously used for growing food crops.
- In some LICs, collecting wood for fuel reduces time spent on food production.

Impacts on industry

- Some countries suffer from shortfalls in electricity production.
- Energy shortages have led to the closure of more than 500 companies in the industrial city of Faisalabad, Pakistan.

Potential for conflict

- Energy insecurity can lead to political conflict. For example, the Iran–Iraq War (1980–88), the Gulf War (1990–91) and the Sudanese Civil War (1983–2005).
- The Gulf and Iraq wars in the 1990s and 2000s were driven in part by the West's fear of a global oil shortage and rising prices.

Six Second Summary

Impacts of energy insecurity include:
- exploration of difficult and environmentally sensitive areas
- economic and environmental costs
- food production • industrial output • conflict

Over to you

Look at the bullet points in the Six Second Summary.

Write one sentence to explain each one.

Student Book
See pages
326–7

You need to know:

- what strategies are used to increase energy supply
- how each strategy works to increase energy supply.

What are the options for increasing energy supplies?

Every day we're using more and more energy!
There are two main options for increasing future energy supplies:

- increase the use of renewable energy sources
- exploit non-renewable fossil fuels and develop the use of nuclear power.

To avoid relying too much on one source, most countries use several energy types – an **energy mix**.
To achieve a sustainable energy mix, countries need to develop the use of renewable energy sources.

Renewable energy sources

Renewable energy source	Can it increase energy supplies?
Biomass	Using land to grow biofuels rather than food crops is controversial. Fuelwood supplies are limited.
Wind	Unpopular with some, but considerable potential.
Hydro (HEP)	In 2018, HEP accounted for 33% of the renewable energy contribution to global energy consumption.
Tidal	There are few tidal barrages due to high costs and environmental concerns.
Geothermal	Limited to tectonically active countries.
Wave	There are many experimental wave farms but costs are high and there are environmental concerns.
Solar	Energy production depends on seasonal availability of light. Solar wind farms need a lot of space.

Non-renewable energy sources

Fossil fuels

Although stocks of fossil fuels are limited, there are still plenty left. But, at some point, the economic and environmental costs of exploiting them will become too high, or they will run out.

- Fossil fuels include coal, gas and oil.
- They remain important for electricity production.
- Carbon capture can help overcome environmental impacts.

Nuclear power

- Radioactive waste can remain dangerous for over 100 years.
- Despite a good safety record, there is considerable opposition, and power stations are expensive to build.
- Low cost of uranium as little is used.

Six Second Summary

Strategies to increase energy supply include renewable and non-renewable sources of energy.

Over to you

Revisit this page in two days' time and remind yourself of anything you have forgotten.

Student Book
**See pages
328–9**

You need to know:

- that natural gas is an **example** of a fossil fuel
- the advantages and disadvantages of extracting natural gas.

EXAMPLE

How is natural gas formed?

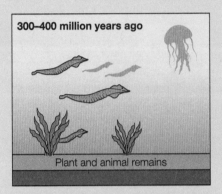

300–400 million years ago

Plant and animal remains

Remains of tiny sea plants and animals are buried on ocean floor. Over time these are covered by sand and sediment.

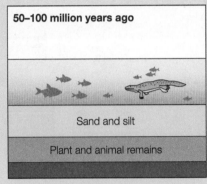

50–100 million years ago

Sand and silt

Plant and animal remains

Over millions of years the remains are buried deeper. Enormous pressure and heat turns them into hydrocarbons (oil and gas).

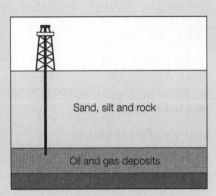

Sand, silt and rock

Oil and gas deposits

Today, oil and gas deposits are reached by drilling through layers of sand, silt and rock.

Figure 1 *The formation of oil and natural gas*

Where is natural gas found?

About 54 per cent of known natural gas reserves are in Russia, Iran and Qatar. Reserves expected to last 53 years at the current rate of production. Recent technology has allowed **shale gas** to be extracted by a controversial process called *fracking* (see 19.7).

Extracting natural gas

Advantages

- Emits 45 per cent fewer CO_2 emissions than other fossil fuels.
- Lower risk of environmental accidents than oil.
- Can be transported easily via pipelines or by tankers.

Disadvantages

- Some gas reserves are in politically unstable countries.
- Wastewater and chemicals from fracking can contaminate groundwater.
- Contributes to global warming by producing CO_2 and methane emissions.

Extracting natural gas in the Amazon

The Camisea project began in 2004 to exploit a huge gas field in the Amazonian region of Peru.

Advantages

- Peru could make several billion dollars in gas exports.
- It provides employment opportunities.
- It could save Peru up to US$4 billion in energy costs.

Disadvantages

- Deforestation will affect the Amazon.
- The project could affect traditional lifestyles of indigenous tribes.
- Local people have no immunity to disease introduced by developers.

Six Second Summary

- Advantages of extracting natural gas include employment and lower risk of environmental accidents.
- Disadvantages include deforestation and contribution to global warming.

Over to you

Create **ten** questions about everything you have learnt about energy. Test yourself in a few days.

Student Book
See pages 330–1

You need to know:

- how different strategies can conserve energy and move towards a sustainable resource future.

What is a sustainable energy supply?

A sustainable energy supply involves balancing supply and demand. Individuals can change their behaviour to reduce their use of energy and their **carbon footprint**.

Energy conservation

Energy conservation is the reduction of energy use. This can be achieved by:

- using technology (e.g. low-energy appliances)
- changing behaviour (e.g. switching off lights)
- more sustainable designs (see Figure **1**)
- encouraging the use of public transport or electric vehicles.

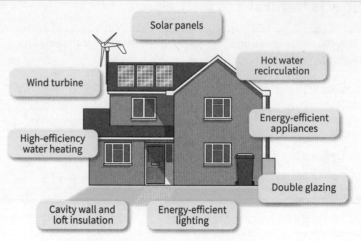

Figure 1 *Energy conservation in the home*

Sustainable energy developments in Malmö, Sweden

Sustainable development is economic development that does not harm or deplete natural resources. In Malmö, Sweden:

- all buildings use 100 per cent renewable energy
- solar tubes on the outside of buildings produce hot water
- energy comes from solar panels, a wind turbine and biogas

- buses run on biogas and natural gas
- cyclists have priority at traffic lights
- buses, water taxis and car sharing have reduced car usage.

Reducing energy demand

Energy demand can be reduced by:

- offering financial incentives to use energy saving devices
- raising public awareness
- encouraging businesses to reduce energy demand.

How can technology increase efficiency of fossil fuels?

Vehicle manufacturers are using technology to design more fuel-efficient cars. These developments include improved engines and aerodynamic designs.

Development of electric and hybrid cars – in the USA, electric cars could reduce the use of oil for transport by up to 95 per cent.

Development of biofuel technology – Brazil has reduced its petrol consumption by 40 per cent since 1993 by using sugar cane ethanol. Around 90 per cent of all new cars in Brazil can run on both ethanol and petrol.

Six Second Summary

Energy can be conserved by designing homes, workplaces and transport for sustainability, reducing demand, and by using technology. Individuals can also reduce their energy use and carbon footprint.

Over to you

Write down **three** ways that energy use could be made more sustainable. For each one, write a reason why that method will make energy use more sustainable.

Student Book
**See pages
332–3**

EXAMPLE

You need to know:

- about the Chambamontera micro-hydro scheme – an **example** of a local renewable energy scheme in an LIC or NEE
- how it provides sustainable supplies of energy.

Why does Chambamontera need a sustainable energy scheme?

Chambamontera is an isolated community in the Andes Mountains of Peru.

- Nearly half the population survives on just US$2 a day.
- Steep slopes and rough roads make Chambamontera very isolated.
- Due to the low population density, it was uneconomic to build an electricity grid to serve the area.

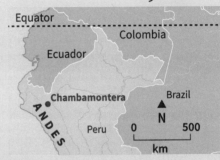

Figure 1 *Location of Chambamontera*

What is the Chambamontera micro-hydro scheme?

The high rainfall, steep slopes and fast-flowing rivers make this area ideal for exploiting water power as a renewable source of energy.

The total cost of the scheme was US$51000. There was some government money invested from Japan, but the community had to pay part of the cost. Credit facilities were made available to pay for this.

How has the local community benefited?

- Provides renewable energy
- Has low maintenance and running costs
- Has little environmental impact
- Used local labour and materials.

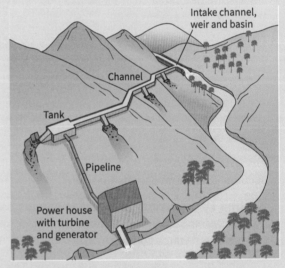

Figure 2 *How the scheme works*

Reduced rural–urban migration, so the population has grown.

Business development is possible, as piped water can drive small machines for coffee de-husking and processing.

Regulating the flow of water has reduced the danger of flooding.

Benefits to the local community

Reliable electricity for refrigeration, light and other uses like computers and entertainment.

Improved school facilities and the possibility of doing schoolwork at home after dark.

Less need to burn wood as a source of heat, so reduced deforestation and risk of soil erosion.

Six Second Summary

- The Chambamontera micro-hydro scheme exploits water power as a renewable source of energy.
- It brings benefits such as electricity and business development.

Over to you

Think of a rhyme or a mnemonic to help you to remember the name or the Chambamontera micro-hydro scheme.

Issue evaluation and Fieldwork

Paper 3 is called 'Geographical applications'. Instead of revising and learning by heart, it is much more practical and you must use your knowledge, understanding and skills. It has two sections:

Your exam

Section A Issue evaluation and Section B Fieldwork is examined by Paper 3: Geographical applications.

Paper 3 is a one-and-a-quarter hour written exam and makes up 30 per cent of your GCSE. The whole paper carries 76 marks (including 6 marks for SPaG) – questions on Section A will carry 37 marks; questions on Section B will carry 39 marks.

In your final exam you will have to answer all questions.

Section A: Issue evaluation

This section involves learning about a new issue which you won't have studied before. It'll be contained in a resource booklet which you'll be given about 12 weeks before the exam.

- The **resource booklet** will consist of maps, diagrams, graphs, statistics, photographs, sketches, text, and quotes from different groups about an issue.

- The **exam** will assess your ability to make sense of the resource booklet. In those 12 weeks, you'll be able to read, understand, and prepare for the exam.

The issue could be about anything, but will be linked to the compulsory sections of subject content. These are:

- **Unit 1:** Tectonic hazards, Weather hazards (see Figure **1**), Climate change, Ecosystems, and Tropical rainforests. An example of an issue based on tectonic hazards appears in 23.2.

- **Unit 2:** Urban issues and challenges and The changing economic world.

Figure 1 *Damage to houses in New Orleans, USA, in September 2021 caused by Hurricane Ida. How should New Orleans try to recover from damage done? This could be the topic of an Issue evaluation.*

Section B: Fieldwork

You must revise your two fieldwork topics. It will help if you practise answering exam questions on fieldwork so that you're used to applying what you learnt on your two topics. Chapter 24 gives you detailed guidance on this.

Your two fieldwork topics will be:

- a physical geography topic, where you carried out an investigation into rivers, coasts or glaciated landscapes and processes

- a human geography topic, where you've investigated a rural or an urban place (like the one in Figure **2**).

The questions will be about two types of fieldwork:

- fieldwork you have carried out yourself – i.e. *familiar* fieldwork

- fieldwork where you apply what you learned to new places – i.e. *unfamiliar* fieldwork.

Figure 2 *A housing estate in East London. This could be the topic of an fieldwork investigation.*

You need to know:

- how to prepare for the exam in Paper 3 (the Issue evaluation and Fieldwork).

What makes Unit 3 different?

Chapters 1 to 22 in this book help you to prepare for Paper 1 (Living with the physical environment) and Paper 2 (Challenges in the human environment). You prepare by revising topics you've done in class and at home.

Unit 3 is different. The exam is less about learning, and more about preparation. Half of it is an *Issue evaluation* – a topic about which different people have different views, which you have to evaluate (or weigh up).

- It's based on a resource booklet which you'll receive 12 weeks before the exam.
- In those 12 weeks, you'll be able to read, understand, weigh up different views, and prepare for the exam.

The other half is based on the two days of *fieldwork* that you've carried out. You can prepare by reading through your fieldwork, and by reading Unit 24 in this book.

The Exam

The exam lasts for 1 hour 15 minutes, which is split between the Issue evaluation and Fieldwork sections.

It has 76 marks in total.

- **Section A** The Issue evaluation, has 37 marks, 3 of which are for spelling, punctuation and grammar.
- **Section B** The Fieldwork section, has 39 marks, 3 of which are for spelling, punctuation and grammar.

So, aim for a mark a minute!

That sounds like a pressurised exam – but remember you'll know the content of the resource booklet already. You'll also probably know which project or option you'll choose for the last question, so you can prepare.

The Issue evaluation

The Issue evaluation is based on a six-page resource booklet. You'll receive this 12 weeks before the exam.

- It will contain geographical information that you probably won't have seen before about an issue somewhere in the world.
- It's likely that you won't know much about this place. Don't worry – it isn't your knowledge of the place that's being assessed, but your ability to understand the issue.
- To help you understand the issue, the resource booklet contains text, maps, photos, diagrams and data. The exam will assess your ability to study these and make sense of them.
- Towards the end of the resource booklet, there will be alternative ways of dealing with the issue in the future. The options will be real ones, not fictional.
- The final question in the exam will ask you to select one of these projects or options. There won't be a 'right' or 'wrong' answer. You'll be marked on how well you argue the reasons you give for your choice.

The resource booklet will also contain key words and concepts that you'll understand from Units 1 and 2. That's intentional – examiners will want you to make links between topics you've studied. This is called being *synoptic* – making links with what you know and understand.

Remember!

It's your ability to understand the issue that's important.

A sample resource booklet follows in 23.2, like the one you'll use in the exam. It's organised into questions.

- The first question introduces you to the place or issue – the example in this topic is Christchurch, New Zealand.
- The next questions will explore the issue – you'll see that Christchurch was hit by several earthquakes in 2010, 2011 and 2016, which seriously damaged some parts of the city. Christchurch now faces an issue – what kind of city should be rebuilt, if at all? The resource booklet will take you through this.

What will the Issue evaluation topics be?

The topic for the Issue evaluation will differ each year. You won't know until the resource booklet is given out. It will always be about *core topics*, not options. Core topics are:

- **Unit 1 Section A** The challenge of natural hazards (natural hazards, tectonic hazards, weather hazards, climate change)
- **Unit 1 Section B** The living world (ecosystems, tropical rainforests)
- **Unit 2 Section A** Urban issues and challenges (case study of a major city in *either* a low-income country *or* a newly emerging economy, *and* a case study of a major city in the UK)
- **Unit 2 Section B** The changing economic world (case study of *either* a low income country *or* a newly emerging economy, *and* economic futures in the UK)
- **Unit 2 Section C** The challenge of resource management (resource management)

Christchurch CBD after the earthquakes of 2010–11. People questioned whether the city was worth rebuilding at all.

The issue

- Christchurch, New Zealand, was affected by a series of earthquakes between 2010 and 2011, with smaller ones in 2016.
- Much of the city centre and suburbs east of the city were destroyed in 2011.
- Over a decade later, with repairs incomplete, there is still debate about how Christchurch should be rebuilt. Who has the best ideas about Christchurch's future?

Figure 1 The earthquakes in Christchurch

Figure 1a Factfile on Christchurch, New Zealand

Fact file

- Christchurch is located on South Island, New Zealand.
- It is New Zealand's third largest city, and the largest city on South Island.
- It is surrounded by a region called Canterbury, which is mainly farmland and small towns (with a lower population density).
- About 395 000 people live in Christchurch itself, and another 210 000 in the Canterbury region.

Figure 1b The earthquakes of 2010, 2011 and 2016

- Several minor earthquakes occur every day in New Zealand.
- There were three big earthquakes between September 2010 and June 2011 (**Figure 1c**), and others that were smaller, including one in 2016.
- Earthquakes that occur in large numbers like this are known as 'earthquake swarms'.

Figure 1c The area around Christchurch

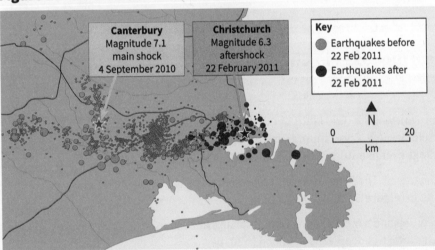

The Christchurch region showing the swarm of earthquakes that occurred between September 2010 and June 2011

Time sequence of the main earthquakes

- First earthquake – September 2010 in Canterbury (7.1 on the Richter scale).
- Second earthquake – February 2011 in Christchurch (6.3) which affected the city itself.
- Third earthquake – June 2011 in Christchurch (also 6.3). Many people and businesses had been evacuated by this time.
- A further earthquake (5.7) occurred in eastern Christchurch in 2016, together with a much larger one (7.8) in the Marlborough region north of Christchurch. Damage was minor in both cases.

Figure 2 What caused the earthquakes?

New Zealand lies across a plate margin. The plates are active and cause thousands of earthquakes every year.

Figure 2a

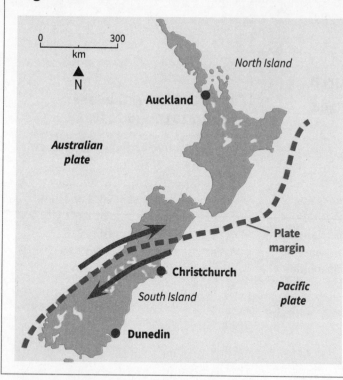

Figure 2b Earthquake prediction and protection

- A lot is known about where earthquakes are likely to happen.
- There is no known way of predicting when they will happen.
- People can prepare for earthquakes in different ways.
- Buildings can be designed to withstand earthquakes in different ways.

The plate margin which caused the earthquakes

Figure 3 Impacts of the earthquakes in Christchurch

Figure 3a

The city centre is the oldest part of Christchurch. Two kinds of buildings suffered most in the earthquakes of 2011: the oldest buildings (e.g. Christchurch Cathedral, **Figure 3b**), and the tallest buildings – out of 220 buildings over five storeys high, half have had to be demolished.

Further east, many houses were destroyed. They had been built on softer sands (which makes poor foundations) near the River Avon (**Figure 3c**).

The 2010–11 earthquakes were New Zealand's most expensive natural disaster costing NZ$20 billion in total. New Zealand's total GDP was NZ$200 billion in 2010.

Figure 3b

Christchurch Cathedral was badly damaged in the 2011 earthquake. Rebuilding is due to complete in 2027.

Figure 3c

Housing in Avonside, east of Christchurch city centre

Figure 3d

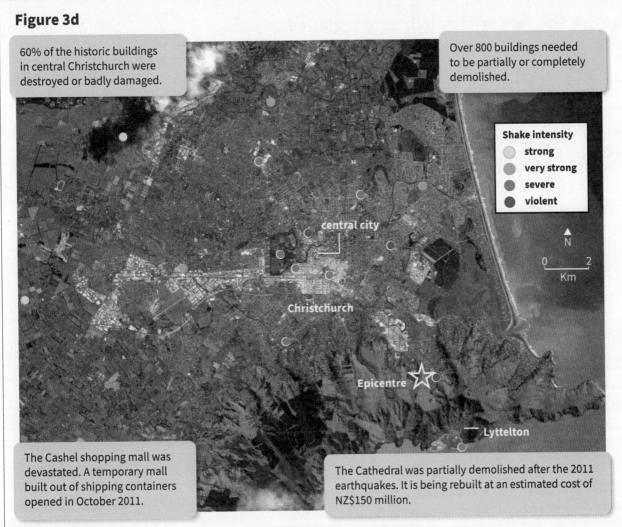

60% of the historic buildings in central Christchurch were destroyed or badly damaged.

Over 800 buildings needed to be partially or completely demolished.

Shake intensity
- strong
- very strong
- severe
- violent

N

0   2
Km

central city

Christchurch

Epicentre

Lyttelton

The Cashel shopping mall was devastated. A temporary mall built out of shipping containers opened in October 2011.

The Cathedral was partially demolished after the 2011 earthquakes. It is being rebuilt at an estimated cost of NZ$150 million.

Areas of Christchurch worst affected by the second earthquake on 21 February 2011

Figure 3e

	3 September 2010	**21 February 2011**	**13 June 2011**
Location	Canterbury	Christchurch urban area	East of Christchurch
Richter Scale	7.1	6.3	6.3
Deaths	0	181 (115 of these were in the Canterbury TV building)	0
Injured	100	6000–7000	46
Cost of damage	NZ$3 billion	NZ$15 billion	NZ$60 million
Buildings	Many buildings were weakened, but only a few were destroyed in the city centre.	Caused major damage. 1000 buildings in the city centre and to the east were destroyed or were demolished later.	Many buildings in the city centre were already damaged or had been evacuated and demolished.
Other points	Affected Canterbury; some damage in Christchurch.	Affected the city centre badly.	

Comparing the effects of the three largest earthquakes 2010–11

Figure 4 Should Christchurch be abandoned?

Figure 4a Future earthquakes

It is very likely that Christchurch will be affected by more earthquakes in future. Its location is in an area of active movement. Around 70000 people – 20 per cent of Christchurch's population – left the city temporarily since the 2010–11 earthquakes, while rebuilding took place. Most had returned by 2020.

- There have been over 100000 aftershocks since September 2010.
- Scientists predicted there was a 72 per cent chance that Christchurch would be struck by an earthquake with a magnitude between 5 and 5.4 between 2012 and 2013.
- Larger earthquakes are less frequent but are much more likely to cause large-scale damage.

Figure 4b Does Christchurch have a future?

An article suggesting that Christchurch should be abandoned

Parker dismisses abandoning city

Christchurch Mayor Bob Parker has hit out at suggestions that rebuilding earthquake-hit Christchurch should be abandoned.

In the Otago Daily Times yesterday, a Dunedin councillor said it was insane to rebuild Christchurch on the same site, and the money should be spent in developing Dunedin instead.

'Rebuilding Christchurch and hoping for no more earthquakes will doom Christchurch and the South Island to long-term loss of investment,' he said. 'It would be foolish to pour money into a city that could be hit by yet another big earthquake.'

Figure 4c Should Christchurch be rebuilt?

The government has divided Christchurch up into four zones: blue, red, orange and white (see map below). These show where rebuilding will or could take place.

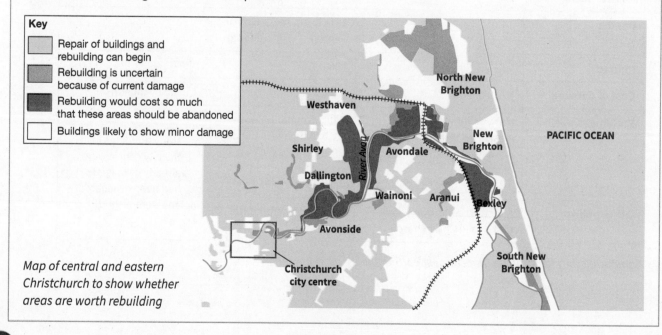

Key
- Repair of buildings and rebuilding can begin
- Rebuilding is uncertain because of current damage
- Rebuilding would cost so much that these areas should be abandoned
- Buildings likely to show minor damage

Map of central and eastern Christchurch to show whether areas are worth rebuilding

Figure 5 How should Christchurch be redeveloped?

Figure 5a Project 1: The Government plan

The New Zealand Government and Christchurch City Council formed the Canterbury Earthquake Recovery Authority (CERA). It believes that Christchurch should be fully rebuilt, but with conditions:

- Rebuilding offices, workplaces and shops is the priority.
- Many heritage buildings were too dangerous and not earthquake-proof – they should be demolished and replaced with earthquake-proof designs.
- The earthquake is a chance to re-plan Christchurch city centre and the economy to attract high salary earners in the quaternary sector.
- All buildings should be built to resist earthquakes.

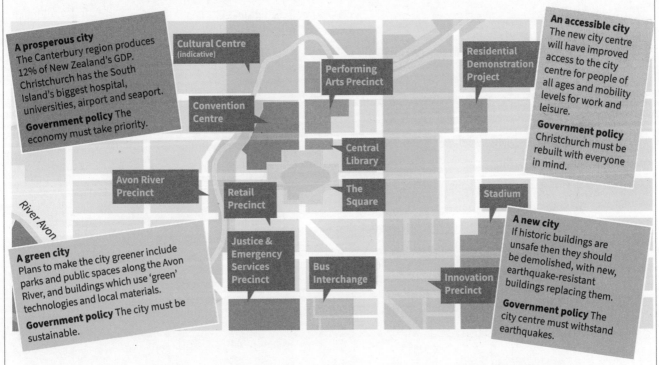

The government plan for rebuilding Christchurch city centre based on 100 000 ideas received from the public

Figure 5b Project 2: The People's plan

We want our city back!

In December 2012 people held a protest march against government plans for Christchurch. They wanted the following:

- **Housing should be rebuilt before businesses**. Although the city centre is being replanned, there are no plans for housing.
- **The red zones (Figure 4c) are unfair**. New homes should be built for people before they are forced to leave.
- **Historic buildings should be rebuilt**. The government has demolished the finest heritage buildings. 'We are losing our heritage and character' said one resident.
- **The city should be sustainable**. Residents want a sustainable city with parks, improved public transport, walkways for pedestrians and cycle paths.

Figure 5c Project 3: Abandon Christchurch and build a new city

This plan claims that no city is earthquake-proof, so rebuilding Christchurch is a waste of money.

- No new building plans should be made for Christchurch – either residential or commercial.
- Companies should be offered new offices in other cities in New Zealand.
- All residents should be compensated for their houses and asked to leave.

Exam-style questions

- These exam-style questions are based on 23.2 in the resource booklet (pages 185–189).
- You should take 37 minutes for this section.
- There are 37 marks, which includes 3 marks for spelling, punctuation and grammar (SPaG).
- Use the mark schemes on the following pages to self-assess your answers – no peeking until you've done the questions!
- When you mark your answers, read the mark scheme carefully to see how you can improve.
- Then answer the questions again to see how close you can get to full marks.

Question 1 (8 marks)

1.1 Christchurch is in which **one** of the following countries?

A Australia ☐

B New Zealand ☐

C France ☐

D Nigeria ☐

[1 mark]

1.2 Christchurch is in which **one** of the following locations?

A In the northern hemisphere ☐

B On the Equator ☐

C In the southern hemisphere ☐

D In Antarctica ☐

[1 mark]

1.3 Suggest why the earthquake in February 2011 had bigger impacts than that of September 2010.

[6 marks]

Question 2 (9 marks)

2.1 The arrows on the diagram of the plate margin (**Figure 2a**) show that this is which type of plate margin?

A Collision ☐

B Conservative ☐

C Constructive ☐

D Destructive ☐

[1 mark]

2.2 Explain **one** way that this kind of plate margin can cause earthquakes.

[2 marks]

2.3 Study **Figure 3**. Assess the impacts of the earthquakes between 2010 and 2011 on Christchurch and the surrounding region.

[6 marks]

Question 3 (20 marks)

3.1 Explain one reason why earthquakes are likely to happen again in Christchurch.

[2 marks]

3.2 'Cities likely to be affected by earthquakes should be abandoned'. Do you agree? YES / NO

Explain your answer.

[6 marks]

3.3 Three projects have been suggested about the future of Christchurch. These are outlined in **Figure 5**.

- Which of the three projects do you think should be adopted for the people, the economy, and the environment of Christchurch?
- Use evidence from this resource booklet and your own understanding to explain why you have reached this decision.

[9 marks]

[+ 3 SPaG marks]

Mark scheme

Question 1 (8 marks)

1.1 **B** New Zealand [1 mark]

1.2 **C** In the southern hemisphere [1 mark]

1.3 Use these points to guide you. Include some (but not all) of the following points:

- The second earthquake in February 2011 was less strong than the first.
- It was in the city itself with a higher density of buildings, unlike the first which was in Canterbury (which is agricultural with a lower population/population density).
- Damage in 2011 was caused by weakening of buildings, roads etc., so the second earthquake destroyed what was already damaged in 2010. Types of damage should be referred to (e.g. cost), or examples (e.g. collapse of Christchurch Cathedral).
- Because city buildings collapsed, the cost was greater than the 2010 earthquake.

You may use or refer to material researched that goes beyond the booklet.

Level	Mark	Description
3 (Detailed)	5–6	• A detailed explanation of the impacts of the different earthquakes; much evidence from the resource booklet. • Communicates ideas with clarity.
2 (Clear)	3–4	• A sound understanding of differences between the two earthquakes. • Demonstrates clear explanation of the impacts of both earthquakes; some evidence from the resource booklet.
1 (Basic)	1–2	• A limited understanding of how or why the two earthquakes differed. May simply identify reasons unrelated to the resource booklet. • Demonstrates limited understanding of the impacts of the earthquakes; little evidence from the resource booklet.
	0	No relevant content.

Question 2 (9 marks)

2.1 **B** Conservative [1 mark]

2.2 Award 1 mark for a factor and 1 mark for development of that point. Answers could include:

- Horizontal movement **(1)** so that 'sticking' can lead to build up of force. **(1)**
- Shallow/not very deep within the crust **(1)** so the force is felt more strongly. **(1)**

2.3 Use the following points to help you. Remember that if you just describe or explain, without saying which were the *biggest impacts*, you cannot reach Level 3.

Your answer should recognise some (but not all) of the following points. It will help to categorise impacts, for example, social, economic and environmental.

- Social impacts – personal injury or death of family members; trauma; loss of housing in eastern part of the city; high repair cost for many houses; need to move away from area, loss of communities.
- Economic impacts – examples of costs of damage; damage to workplaces; jobs lost; potential for the city to lose jobs if companies decide to leave.
- Environmental impacts – for example, on the heritage buildings within Christchurch; loss of character (e.g. quotes in **Figure 5b**).

You may use or refer to material researched that goes beyond the booklet.

Level	Mark	Description
3 (Detailed)	5–6	• A detailed assessment of the most important impacts, with supporting evidence from the resource booklet. • Communicates ideas with clarity.
2 (Clear)	3–4	• A sound understanding of impacts of the earthquakes. • Demonstrates clear assessment of the relative importance of different impacts. Uses some supporting evidence from the resource booklet.
1 (Basic)	1–2	• A limited understanding of different impacts. May simply describe impacts in general terms. • Demonstrates limited or no assessment of the importance of different impacts. Little evidence from the resource booklet.
	0	No relevant content.

Question 3 (20 marks)

3.1 Award **1 mark** for a factor and **1 mark** for development of that point Answers could include:

- There have been over 10 000 aftershocks since September 2010 **(1)** so there will be more! **(1)**
- Scientists predicted a 72 per cent chance of an earthquake with a magnitude of 5–5.4 between 2012 and 2013 **(1)** – so the odds against that happening are only 28 per cent. **(1)**
- An earthquake occurred in 2016 **(1)** which was even bigger that 2010–11. **(1)**

3.2 Use the following points to help you. Remember that if you just describe or explain (without making a judgement on either side) you cannot reach Level 3.

Your answer should recognise some (but not all) of the following points.

- Reasons for abandoning – more earthquakes may occur in future, destroying any rebuilding that may have take place; compensation costs high; cost of continuous rebuilding; human dangers.
- Reasons for not abandoning (or for rebuilding) – rebuilding maintains communities; provides jobs and creates economic growth; new buildings may resist damage (earthquake-proof designs); a chance to redesign the city.

You may use or refer to material researched that goes beyond the booklet.

Level	Mark	Description
3 (Detailed)	5–6	• A detailed discussion of the reasons on both sides, with supporting evidence from the resource booklet. • Communicates ideas with clarity.
2 (Clear)	3–4	• A sound explanation of both sides of the argument. • Demonstrates clear discussion using some supporting evidence from the resource booklet.
1 (Basic)	1–2	• A limited discussion of different arguments. May be one-sided. • Demonstrates limited or no explanation. Little evidence from the resource booklet.
	0	No relevant content.

3.3 Your answer should include material from your course as well as from the *resource booklet*. You should:

- give at least three detailed reasons to reach the top of level 3, quoting evidence from the resource booklet
- refer to each of people, the economy and the environment to reach Level 3
- refer to all the options, about what is most appealing about one and why you rejected the other two
- include detailed evidence from the resource booklet to support your case
- include any evidence from the course to support your case.

You may use or refer to material researched that goes beyond the booklet.

Level	Mark	Description
3 (Detailed)	7–9	• A thorough evaluation of the effectiveness of the chosen project in terms of its benefits. • Uses a wide range of evidence to support the decision, using detailed content from different areas of the course.
2 (Clear)	4–6	• A reasonable evaluation of the effectiveness of the chosen project in terms of its benefits. • Uses some evidence from the resource booklet to support the decision, and content from different areas of the course.
1 (Basic)	1–3	• A basic evaluation of the effectiveness of the chosen project in terms of its benefits. • Uses limited evidence from the resource booklet to support the decision, using basic content from different areas of the course.
	0	No relevant content.

Spelling, punctuation and grammar [3 marks]

- **3 marks** if you spell and punctuate accurately, use rules of grammar with effective control of meaning, and use a wide range of specialist terms.
- **2 marks** if you generally spell and punctuate accurately, use rules of grammar with general control of meaning, and use a good range of specialist terms.
- **1 mark** if you spell and punctuate reasonably accurately, use rules of grammar with some control of meaning, and any errors you make do not significantly hinder meaning, and use a limited range of specialist terms.
- **0 marks** if you write nothing, or do not relate to the question, with a basic grasp of spelling, punctuation and grammar which prevents any meaning being clear.

Student Book
See pages
340–1

You need to know:

- the six strands (stages) of a fieldwork enquiry.

Getting to know Paper 3

Paper 3 is called Geographical Applications and Skills. It has two sections; Section A, Issue evaluation and Section B, Fieldwork.

Geographical skills run through the whole paper.

How is fieldwork assessed?

You should have carried out two days fieldwork:

- One day on a **physical** topic, e.g. a river study.
- One day on a **human** topic, e.g. a local town study.

Both topics involve **primary data** (data you collect yourself).

One topic will study links between physical and human geography, e.g. how flood defences have developed along a river.

> **Checklist!**
>
> - The topic we studied for our **physical** fieldwork was _____.
> - The place we went to was _____.
> - The data we collected included _____.
> - The topic we studied for our **human** fieldwork was _____.
> - The place we went to was _____.
> - The data we collected included _____.

Understanding geographical enquiry

Fieldwork has six *strands*, or *stages of enquiry* used in investigating a geographical question. Each strand follows on from an earlier one, so the enquiry develops through each strand.

Strand or Stage	Focus
1	Setting up a suitable question for investigation (see 24.2)
2	Selecting, measuring and recording data that are appropriate to the chosen enquiry (see 24.3)
3	Selecting appropriate ways of processing and presenting the fieldwork data (see 24.4)
4	Analysing results – describing, analysing and explaining the fieldwork data (see 24.5)
5	Reaching conclusions that are supported by the data (see 24.6)
6	Evaluating the enquiry – what went well? What didn't go so well? (see 24.7)

Figure 1 *The six strands (stages) of enquiry*

Fieldwork in the exam

Paper 3 Section B is a compulsory section on fieldwork. It has two questions, in total worth 39 marks, including three marks for SPaG.

Question 4 is about *unfamiliar fieldwork* (fieldwork done by others).

- These are skills-based questions; use your skills to interpret data.
- It has 16 marks, consisting of short questions worth 1–4 marks.

Question 5 is about *familiar fieldwork* (fieldwork that you've done).

- These are about your physical and human fieldwork.
- It has 23 marks, including one 6-mark and one 9-mark question plus 3 marks for SPaG.

Before you begin revising your fieldwork, make sure you know about the fieldwork you have carried out and how it will be assessed. Complete a checklist like the one above.

Strand 1 – Developing questions for your enquiry

Student Book
See pages
342–3

You need to be able to:

- develop a suitable enquiry focus for your fieldwork.

What's Strand 1 about?

Strand 1 involves focusing your fieldwork. It has four parts:

1 Selecting an enquiry question or hypothesis.

2 The idea, concept or theory that supports your enquiry.

3 What primary and secondary data you'll collect, and suitable locations.

4 Identifying risks.

1 Selecting an enquiry question or hypothesis

Your fieldwork title will be a question or hypothesis. Figure **1** shows examples.

- Questions are used when a 'maybe' answer is likely, e.g. 'Has regeneration been a success in Cardiff?'.
- Hypotheses are used when data collection is like an experiment, e.g. 'River velocity gets faster downstream'.

Question	Hypothesis
How does the velocity of River X change downstream?	The discharge of River X increases downstream
How successful has the regeneration been in Cardiff?	The regeneration of Cardiff has been successful.

Figure 1 Comparing questions and hypotheses.

2 The geographical idea, concept or theory that supports your enquiry

Geographical concepts or theories are useful because they help to:

- test your fieldwork against an idea
- compare your data with a theory
- judge the reliability and accuracy of data compared to a theory.

Checklist!

- My fieldwork question/hypothesis _____.
- The theory or concept I used was _____.
- The location was suitable for this fieldwork because ____.
- Two risks that we faced were _____.
- We overcame these risks by_____.

3 Primary and secondary evidence and selecting locations for fieldwork

- Primary data are data you collect yourself. They have to be suitable for a particular location.
- Secondary data are data collected by someone else. They help with background (see 24.3).

4 Identifying and managing risks in fieldwork

Both physical and human fieldwork locations must be safe. You need to know the risks you face in collecting data – called a risk assessment. This means identifying the risks, and who they affect; and working out how severe the risks are and how to reduce them.

Figure **2** is part of a risk assessment. Risks are rated between 1 (low) and 5 (high).

Risk/Hazard	Who might be harmed	Level of risk	Management/precautions
Sand dunes – injury through climbing and jumping	Students	2	Students are warned of hazard and told not to jump/play in dunes

Figure 2 Part of a risk assessment

Student Book
See pages
344–5

You need to be able to:

- develop suitable data collection methods for your fieldwork.

What's Strand 2 about?

Strand 2 is about choosing the data you need for your investigation. It has four parts:

1 Primary and secondary data.

2 Selecting appropriate data.

3 Using different sampling methods.

4 Describe and justify data collection methods.

1 Differences between data

- **Primary data** means data collected that you have collected yourself (by fieldwork).
- **Secondary data** means data collected by someone else. It might be published.

For your fieldwork, you need to know:

- examples of primary and secondary data
- limitations of each (e.g. accuracy, relevance, age).

Checklist!

- One example of primary quantitative data I collected

  _____ ;

  I collected this to help me find out _____ .

- One example of primary qualitative data I collected was

  _____ ;

  I collected this to help me find out _____ .

- One example of secondary data I collected

  _____ ;

  I collected this to help me find out _____ .

- A sampling method I used was _____ ,

  which I used to collect data on _____ .

2 Selecting appropriate data

Think how relevant your data are to your aim. For example, a questionnaire will help you investigate the success of a shopping centre, because you can collect data about people's opinions. Figure **1** shows examples of relevant data for physical and human topics.

Fieldwork Focus	Possible fieldwork data collection techniques
Success of a new shopping centre	*Pedestrian counts, questionnaires, interviews*
Downstream changes in a river channel	*Channel width, depth, cross-sectional area, velocity / speed of the river*
Shape of storm beach	*Gradient (across and long the beach)*

Figure 1 *Examples of relevant fieldwork data collection techniques*

3 Using different sampling methods

Sampling helps to collect data that are representative of a bigger number, such as data about a number of people, or stones on a beach. The larger the sample, the more reliable your conclusions (see 24.7). Figure **2** shows the three main types of sampling.

Random	**Every person or place has an equal chance of being selected.** Used when sampling is the same throughout, e.g. a woodland where trees are the same type and age.
Stratified	**Where the data are collected in proportion to a population**, e.g. choosing numbers of people to interview in different age groups, in proportion to numbers in the actual population.
Systematic	**A sample taken at regular intervals,** e.g. every 50 m along a footpath.

Figure 2 *Three types of sampling.*

4 Justifying your data collection methods

Justifying fieldwork methods means knowing why you're doing them, such as how and why you measure the velocity of a stream at several places across its width.

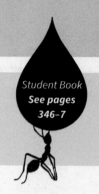

Student Book
See pages
346–7

You need to be able to:

- present your fieldwork data in different ways.

What's Strand 3 about?

Strand 3 is about how you present fieldwork data. It has three parts:

1 Understanding different ways of presenting data.

2 Selecting the most appropriate way of presenting data.

3 Justifying chosen methods of presenting data.

1 Different ways of presenting fieldwork data

You have a wide choice of methods you can use to present your data. It's a matter of choosing the best one and being able to justify your choice. Figure **1** shows different geographical data presentation methods.

Visual	Graphical (graphs)	Cartographic (maps)
Good for showing change in an area or evidence of processes	Good for showing patterns in data, e.g. trends over time and space	Good for showing patterns at locations and to make comparisons between places
Examples: photographs, (field) sketches, video, diagrams, and personal theories or models	Examples: bar charts, pie charts, pictograms, histograms, scattergraphs, population pyramids, dispersion graphs Graphs are even more useful when located on a map to show changes or patterns.	Examples: sketch maps, choropleth maps, isoline maps, dot maps, desire lines and flow lines, proportional symbols All of these are presented on a base map.

Figure 1 Ways of classifying data presentation techniques

2 Selecting the most appropriate presentation method

The best ways of presenting data are those which show meaning. Figure **2** gives some examples of different of graphs. When you choose a method, make sure you know:

- why you made your choice
- why it was appropriate
- its advantages and disadvantages.

Using Geographical Information Systems (GIS)

Geographical Information Systems (GIS) are useful because you can overlay different types of data on one image, e.g. a cross-section of river channels onto a relief map to show how these change downstream.

Justifying ways of presenting fieldwork data

You need to be able to describe a presentation method and explain why it is suitable for the data, or why it could be improved.

	Scattergraph	Usually used to show the relationship between two variables, each of which has its own axis
	Dot range plot	A simple way of showing the range (maximum and minimum) for a number of contrasting variables or categories of data
	Gain-loss bar chart	An adaptation of the standard bar chart, which can show both negative and positive values

Figure 2 Three graphical methods of presenting data

Checklist!

- One method I used to present my primary **physical** data was _____;

  I chose this method because _____.

  An alternative method I could have used was _____,
  which might have been better because _____.

- One method I used to present my primary **human** data was _____;

  I chose this method because _____.

  An alternative method I could have used was _____,
  which might have been better because _____.

Student Book
**See pages
348–9**

You need to be able to:

- describe, analyse and explain your fieldwork data.

What's Strand 4 about?

Strand 4 is about analysing data. It has four parts:

1 Describing, analysing and explaining results.

2 Making links between different sets of data.

3 Using statistical techniques to understand data.

4 Spotting anomalies in data.

Describing, analysing and explaining your results

Describing data means:

- saying what data show, e.g. biggest? smallest?
- spotting highest and lowest values
- giving examples to illustrate your description.

Analysing data means:

- looking for patterns, e.g. does pebble size get smaller along a beach?
- finding examples which do not fit the pattern
- calculating the range between highest and lowest
- identifying trends, e.g. how values go up or down over time.

Explaining data means:

- asking the question 'why?'
- linking trends to a process, such as longshore drift
- explaining difficult trends, e.g. why results change unexpectedly.

Use phrases in Figure **1** to help you.

Linking sets of data

- Linking means whether what happens in one set of data also happens in another.
- A questionnaire about how people travelled to a town centre could be compared with a land use map. People questioned in one area might have travelled by train because it was near the train station!

Using statistical techniques

Techniques such as mean, median, mode, range, quartiles, percentage change and trend lines can be used to analyse data. See pages 374–7 of the Student Book for more detail.

Spotting anomalies in data

Anomalies are data that don't fit the pattern. Possible reasons are:

- errors in data collection
- a change in the environment, e.g. a riverbed becomes steeper, so the river speeds up
- data are correct but just different.

Checklist!

- One method used to analyse my physical fieldwork data was _____;
  It showed that _____.
  An alternative method I could have used was _____;
  which might have showed _____.
- One method used to analyse my human fieldwork data was _____;
  It showed that _____.
  An anomaly occurred which showed that _____;
  A reason for this was _____.

Cause and effect	Emphasis
As a result of …	above all …
this results in …	mainly …
triggering this …	mostly …
consequently …	most significantly …
the effect of this is …	usually …

Explaining	Suggesting
This shows …	could be caused by …
because …	this looks like …
similarly …	points towards …
therefore …	tentatively …
as a result of …	the evidence shows …

Figure 1 *Explanation and analysis – some useful words and short phrases*

Student Book
See pages
350–1

> **You need to be able to:**
>
> • draw conclusions from your fieldwork data.

What's Strand 5 about?

Strand 5 is about developing conclusions linked to the aims of your fieldwork.

• This applies to *both your physical and human fieldwork*.
• You need to quote evidence from your fieldwork to support your conclusions.

Developing evidenced conclusions based on your original aims

Conclusions are one of the final stages of enquiry. They answer your main question or hypothesis, e.g. *How does the velocity of a river change downstream?*

• The best ones are supported by data from your fieldwork.
• You should revise your conclusions, with data to support it.

Writing your conclusion

To write your conclusion:

• Refer back to the aim of your investigation. Can you answer your aim?
• Is your conclusion different to what you expected?
• Which primary and secondary data support your conclusion?
• Is your conclusion strong, based on reliable and accurate data? Or is it inconclusive, based on less reliable or less accurate data?
• Were there anomalies or unexpected results? Do anomalies affect your conclusion?
• Do geographical theories support your conclusions?
• Could your results and conclusion be useful to others?

Question:

• How does the number of pedestrians change over the day in a city centre?

Conclusion:

• We found big variations in the number of pedestrians over 5-minute intervals and during the day

Evidence

• The peak number of pedestrians was 500 per minute at one location.

Figure 1 *How a photo can help you to remember short conclusions*

whereas	overall	most significantly
notably	above all	especially
in particular	in the same way	also
alternatively	revealed by	as a consequence
the result is	triggering	initiating
although	nonetheless	this shows
to sum up	similarly	the effect of this is
likewise	this, in turn, causes	

Figure 2 *A word bank to help you write your conclusions*

Checklist!

• The conclusion I can draw from my **physical** fieldwork is _____.

• This conclusion is firm/tentative (*cross out one*) because _____.

• The data which support my conclusion most are

_____.

• The anomaly which makes my conclusion less certain is _____.

• My conclusion would be even firmer if I could find out _____

_____

_____

Now repeat this for your **human** fieldwork investigation.

Student Book
See pages
352–3

You need to be able to:

- identify problems and limitations of any methods you used
- identify any limitations of your data
- be able to judge the reliability of your conclusions.

What does 'evaluation' mean?

The evaluation is the last part of your fieldwork investigation, and it's probably the hardest. Remember that no study is perfect. You need to look back over the investigation and think about:

- how and when you collected data
- how the methods you used might have affected your results
- whether your conclusion is reliable – if you did it again in the same way, on a different day, would you get similar results?

Figure **1** should give you some ideas.

Checklist!

1   A possible source of error in my physical investigation was

    _____

2   The ways in which these errors might have affected our results are

    _____

3   My conclusions might be affected because

    _____

Possible sources of error	Impacts on quality	Tick if this applies
Sample size	Were your sampling sizes large enough? • *Smaller sample sizes usually mean lower quality data.*	
Frequency of sample	Did you have enough sampling points (e.g. every 10 m instead of every 100 m)? • *Fewer sites reduce frequency and quality.*	
The type of sampling used (see 24.5)	Did you use random, systematic or stratified samples? • *The method you chose might create 'gaps' and introduce bias (e.g. if you only questioned people aged over 65).*	
Using the right equipment	The wrong/inaccurate equipment can affect overall quality by producing incorrect results. • *Is a dog biscuit the best way to record river velocity?* • *Did your questionnaire ask questions that gave you the answers you needed?*	
Time of survey	Times affect results (e.g. tides might influence beach accessibility or the measurable width of a river). • *11.30 a.m. on a Monday in January may not give a sample of the whole population.*	
Location of survey	Big variations in beach profiles and sediment can occur in locations close to each other. • *Where you collect data matters.*	
Quality of secondary data	Did you find up-to-date secondary sources? • *Age and reliability of secondary data affect its quality.*	

Figure 1 *Possible sources of error in a geographical enquiry*

 Six Second Summary

Evaluation means looking critically at:
- how and when you collected data
- how methods might have affected results
- whether conclusions are reliable.

 Over to you

Copy and complete the checklist for **each** of your fieldwork investigations.

Student Book
See pages
354–5

You need to know:

- the different types of skills-based exam question used to assess fieldwork in Paper 3.

Understanding the range of exam questions

- Fieldwork and geographical skills are assessed in Section B of Paper 3.
- Together, they are worth 39 marks (including 3 for SPaG).
- Questions are based on either **familiar** fieldwork (that you have done) or **unfamiliar** fieldwork (which someone else has done).
- *Unfamiliar* fieldwork questions occur in *Question 4* and *familiar* fieldwork questions in *Question 5*.

Figure 1 shows more detail.

Section and Questions	Details
Section B, Question 4 - Based on unfamiliar fieldwork. - Some questions test your skills in interpreting data. - Others test your ability to apply knowledge and understanding.	- A mix of shorter and longer questions, worth 1–4 marks. - Includes multiple choice, explain/suggest, and maths calculations. - Resources (data, maps etc) create an 'unfamiliar' context - Skills and fieldwork questions are mixed together.
Section B, Question 5 - Based on familiar fieldwork. - There are no recall questions. - Questions test your ability to apply knowledge and understanding.	- Questions usually range from 2 to 9 marks, and include one 6-mark and one 9-mark question (plus 3 for SPaG). - 6- and 9-mark questions demand evaluation and judgment. These are marked using levels. - 6- and 9-mark questions are based on Strands 5 and 6 (drawing conclusions and evaluating your fieldwork).

Figure 1 *How fieldwork and skills are usually tested in Paper 3*

Short-answer unfamiliar skills questions

These occur in Section B, Question 4. There are two types:

- Some are about strands of fieldwork, e.g. how data collection or methods of presentation could be improved
- Others are skills based, such as completing graphs and maps, doing calculations, or using statistics.

 Six Second Summary

Check that you can recognise:

- exam questions based on unfamiliar fieldwork
- exam questions based on the six strands of fieldwork enquiry.

 Over to you

Based on your fieldwork, be clear about:

- what makes a suitable location
- how to set fieldwork aims
- methods of collecting data
- methods of presenting data
- analysing, concluding and evaluating fieldwork.

Student Book
See pages
356–7

- how to answer familiar fieldwork questions in Paper 3.

Levels marking

- All questions carrying 4 marks or more are marked using 'levels'.
- Levels-based marking means that examiners match your answer to a set of descriptors.
- Level 1 is easiest to achieve, and Level 3 most difficult.
- Fieldwork questions are marked on your ability to apply what you know and understand to new situations (Assessment Objective 3 (AO3) in Figure **1**) and your ability to use skills (Assessment Objective 4 (AO4) in Figure **1**).

Level	Marks	Description
2 (Clear)	3–4	AO3 – Demonstrates clear application of knowledge and understanding.
		AO4 – Clear reference made to the data.
1 (Basic)	1–2	AO3 – Demonstrates limited application of knowledge and understanding.
		AO4 – Some reference made to the data.
	0	No relevant content.

Figure 1 An example of a levels-based mark scheme used in fieldwork questions

Answering 4-mark questions

These levels-based questions usually use commands words such as 'assess' or 'compare'. Expect to have to use a resource on unfamiliar fieldwork in Question 4. There is a sample 4-mark question on page 356 of the Student Book.

Answering 6-and 9-mark questions

- 6- and 9-mark questions are marked using levels, in questions about familiar fieldwork in Question 5, Section B.
- Figure **2** shows examples of exam-style questions, linked to different 'strands'.

Example 6- or 9-mark question	Link to Strand(s)
Assess the suitability of your sites used for your **physical** geography enquiry.	Strand 2
Explain how the data presentation techniques used in your **physical** geography enquiry helped you reach conclusions.	Strand 3, Strand 5
Assess the effectiveness of **one** technique you used to analyse your data in your **human** geography enquiry.	Strand 2

Figure 2 Examples of 6-mark and 9-mark familiar fieldwork questions, and their links to enquiry strands

Handy hints on fieldwork questions

- Watch the time – a mark a minute!
- Don't overwrite – only use the extra space if you need it.
- Watch the question wording, e.g. 'one technique' or 'physical enquiry'.
- Don't describe – remember most questions are evaluative.

Six Second Summary

Check that you can recognise:

- exam questions based on unfamiliar fieldwork
- exam questions based on the six strands of fieldwork enquiry.

Over to you

Based on your fieldwork, be clear about:

- what makes a suitable location
- how to set fieldwork aims
- methods of collecting data
- methods of presenting data
- analysing, concluding and evaluating fieldwork.

Glossary

Abiotic Related to non-living things

Abrasion (1) Rocks carried along a river wear down the river bed and banks; (2) the sandpaper effect of glacial ice scouring a valley floor and sides

Adaptation Actions taken to adjust to natural events, such as climate change, to reduce damage, limit the impacts, take advantage of opportunities, or cope with the consequences

Aeroponics Growing plants in air and providing nutrients through mist without the use of soil

Agribusiness Application of business skills to agriculture

Appropriate (or intermediate) technology Technology suited to the needs, skills, knowledge and wealth of local people and their environment

Arch A wave-eroded passage through a small headland. This begins as a cave which is gradually widened and deepened until it cuts through

Arête A sharp, knife-like ridge formed between two corries cutting back by processes of erosion and freeze-thaw weathering

Attrition Rocks being carried by the river smash together and break into smaller, smoother and rounder particles

Bar Where a spit grows across a bay, a bay bar can eventually enclose the bay to create a lagoon

Beach A zone of deposited material that extends from the low water line to the limit of storm waves

Beach nourishment Adding new material to a beach artificially, through the dumping of large amounts of sand or shingle

Beach reprofiling Changing the profile or shape of the beach

Biodiversity The variety of life in the world or a particular ecosystem

Biomass Renewable organic materials, such as wood, agricultural crops or wastes, especially when used as a source of fuel or energy

Biotechnology The genetic engineering of living organisms to produce useful commercial products

Biotic Related to living things

Birth rate The number of births a year per 1000 of the total population

Brownfield site Land that has been used, abandoned and now awaits reuse; often found in urban areas

Bulldozing The pushing of deposited sediment by the snout (front) of the glacier as it advances

Business park An area of land occupied by a number of businesses

Carbon footprint A measurement of the greenhouse gases individuals produce through burning fossil fuels

Cave A large hole in a cliff caused by waves forcing their way into cracks in the cliff face

Channel straightening Removing meanders from a river to make it straighter

Chemical weathering The decomposition (or rotting) of rock caused by a chemical change within that rock

Cliff A steep high rock face formed by weathering and erosion

Climate change A long-term change in the Earth's climate, especially a change due to an increase in the average atmospheric temperature

Commercial farming Growing crops or raising livestock for profit, often involving vast areas of land

Commonwealth The Commonwealth is a voluntary association of 54 independent and equal sovereign states, most being former British colonies

Conservation Managing the environment in order to preserve, protect or restore it

Conservative plate margin Two plates sliding alongside each other, in the same or different directions – sometimes known as a transform plate margin

Constructive plate margin A tectonic plate margin where rising magma adds new material to plates that are diverging or moving apart

Consumer An organism that eats animals and/or plant matter

Corrie or cirque An armchair-shaped hollow in the mountainside formed by glacial erosion, rotational slip and freeze-thaw weathering – this is where the valley glacier begins

Cross profile The side-by-side cross-section of a river channel and/or valley

Dam and reservoir A barrier built across a valley to interrupt river flow and create a man-made lake to store water and control river discharge

Death rate The number of deaths in a year per 1000 of the total population

Debt reduction Countries are relieved of some of their debt in return for protecting their rainforests

Decomposer Organisms, such as bacteria or fungi, that break down plant and animal material

Deforestation The cutting down and removal of forest

Deindustrialisation The decline of a country's traditional manufacturing industry due to exhaustion of raw materials, loss of markets and overseas competition

Demographic Transition Model A model showing how populations should change over time in terms of their birth rates, death rates and total population size

Deposition Occurs when material being transported by the sea is dropped due to the sea losing energy

Dereliction Abandoned buildings and wasteland

Desertification The process by which land becomes drier and degraded, as a result of climate change or human activities, or both

Destructive plate margin Tectonic plate margin where two plates are converging and the oceanic plate is subducted – there could be violent earthquakes and explosive volcanoes

Development The progress of a country in terms of economic growth, the use of technology and human welfare

Development gap The difference in standards of living and wellbeing between the world's richest and poorest countries

Discharge The quantity of water that passes a given point on a stream or riverbank within a given period of time

Drumlin An egg-shaped hill of moraine material deposited in a glacial trough

Dune regeneration Building up dunes and increasing vegetation to prevent excessive coastal retreat

Earthquake A sudden or violent movement within the Earth's crust followed by a series of shocks

Economic impact The effect of an event on the wealth of an area or community

Economic opportunities Chances for people to improve their standard of living through employment

Glossary

Ecosystem A community of plants and animals that interact with each other and their physical environment

Ecotourism Nature tourism usually involving small groups with minimal impact on the environment

Embankment An artificially raised riverbank often using a concrete wall

Energy conservation Reducing energy consumption by using less energy and existing sources more efficiently

Energy exploitation Developing and using energy resources to the greatest possible advantage, usually for profit

Energy mix A range of energy sources of a region or country, both renewable and non-renewable

Energy security The uninterrupted availability of energy sources at an affordable price

Environmental impact The effect of an event on the landscape and ecology of the surrounding area

Erosion Wearing away and removal of material by a moving force, such as a breaking wave

Erratic A rock that has been transported by glacial ice to a different location and deposited, often hundreds of kilometres away

Estuary The tidal mouth of a river where it meets the sea – wide banks of deposited mud are exposed at low tide

European Union A politico-economic union of 27 European countries

Extreme weather When a weather event is significantly different from the average or usual weather pattern and it is especially severe or unseasonal

Fair trade Producers in LICs are given a better price for their goods, such as cocoa, coffee and cotton

Famine A widespread, serious, often fatal shortage of food

Flood Where river discharge exceeds river channel capacity and water spills onto the floodplain

Floodplain A relatively flat area forming the valley floor either side of a river channel that is sometimes flooded

Floodplain zoning Identifying how a floodplain can be developed for human uses

Flood relief channels Artificial channels that are used when a river is close to maximum discharge; they take the pressure off the main channels when floods are likely

Flood risk The likelihood of a flood event or vulnerability of an area to flooding.

Flood warning Providing reliable advance information about possible flooding

Fluvial processes Processes relating to deposition, erosion and transportation by a river

Food chain Connections between different organisms (plants and animals) that rely upon one another as their source of food

Food insecurity Being without reliable access to enough affordable, nutritious food

Food miles The distance covered when supplying food to consumers

Food security Access to sufficient, safe, nutritious food to maintain a healthy and active life

Food web A complex hierarchy of plants and animals relying on each other for food

Fossil fuel A natural fuel, such as coal or gas, formed in the geological past from the remains of living organisms

Fragile environment An environment that is both easily disturbed and difficult to restore

Freeze-thaw weathering (or frost shattering) A common process of weathering in a glacial environment involving repeated cycles of freezing and thawing that can make cracks in rock bigger

Gabion A steel wire mesh filled with boulders – used in coastal defences

Geothermal energy Energy generated by heat stored deep in the Earth

Glacial trough A wide, steep-sided valley eroded by a glacier

Global atmospheric circulation The worldwide system of winds, which transports heat from tropical to polar latitudes

Global ecosystem Very large ecological areas on the Earth's surface (or biomes), with fauna and flora (animals and plants) adapting to their environment, e.g. tropical rainforest and hot desert

Globalisation The process of creating a more connected world, with increases in the global movements of goods (trade) and people (migration and tourism)

Gorge A narrow steep-sided valley – often formed as a waterfall retreats upstream

Greenfield site A plot of land, often in a rural area or on the edge of an urban area that has not been built on before

Grey water Recycled domestic waste water

Gross National Income (GNI) A measurement of economic activity calculated by dividing the gross (total) national income by the size of the population

Groundwater management The regulation and control of water levels, pollution, ownership and use of groundwater

Groyne A wooden barrier built out into the sea to stop the longshore drift of sand and shingle, and allow the beach to grow

Hanging valley A tributary glacial trough on the side of a main valley – often with a waterfall

Hard engineering Using concrete or large artificial structures to defend against natural processes – coastal, fluvial or glacial

Hazard risk The probability or chance that a natural hazard may take place

Headlands and bays A rocky coastal promontory (high point of land) made of rock that is resistant to erosion: headlands lie between bays of less resistant rock where the land has been eroded by the sea

High income country (HIC) A country with GNI per capita higher than $12 696 (World Bank, 2020)

Hot desert An area of the world that has high average temperatures and very low precipitation

Human Development Index (HDI) A method of measuring development in which GDP per capita, life expectancy and adult literacy are combined to give an overview

Hydraulic action The power of the water eroding the bed and banks of a river

Hydraulic power The process where breaking waves compress pockets of air in cracks in a cliff; the pressure may cause the crack to widen, breaking off rock

Hydro-electric power (HEP) Electricity generated by turbines that are driven by moving water

Glossary

Hydrograph A graph which shows the discharge of a river, related to rainfall, over a period of time

Hydroponics Growing plants in water using nutrient solutions, without soil

Immediate responses The reactions of people as the disaster happens and in the immediate aftermath

Industrial structure The relative proportion of the workforce employed in different sectors of the economy

Inequality The difference between poverty and wealth, as well as wellbeing and access to jobs, housing, education, etc.

Infant mortality The number of babies that die under one year of age, per 1000 live births

Information technology Computer, Internet, mobile phone and satellite technologies

Infrastructure The basic equipment and structures (such as roads, utilities, water supply and sewage) that are needed for a country or region to function properly

Integrated transport system Different forms of transport are linked together to make it easy to transfer from one to another

Interlocking spur An outcrop of land in a valley along the river course

Intermediate (or appropriate) technology Simple, easily learned and maintained technology used in LICs for a range of economic activities

International aid Money, goods and services given by single governments or an organisation, like the World Bank or IMF, to help the quality of life and economy of another country

Irrigation The artificial application of water to the land or soil

Landscape An extensive area of land regarded as being visually and physically distinct

Land use conflict A disagreement between interest groups who do not agree on how land should be used

Lateral erosion Erosion of river banks rather than the riverbed – helps to form the floodplain

Levée A raised bank found on either side of a river, formed naturally by regular flooding or built up by people to protect the area against flooding

Life expectancy The average number of years a person is expected to live

Literacy rate The percentage of people in a country who have basic reading and writing skills

Local food sourcing Food production and distribution that is local, rather than national and/or international

Logging The business of cutting down trees and transporting the logs to sawmills

Long profile The gradient of a river, from its source to its mouth

Longshore drift The transport of sediment along a stretch of coastline caused by waves approaching the beach at an angle

Long-term responses Later reactions that occur in the weeks, months and years after the event

Low income country (LIC) A country with GNI per capita lower than $1025 (World Bank, 2018)

Managed retreat Controlled retreat of the coastline, often allowing flooding to occur over low-lying land

Management strategies Techniques of controlling, responding to, or dealing with an event

Mass movement The downhill movement of weathered material under the force of gravity

Meander A wide bend in a river

Mechanical weathering The physical disintegration or break-up of exposed rock without any change in its chemical composition, i.e. freeze–thaw

Megacity An urban area with a total population of more than ten million people

Microfinance loans Very small loans which are given to people in LICs to help them start a small business

Migration When people move from one area to another; in many LICs people move from rural to urban areas (rural–urban migration)

Mineral extraction The removal of solid mineral resources from the Earth

Mitigation Action taken to reduce the long-term risk from natural hazards, such as earthquake-proof buildings or international agreements to reduce greenhouse gas emissions.

Monitoring (1) Recording physical changes, i.e. tracking a tropical storm by satellite, to help forecast when and where a natural hazard might strike; (2) using scientific methods to study coastal processes to help inform management options.

Moraine Frost-shattered rock debris and material eroded from the valley floor and sides, transported and deposited by glaciers

Natural hazard A natural event (e.g. earthquake, volcanic eruption, tropical storm, flood) that threatens people or has the potential to cause damage, destruction and death

Natural increase The birth rate minus the death rate of a population

New green revolution A combination of modern technology and traditional knowledge focusing on sustainability and community while maximising yields

Newly emerging economy (NEE) A country that has begun to experience high rates of economic development, usually along with rapid industrialisation

North–south divide (UK) Real or perceived economic and cultural differences between southern England and northern England

Nuclear power Energy released by a nuclear reaction, especially by fission or fusion

Nutrient cycling The on-going recycling of nutrients between living organisms and their environment

Orbital change Changes in the pathway of the Earth around the Sun

Organic produce Food produced without the use of chemicals such as fertilisers and pesticides

Outwash Well sorted and rounded sediment that has been deposited by meltwater in front of a glacier

Over abstraction When water is used more quickly than it is replaced

Over-cultivation Where the intensive growing of crops exhausts the soil leaving it barren

Overgrazing Feeding too many livestock for too long on the land, so the vegetation unable to recover

Ox-bow lake An arc-shaped lake on a floodplain formed by a cut-off meander

Permaculture A system of food production which follows the patterns and features of natural ecosystems; it aims to be sustainable, productive, non-polluting and healthy

Permafrost Permanently frozen ground, found in polar and tundra regions

Planning Actions taken to enable communities to respond to, and recover from, natural disasters

Glossary

Plate margin The border between two tectonic plates

Plucking A process of erosion – rocks are pulled from the valley floor as water freezes them to a glacier

Polar The most extreme cold environment with permanent ice, i.e. Greenland and Antarctica

Pollution Chemicals, noise, dirt or other substances which have harmful or poisonous effects on an environment

Post-industrial economy The shift of some HIC economies from producing goods to providing services

Precipitation Moisture falling from the atmosphere – rain, sleet or snow

Prediction Attempts to forecast when and where a natural hazard will strike, based on current knowledge

Primary effects The initial impacts of a natural event on people and property, caused directly by it, i.e. the buildings collapsing following an earthquake

Producer An organism or plant that is able to absorb energy from the Sun through photosynthesis

Protection Actions taken before a hazard strikes to reduce its impact, such as educating people or improving building design

Pyramidal peak Where several corries cut back to meet at a central point, the mountain takes the form of a steep pyramid

Quaternary period The period of geological time from about 2.6 million years ago to the present, characterised by the appearance and development of humans

Renewable energy sources A resource that cannot be exhausted, i.e. wind, solar and tidal energy

Resource management The control and monitoring of resources so that they do not become exhausted

Ribbon lake A long narrow lake in the bottom of a glacial trough

Rock armour Large boulders deliberately dumped on a beach as part of coastal defences

Rotational slip The slippage of ice along a curved surface

Rural-urban fringe A zone of transition between a built-up area and the countryside, where there is often competition for land use

Saltation The hopping movement of pebbles along a river or seabed

Sand dune A coastal sand hill above the high-tide mark, shaped by wind action

Sanitation Measures designed to protect public health, such as providing clean water and disposing of sewage and waste

Science park A collection of scientific and technical knowledge-based businesses located on a single site

Sea wall A concrete wall that aims to prevent erosion of the coast by reflecting wave energy

Secondary effects The after-effects that occur as indirect impacts of a natural event, sometimes on a longer timescale, i.e. fires due to ruptured gas mains, resulting from the ground shaking

Selective logging Sustainable forestry management in which only carefully selected trees are cut down

Service (tertiary) industries The economic activities that provide various services – commercial, professional, social, entertainment and personal

Sliding Rapid mass movement where a whole segment of a cliff moves downslope along a saturated shear plane or line of weakness

Slumping Loose surface material becomes saturated and the extra weight causes the material to become unstable and move rapidly downhill

Social deprivation The extent to which an individual or an area lacks services, decent housing, adequate income and employment

Social impact The effect of an event on the lives of people or communities

Social opportunities The chances available to improve quality of life, e.g. access to education and health care

Soft engineering Managing erosion by working with natural processes to help restore beaches and coastal ecosystems or to reduce the risk of river flooding

Soil erosion The removal of topsoil faster than it can be replaced, due to natural (water and wind action), animal and human activity

Solar energy Energy from the Sun exploited by solar panels, collectors or cells to heat water or air, or to generate electricity

Solution Chemical erosion caused by the dissolving of rocks and minerals by river or sea water

Spit A depositional landform formed when a finger of sediment extends from the shore out to sea, often at a river mouth

Squatter settlement An area of (often illegal) poor-quality housing, lacking in services like water supply, sewerage and electricity

Stack An isolated pillar of rock left when the top of an arch has collapsed

Subsistence farming A type of agriculture producing only enough food and materials for the benefit of a farmer and their family

Suspension Small particles carried in river flow or sea water, i.e. sands, silts and clays

Sustainability Actions that meet the needs of the present without reducing the ability of future generations to meet their needs

Sustainable development Development that meets the needs of the present without limiting the ability of future generations to meet their own needs

Sustainable energy supply Energy that can potentially be used well into the future without harming future generations

Sustainable food supply Food production that avoids damaging natural resources, and provides good quality produce and social and economic benefits to local communities

Sustainable urban living A way of life where there is minimal damage to the environment, the economic base is sound with resources allocated fairly and jobs secure, and there is a strong sense of community, with local people involved in decisions that are made

Sustainable water supply Meeting the present-day need for safe, reliable and affordable water without reducing supply for future generations

Tectonic hazard A natural hazard caused by the movement of tectonic plates (i.e. volcanoes and earthquakes)

Tectonic plate A rigid segment of the Earth's crust which can 'float' across the heavier, semi-molten rock below

Glossary

Till Sediment deposited by a glacier that is unsorted and angular

Traction Where material is rolled along a river bed or by waves

Trade The buying and selling of goods and services between countries

Traffic congestion When there is too great a volume of traffic for roads to cope with, and traffic slows to a crawl

Transnational corporation (TNC) A company that has operations (factories, offices, research and development, shops) in more than one country

Transportation The movement of eroded material

Tropical storm (hurricane, cyclone, typhoon) An area of low pressure with winds moving in a spiral around a calm central point called the eye of the storm – winds are powerful and rainfall is heavy

Truncated spur A former river valley spur which has been sliced off by a valley glacier, forming steep edges

Tundra A vast, flat, treeless Arctic region of Europe, Asia, and North America where the subsoil is permanently frozen

Undernutrition When people do not eat enough nutrients to cover their needs for energy and growth, or to maintain a healthy immune system

Urban farming Growing food and raising animals in towns and cities; processing and distributing food; collecting and reusing food waste

Urban greening The process of increasing and preserving open spaces in urban areas, i.e. public parks and gardens

Urbanisation When an increasing percentage of a country's population comes to live in towns and cities

Urban regeneration Reversing the urban decline by modernising or redeveloping, aiming to improve the local economy

Urban sprawl Unplanned growth of urban areas into the surrounding rural areas

Vertical erosion The downward erosion of the river bed

Volcano An opening in the Earth's crust from which lava, ash and gases erupt

Waste recycling The process of extracting and reusing useful substances found in waste

Waterborne diseases Diseases, such as cholera and typhoid, caused by micro-organisms in contaminated water

Water conflict A dispute between different regions or countries about the distribution and use of freshwater

Water conservation The preservation, control and development of water resources, both surface and groundwater, and the prevention of pollution

Water deficit When demand for water is greater than supply

Waterfall A step in the long profile of a river usually formed when a river crosses over a hard (resistant) band of rock

Water insecurity When water availability is insufficient to ensure the good health and livelihood of a population, due to short supply or poor quality

Water quality Measured in terms of the chemical, physical and biological content of the water

Water security The availability of a reliable source of water that is of an acceptable quantity and quality

Water stress When the demand for water exceeds supply in a certain period or when poor quality restricts its use

Water surplus When water supply is greater than demand

Water transfer Matching supply with demand by moving water from an area with water surplus to another with water deficit

Wave-cut platform A rocky, level shelf at or around sea level representing the base of old, retreated cliffs

Waves Ripples in the sea caused by the transfer of energy from the wind blowing over the surface of the sea

Wilderness area A natural environment that has not been significantly modified by human activity

Wind energy Electrical energy produced from the power of the wind, using windmills or wind turbines

Command words

It's important to answer questions properly. When you first read a question, check out the command word – that is, the word that tells you what to do.

The following is a list of command words and their meanings that are relevant to GCSE 9-1 Geography AQA.

For more detailed explanations of command words, see pages 8–9 of the Student Book.

Command word	What is it asking you to do?	Here's an example...
Assess	Weigh up which is the most/least important.	Choose either an earthquake or a volcanic eruption. Assess the extent to which primary effects are more significant than secondary effects.
Calculate	Work out.	Using the data in Figure 9, calculate the interquartile range of the pebble size data.
Compare	Identify similarities and differences.	Using Figure 4, compare HDI values in Africa and South America.
Complete	Add information to finish the task.	Using Figure 10, complete the graph for Dartmoor using the following data for rainfall.
Describe	Say what something is like.	No explanation is needed. Describe the distribution of hot deserts shown in Figure 6.
Discuss	Give the points on both sides of an argument and come to a conclusion.	Discuss the effects of urban sprawl on people and the environment.
Evaluate	Make judgements about which is most or least effective.	Evaluate the effectiveness of an urban transport scheme you have studied.
Explain	Give reasons why something is the case.	Explain how food security can be improved.
Give	Recall one or more pieces of geographical information.	Give one physical factor that affects flooding.
Identify	Name an example, sometimes from a map, photo or graph.	Identify two data collection techniques that could be used to carry out a geographical fieldwork investigation in one of the areas shown.
Justify	Give evidence to support your ideas.	Do you agree with this statement? Justify your decision.
Outline	Summarise the main points.	Outline one reason why the concentration of carbon dioxide in the atmosphere has changed over time.
State	Write a short, factual answer.	State the grid reference of the church with a tower.
Suggest	Give a well-reasoned guess to explain something where you can't be sure of the answer.	Using Figures 11 and 12, suggest why there might be a need for water transfer from one part of the UK to another.
To what extent...?	Judge the importance of something.	To what extent do urban areas in LICs or NEEs provide social and economic opportunities for people?
Use evidence to support this statement	Choose information to prove or disprove something.	'Weather in the UK is becoming more extreme.' Use evidence to support this statement.

Please note that this our interpretation of AQA's guidance and is not an exhaustive list of all command words that might be used in exams

Ordnance Survey map symbols

Symbols on Ordnance Survey maps (1:50 000 and 1:25 000)

ROADS AND PATHS

M1 or A 6(M)	Motorway
A 35	Dual carriageway
A 31(T) or A 35	Trunk or main road
B 3074	Secondary road
	Narrow road with passing places
	Road under construction
	Road generally more than 4 m wide
	Road generally less than 4 m wide
	Other road, drive or track, fenced and unfenced
	Gradient: steeper than 1 in 5; 1 in 7 to 1 in 5
Ferry	Ferry; Ferry P – passenger only
	Path

PUBLIC RIGHTS OF WAY

(Not applicable to Scotland)

1:25 000	1:50 000	
		Footpath
		Road used as a public footpath
+++++		Bridleway
	-+-+-+-+-	Byway open to all traffic

RAILWAYS

	Multiple track
	Single track
	Narrow gauge/Light rapid transit system
	Road over; road under; level crossing
	Cutting; tunnel; embankment
	Station, open to passengers; siding

BOUNDARIES

	National
	District
	County, Unitary Authority, Metropolitan District or London Borough
	National Park

HEIGHTS/ROCK FEATURES

50	Contour lines
·144	Spot height to the nearest metre above sea level

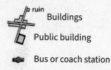

outcrop, cliff, scree

ABBREVIATIONS

P	Post office	PC	Public convenience (rural areas)
PH	Public house	TH	Town Hall, Guildhall or equivalent
MS	Milestone	Sch	School
MP	Milepost	Coll	College
CH	Clubhouse	Mus	Museum
CG	Coastguard	Cemy	Cemetery
Fm	Farm		

ANTIQUITIES

Roman	✕ Battlefield (with date)
Non-Roman	✲ *Tumulus/Tumuli* (mound over burial place)

LAND FEATURES

ruin	Buildings
	Public building
	Bus or coach station
	Place of Worship — with tower / with spire, minaret or dome / without such additions
○	Chimney or tower
	Glass structure
	Heliport
△	Triangulation pillar
	Mast
	Wind pump / wind generator
	Windmill
+	Graticule intersection
	Cutting, embankment
	Quarry
	Spoil heap, refuse tip or dump
	Coniferous wood
	Non-coniferous wood
	Mixed wood
	Orchard
	Park or ornamental ground
	Forestry Commission access land
	National Trust – always open
	National Trust, limited access, observe local signs
	National Trust for Scotland

TOURIST INFORMATION

P	Parking
P&R	Park & Ride
V	Visitor centre
i	Information centre
☎	Telephone
	Camp site/ Caravan site
	Golf course or links
	Viewpoint
PC	Public convenience
	Picnic site
	Pub/s
	Museum
	Castle/fort
	Building of historic interest
	Steam railway
	English Heritage
	Garden
	Nature reserve
	Water activities
	Fishing
☆	Other tourist feature
	Moorings (free)
	Electric boat charging point
	Recreation/leisure/ sports centre

WATER FEATURES

Marsh or salting, Towpath, Lock, Slopes, Cliff, High water mark, Low water mark, Flat rock, Lighthouse (in use), Aqueduct, Canal, Ford, Sand, Lighthouse (disused), Beacon, Weir, Normal tidal limit, Dunes, Bridge, Footbridge, Lake, Mud, Shingle, Canal (dry)